GLOBAL SOCIAL
IN THE MAK

The foundations of the
social protection floor

Bob Deacon

First published in Great Britain in 2013 by

Policy Press
University of Bristol
6th Floor
Howard House
Queen's Avenue
Clifton
Bristol BS8 1SD
UK
t: +44 (0)117 331 4054
f: +44 (0)117 331 4093
tpp-info@bristol.ac.uk
www.policypress.co.uk

North America office:
Policy Press
c/o The University of Chicago Press
1427 East 60th Street
Chicago, IL 60637, USA
t: +1 773 702 7700
f: +1 773 702 9756
sales@press.uchicago.edu
www.press.uchicago.edu

British Library Cataloguing in Publication Data
A catalogue record for this book is available from the British Library.

Library of Congress Cataloging-in-Publication Data
A catalog record for this book has been requested.

ISBN 978 1 44731 234 5 paperback
ISBN 978 1 44731 233 8 hardcover

Cover design by Qube Design Associates.
Front cover: image kindly supplied by Jupiter Images.
Printed and bound in Great Britain by Hobbs, Southampton.
The Policy Press uses environmentally responsible print partners.

FSC
www.fsc.org
MIX
Paper from
responsible sources
FSC® C020438

For Bodhi Alexander Phoenix Deacon-Slater,
born September 2012;
that he might thrive in a more socially just world

"The Recommendation is a breakthrough in global social policy. National Social Protection Floors can be a major tool to achieve the targets of the United Nations' Millennium Development Goals." (Michael Cichon, director of the International Labour Organization's Social Security Department, 13 June 2012)

"*Social security for all: Building social protection floors and comprehensive social security systems* is the result of a decade of research, economic, fiscal and actuarial studies, legal analyses, tripartite consultations at global, regional and national levels, consultation and collaboration with our sister organizations in the UN [United Nations] system, dialogue with the international financial institutions as well as with a large number of civil society organisations and, most prominently, intense discussions during three sessions of the International Labour Conference (2001, 2011 and 2012). The consensus that emerged from these consultations and discussions was finally, in June 2012, promulgated in the form of a new international labour standard: the ILO [International Labour Organization] Social Protection Floors Recommendation, 2012 (No. 202). Consensus documents that have to be adopted in international or, as in this case, global decision-making processes, often lose their 'bite', yet this document stands out as an exception....At the heart of these messages is this: there is no excuse for any society to put off building social security for its members, and it can be done at any stage of development, even if gradually. All societies can grow with equity." (Guy Ryder, director-general of the ILO, November 2012)

Contents

List of tables, figures and boxes

Tables

Figures

Boxes

List of abbreviations

ACTEMP	Bureau for Employers' Activities
ACTRAV	Bureau for Workers' Activities
ASEM	Asia–Europe Meeting
ASID	Agency, Structure, Institution and Discourse framework
BIEN	Basic Income Earth Network
BMZ	German Federal Ministry for Economic Development Cooperation
BRICS	Brazil, Russia, India, China and South Africa
CESCR	Committee on Economic, Social and Cultural Rights
DFID	Department for International Development
ECOSOC	Economic and Social Council
FAO	Food and Agriculture Organization
GASPP	Globalism and Social Policy Programme
GDP	gross domestic product
GESS	Global Extension of Social Security
GTZ	German Organisation for Technical Cooperation
ICFTU	International Confederation of Free Trade Unions
ICSW	International Council on Social Welfare
IFPSES	InFocus Programme on Socio-Economic Security
ILC	International Labour Conference
ILO	International Labour Organization
IMF	International Monetary Fund
INGO	international non-governmental organisation
IOE	International Organisation of Employers
IPC-IG	International Policy Centre for Inclusive Growth
ISSA	International Social Security Association
ITUC	International Trade Union Confederation
MDG	Millennium Development Goal
NGO	non-governmental organisation
OECD	Organisation for Economic Co-operation and Development
PAHO	Pan American Health Organization
PAYG	Pay As You Go
REO	resilience, equity, opportunity
SEWA	Self-Employed Women's Movement
SIDA	Swedish International Development Cooperation Agency
SOC/POL	Social Security Policy and Development Branch of the ILO
SPF	social protection floor
SPF-I	Social Protection Floor Initiative

SPIAC-B	Social Protection Inter-Agency Cooperation Board
STEP	Strategies and Tools against Social Inclusion and Poverty
UK	United Kingdom
UN	United Nations
UNCEB	United Nations System Chief Executives Board
UNCTAD	United Nations Conference on Trade and Development
UNDESA	United Nations Department of Economic and Social Affairs
UNDP	United Nations Development Programme
UNESCO	United Nations Educational, Scientific and Cultural Organization
UNFPA	United Nations Population Fund
UNHRC	United Nations Human Rights Council
UNICEF	United Nations Children's Fund
UNRISD	United Nations Research Institute for Social Development
US	Unites States
WFP	World Food Programme
WHO	World Health Organization
WTO	World Trade Organization

About the author

Bob Deacon is emeritus professor of international social policy at the University of Sheffield, UK, and currently holds the UNESCO-UNU Chair in Regional Integration, Migration and the Free Movement of People at UNUCRIS in Bruges. His most recent books are *Global Social Policy and Governance*; *World-Regional Social Policy and Global Governance* (co-edited with Nicola Yeates, Maria Cristina Macovei and Luk Van Langenhove); *Social Policy and International Interventions in South-East Europe* (co-edited with Paul Stubbs); and *Global Social Policy: International Organisations and the Future of Welfare* (co-authored with Paul Stubbs and Michelle Hulse). He is founding editor of the journals *Critical Social Policy* and *Global Social Policy* (GSP). He contributes to the Global Social Policy Digest, published in GSP, and online at www.gsp-observatory. org. He has acted as consultant or advisor to the ILO, UNICEF, UNDP, UNDESA, UNRISD, World Bank, European Commission, Council of Europe, ICSW, CROP and the social security ministries of several countries. He now lives in Hebden Bridge, West Yorkshire, UK.

Acknowledgements

This book would not have been able to be written but for the cooperation and support of a large number of individuals. First and foremost my thanks must go to the staff of the Social Security Department of the International Labour Organization (ILO) for having me reside with them for six months between September 2011 and February 2012. It could not have been easy befriending me knowing I was also writing about them. In particular I want to thank Christina Behrendt, Christine Bockstal, Michael Cichon, Krzysztof Hagemejer, Christian Jacquier, Clara Van Panhuys, Xenia Scheil-adlung, Veronika Wodsak and John Woodall of that department for their support given in various ways, from finding me a flat through chats over coffee to enjoying Serbian beer at my local. I hope none of you feels I abused your cooperation too much in the final revised telling of this social protection floor story. Michael Cichon, Frank Hoffer, Guy Standing and Krzysztof Hagemejer are to be thanked for reading the first or second draft of the book and having the patience to send me detailed comments and suggestions for change even though there was much in the first draft that they were most unhappy about. I can only hope that the revised version is seen by them as acknowledging many of their criticisms. Thanks also go to members of the Social Dialogue Sector with whom I was also formally linked and in particular to Youcef Ghellab of that sector. I must also acknowledge the help of members of both the Bureau for Workers' Activities (ACTRAV) and the Bureau for Employers' Activities (ACTEMP) of the ILO. Many current and former ILO staff from these and other departments were helpful in responding to requests for interviews or in other ways. Among these, in no particular order, were Philippe Marcadent, Wouter van Ginneken, Emmanuel Reynaud, Guy Standing, Stephen Pursey, Vinicius Pinheiro, Frank Hoffer, Anna Biondi, Alexander Egorov, Susan Hayter, Griet Cattaert, Eddy Lee, Raymond Torres, Gerry Rodgers, Rafael Gijon, Ana Sanchez, May Ontal, Charlotte Beauchamp, Samia Kazi Aoul, Anne Sullivan, Margret Antosik and Ian Orton. None of this would have happened had I not been awarded a competitive ILO research fellowship, which covered my costs while in Geneva. I thank the ILO for this and hope they do not regret their decision.

In terms of support from those outside the ILO, I have to put at the top of the list Isabel Ortiz, who at the time was at UNICEF and a key player in the original Campaign for a Global Social Floor and an important player in the United Nations (UN) Social Protection Floor

Initiative. Her willingness to share her knowledge of the UN process as far as the non-ILO dimensions were concerned was fundamental in enabling me to better understand the policy-making processes I was observing. She too took a weekend out of her busy life to correct the first draft of the book. Others involved in some small way with the events analysed in this book and whose knowledge helped me to clarify things were Sarah Cook of UNRISD, Shahra Razavi then of UNRISD, Gabriele Kohler of the Institute of Development Studies at Sussex and Jomo K. Sundaram then of UNDESA.

In terms of my efforts to frame the story theoretically and to offer an explanation of an example of global social policy making, I have to thank first and foremost my long-time friend and collaborator Paul Stubbs whose ideas I have stolen and whose inspiration and support I have depended on. Paul, for all the times shared at jazz events, over excellent food and over a pint, I am truly grateful. Without your critical support my contribution to the global social policy literature would have been even less useful.

Others who have helped in this intellectual endeavour during the writing of this book include my PhD student turned firm critic Alexandra Kaasch, Rianne Mahon, Daniel Beland and Timo Voipio. Chapter Three of the book was first presented as a paper at the RC19 Research Committee of the International Sociological Association in Oslo in August 2012. The ideas in Chapter Six were first articulated at a workshop at Bremen University in 2010 and subsequently developed with Paul Stubbs for a paper to be published jointly with him in *Global Social Policy* in 2013. I thank participants at both events for useful feedback.

Finally, let me thank my good friend of many years, Gerry Lavery and the new network of friends in Hebden Bridge who now sustain me as do my children and grandchildren who continue to delight. The book is dedicated to Bodhi Alexander Phoenix Deacon-Slater, born 12 weeks ago and just home from intensive care after a serious illness.

Hebden Bridge, December 2012

ONE

Introduction

This is the story of how the International Labour Organization (ILO) came in 2012 to use its standard setting and soft law powers to resolve upon a recommendation to all countries that they should establish a 'social protection floor' (SPF) containing basic social security guarantees that would ensure that over the life cycle all in need could afford and have access to essential health care and have income security. It is the story of how the concept of a 'social floor under the global economy' or the 'global social floor' was transformed from a term used by global social reformists challenging neoliberal globalisation at the turn of the century into a concrete global social policy measure. It is also the story of the compromises that needed to be made en route, which, in the view of some critics, meant that the initial concept of a 'global social floor' became watered down into the concept of 'nationally variable social protection floors'. In part therefore it is a story of the internal politics of one of the major international organisations of the United Nations (UN). It throws light on the respective roles of governments, employers and trades unions on the one hand, who sit on the ILO's governing body and attend the annual International Labour Conference (ILC), and the permanent secretariat of the ILO on the other. It is therefore also the story of individuals who occupied positions within that context. It reveals who had influence inside the ILO and how it was used in order to win the institution over to promulgating the SPF Recommendation. The story throws light in particular on the role of the secretariat of the ILO. One of the first books to be published in the context of the ILO Century Project, a programme of work to write the history of the ILO as it approaches its 100th year in 2019, notes in its review of all the existing texts on ILO history (van Daele, 2010: 38) that:

> In addition to the three constituent groups [government, workers, employers], the ILO is driven by the work of officials and experts, which in historical research are far too often represented as invisible and anonymous actors in international bureaucracy. Consequently their ideas and (non-) decisions through contacts and expert networks worldwide merit greater attention in historical research.

This contemporary history story makes up a little for this lack of attention to the role of the so-called 'technical' secretariat.

It is also a story of the ways in which the ILO struggled to win other agencies in the system of global social governance over to supporting this global social policy idea. In 2009 the United Nations System Chief Executives Board for coordination (UNCEB) endorsed the concept of a global 'Social Protection Floor Initiative' (SPF-I) led by the ILO and the World Health Organization (WHO) but involving the active participation of several other international agencies and other actors. In 2011 the G20 communiqué after the Cannes meeting endorsed the call for SPFs to be laid down in all countries and called on the several international organisations to work together on the social impacts of globalisation (G20, 2011b). During 2011 and 2012 the World Bank was formulating its new Social Protection and Labor Strategy for the period 2012-20. We shall learn how far the SPF concept became endorsed by the World Bank and to what extent the World Bank was brought more firmly into the UN fold. Similarly in 2010 the International Monetary Fund (IMF) and the ILO held their first ever meeting. We discuss what was to become of this. And in 2012 the European Commission published its first Communication on social protection policy in the context of its evolving development agenda. Most significantly, in 2012 a new UN Social Protection Inter-Agency Cooperation Board was established. The book analyses the players and the means they used to succeed, to some extent, in generating greater policy synergy between international actors around the concept of the SPF.

There are several aspects of the development of the SPF policy that demanded an explanation. An earlier attempt by United Kingdom's (UK) Gordon Brown in 2000 to get the UN to agree to a set of global social policy principles was unacceptable to much of the Global South. What changed between 2000 and 2012? Furthermore, these new principles for a SPF for all residents and children of all countries went far beyond the traditional concern of the ILO to fashion standards only for the 20% of the world's population; workers covered by contributory social security systems. Why? Moreover, how did such a policy become endorsed by the UN normally resistant to acting as one and by the G20 not hitherto known for its concern with social protection? The World Bank's endorsement of the SPF also needed explaining given the history of ILO–World Bank contestation on issues of social protection (Deacon, 2007). Finally, the willingness of the ILO and the World Bank to jointly chair a new Social Protection Inter-Agency Cooperation Board (SPIAC-B) would need explaining against the backcloth of ILO–World Bank antagonisms.

A story of the internal dynamics and external influence of international institutions can not be complete without an account of the global economic, social, structural and historical context within which the story unfolds and by which it is shaped. This broader context must also include the pressures on such international organisations exerted by national and international social movements, global civil society organisations and countries.

This is a story of:

- global *structural* dynamics and global political processes as global neoliberalism became challenged, of the
- dynamics and processes inside and between international *institutions* and how such institutions both frame and limit what is possible but are also open to the influence of
- global *actors* and players, sometimes individuals occupying particular positions, who use their positions to make change by shifting
- *discourse* about, in this case social security and social protection.

Indeed, the story supports, I believe, the case I have made elsewhere (Deacon, 2010; see also Deacon and Stubbs, 2013) for the usefulness of the agency, structure, institution and discourse (ASID) framework in the task of understanding and explaining global social policy change. This little volume is not primarily a theoretical text, although I do believe that it contributes to some important debates about path dependency, discursive institutionalism, the nature of complex multilateralism, the role of individuals and the accidental or contingent nature of some policy changes. It also, in my view, challenges accounts of the development of the SPF couched in terms of world society theory within which global social policy developments are 'not attributed to (individual) actors but to larger cultural processes, logics, and mechanisms' (Tag, 2013).

In summary, it is suggested in this book that the SPF resulted from the intersection of the *biographies* and careers of three individuals – the head of the Social Security Department at the ILO, the director-general of the ILO and his social protection advisor in his Cabinet (obviously supported by others in their teams) – with the *idea* that the world needed a global social floor, which had for some time been advanced by a policy advocacy coalition, an idea whose time came with the new *circumstances* of the 2008 global economic crisis. This provided the opportunity for UNCEB to act, an idea that could find an unlikely home inside the *institution* of the ILO, which was open to a degree of policy change (a) because of the de facto *circumstance* of the development of forms of social protection in Latin America and Africa and (b) through the skill-full development of alliances within the ILO's tripartite governing process. The subsequent endorsement by the G20 was due entirely to determined work by one of the individuals working in the context of an earlier G8 focus on social protection and the fortuitous interest by France in having social protection on the G20 agenda in 2011. Not unimportant to ensuring the involvement of other UN agencies in the SPF-I was the *biography* of Isabel Ortiz, a key player within the United Nations Children's Fund (UNICEF) social and economic policy division at the time.

The motivation for writing the text was political or rather it was written for advocacy reasons. It advocates the case for the SPF. It advocates the case for the supporting international social movements and international non-governmental organisations (INGOs) that have helped to put universal social protection on the global agenda. It advocates the case for the positive role that the UN system can still play in mending the global economy (and in this case contributing to laying the foundation for a social floor under it). It advocates supporting the ILO as an agent of change despite the rigidities of its governing structures. This point is strongly felt as at the start of researching this topic my own country had, after a review of its support to international agencies, downgraded its support to the ILO on the basis of an inappropriate short-sighted criteria related to immediate anti-poverty impacts in countries. It advocates giving more attention to the functionaries and office holders in international organisations who against all odds stick to their purpose of improving the world. Finally, it advocates support for the recent October 2012 call by UN human rights rapporteurs for a Global Fund for Social Protection. I was taught by Richard Titmuss in 1965 that social policy as a subject was imbued with a 'commitment to welfare'. Today that commitment to welfare has to become global. The story of the SPF policy is an example of the commitment to global welfare of a number of individuals working within the UN system.

Why do I characterise the SPF Recommendation as historic? The Recommendation is historic because, in the words of its main protagonist inside the ILO:

- it asserts that the ILO has a role in formulating social protection policy for residents and citizens, not just workers;
- it challenged the growth-first economists with the priority of social protection whatever the level of the economy;
- it argues for redistribution nationally and internationally;

- it challenged the equity-efficiency trade-off economists with the case that equity supports efficiency;
- it saw off the initial objections of countries such as the UK and the United States (US), and won support from the wiser councils of Brazil, France, many Latin America and African countries and, perhaps reluctantly, even India.

Just as I am not primarily a theorist, nor am I primarily a methodologist. But convention dictates that I should explain how I undertook this study. The methods used to obtain material for the analysis extend from participant observation, through observation, documentary analysis, interviews, casual conversations and eves-dropping. I participated in some of the meetings referred to in Chapter Two describing the emergence of a broad case and coalition for universal social policies designed to counter the negative impacts of globalisation. I have interviewed, had lunch with or otherwise obtained information from key individuals who were working for or had worked or acted as consultants for the World Bank, UNICEF, WHO, United Nations Development Programme (UNDP), ILO European Commission and elsewhere. However, the core of the research undertaken for this book was carried out during a period of six months spent at the ILO between September 2011 and February 2012, the period when the draft SPF Recommendation was being formulated and countries were being consulted about its content. This period also coincided with the publication of the Bachelet Report (ILO, 2011d) advocating the SPF and also relevant meetings of the G20, World Bank and UNDP, with which the ILO was closely linked. Subsequently, I attended the historic 2012 ILC as an observer. The residence within the Social Security Department was made possible by an ILO Social Dialogue Department visiting research fellowship, which I happened to win through open competition for which I am most grateful. During those six months I had access to some, although not all, papers I would not have been able to access otherwise. The ILO still kept some of its internal meetings closed, such as for example those between the Social Security Department and the Workers' and Employers' Bureaus and the one in which the final details of the SPF Recommendation to be put to the 2012 conference was written. As the liaison person for the Workers' Bureau said quoting Bismarck: there are two things you should never see being made, sausages and law. Equally I was not of course able to attend the Sherpa meetings with which the ILO was involved in the run-up to the G20 at Cannes and subsequently Mexico. On a day-to-day basis in regular conversations with individuals within the Social

Security Department and some from outside it I think I was able to build up a reasonably accurate picture of processes, policies, priorities and roles pertaining to the SPF emerging Recommendation.[1] It is for others to modify and improve on my account or to challenge it.

While the focus of this book is often the words in documents about the SPF, the understanding of the meaning of these words becomes apparent only by complementing their study either with interviews with their authors or by ethnographic study of the locations and contexts within which the words were drafted: 'Documents are not to be analyzed as dead artifacts; they are alive with the social processes that produced them.... Documents contain hidden relational baggage; statements are best understood as bargaining positions in ongoing disputes over policy within or between professional teams or as negotiating positions for future disagreements' (Mosse, 2011: 12–17). While sitting inside the offices of the ILO I tried to apply this approach to my examination of the texts being drafted and redrafted before me.

Subsequently, drafts of the sections of this book were commented on by Social Security Department members by which process greater accuracy was ensured. If I became aware of anything about the problems of researching processes such as these it was that even being resident does not give the researcher insight into the myriad informal meetings, lunch-time and toilet conversations, telephone calls and email exchanges that take place and *do* influence events and policy content. *Researchers are impossibly outside the loops and those in the loops do not see from inside one loop other equally significant loops and rarely have the time to reflect on their own role.* This account will reflect only some of what happened but I believe that it captures enough of it to be a plausible account of the dynamics of making global social policy on which theorising is possible and evaluation can be made.

To recap, the questions posed that this study sought to provide answers to were:

- Who had influence inside the ILO and how was it used in order to win the institution over to promulgating the SPF Recommendation for all residents?
- Who were the players and what were the means used so that the ILO did to some extent succeed in generating greater policy synergy between international organisations in the UN around the concept of the SPF?
- What shifted in the global political context between 2000 and 2012 to overcome, in effect, the objection of many in the Global South to

a set of global social policy principles perceived earlier as emerging from and reflecting only the interests of the Global North?

This book is, however, more than a case study. It has enabled me to revisit my book *Global Social Policy and Governance* (Deacon, 2007) and reassess both the explanations I offered then about how global social policy is formed and changed and the predictions I made then about the likely developments that were to take place in global social governance. While not a second edition of *Global Social Policy and Governance*, the present book is a sequel addressing in an updated way the concerns of that book. In the final chapter I examine some of what I predicted then in the light of subsequent events.

The structure of the book is as follows. Chapter Two recalls the global economic, social structural and social policy context within which this story is set. It revisits briefly the lost years of neoliberal globalisation, the setbacks of structural adjustment, the failed efforts to establish a social reformist globalisation and the economic crisis beginning in 2008. It contrasts the emergence since 2000 of a social protection revolution in the Global South with the limitation of the poverty focused Millennium Development Goals (MDGs). It also describes the diverse ways in which professionals and technical experts inside the ILO between 2000 and 2005 sought to address the problem that wage-related formal contributory social security schemes covered only a small minority of the world's workers. The chapter draws attention to three ideas that existed then for extending social security, namely one that would extend social security using micro finance and cooperative forms of insurance, a second that argued for a basic income as the underpinning of socioeconomic security replacing conventional social security and third the strategy that was to be pursued of focusing on the promulgation of an ILO convention or recommendation on a SPF for residents.

Chapter Three tells the story of the development of the SPF concept from initial conceptualisation in the context of debates about the need for a global social floor through to its being accepted as ILO policy. It examines how, en route to acceptance, compromises had to be made and changes in thinking introduced. These shifts included the shift of the SPF from being a defined *benefit package* to a set of *guarantees*, the shift from the SPF being a *global social floor* to being a set of *national social protection floors* and from it being a *global social contract* to something that would be essentially a *national responsibility*.

Chapter Four tells the story of the passage through the ILO decision-making processes of the SPF from concept to ILO recommendation.

There is an initial discussion of why getting agreement of the ILO to the SPF would be a challenge in the context of the tripartite governance structure of the ILO. It then describes and analyses how the policy was steered through the 2011 and 2012 ILCs to final acceptance.

Chapter Five looks outwards from the ILO and asks and demonstrates how the SPF became a rallying point for the struggle for global social policy synergy, that is for the struggle to ensure that all UN agencies, including the World Bank and the IMF, sung from the same songbook and lined up behind tackling the shortcomings of market-driven globalisation with a plan to construct a social floor under the global economy. It shows how the ILO influenced the UN initially through UNCEB; how it influenced the G8 and then the G20 under the French Presidency of 2011; and how as a consequence it came to be able to try to influence the World Bank and the IMF. It ends by explaining how the ILO was able to play a major role, alongside UNICEF and the UNDP, in bringing it all together in the form of a new UN Social Protection Inter-Agency Cooperation Board. The limitations of this apparent success are also noted.

Chapter Six then uses this case study to address the theoretical and analytical questions concerned with how we can explain global social policy change and development. The chapter suggests that the emergence of the SPF can be understood as an outcome of the interplay of specific *actors and agencies*, often individuals, working within constraining and influencing *social structures* and more importantly path-dependent *institutional pressures* and shifting *discourses* to bring about both institutional and policy change, often helped by a good dose of contingent luck.

Chapter Seven concludes by evaluating the SPF Recommendation and examines the extent to which the concept is now embedded within the UN system and is informing the post-2015 MDG agenda. It reviews the emergence of a broad civil society Coalition for the Social Protection Floor and advances the case for a Global Fund for Social Protection. The developments described in this book are then used as a basis for reflecting on the predictions made about the future of global social governance and the prospects for the global social reformist project argued for in my 2007 book on *Global Social Policy and Governance* (Deacon, 2007).

The two parallel stories told in this book – the internal ILO process and the external ILO context and influences – refer to a very large number of meetings, events, official publications and initiatives. To help the reader through this is a summary table of the key events and dates (see Table 1.1). It might help to refer back to it when lost in some detail or other, especially within Chapters Two, Three, Four and Five.

Table 1.1: Timeline of key events associated with the SPF

Year: month	SPF ILO internal process	SPF ILO external influence and context
1999-2005	Socio-Economic Security Programme	
2000		"Social floor of global economy" and "global social floor" terms first used by ILO DG and member of Social Security dept in separate external communications.
2001	ILC decides to launch a campaign to extend social security	
2003	Extension of social security campaign launched	
2004		ILO's World Commission on Social Dimension of Globalization Report published calling for a "global socio-economic floor"
2005	"Basic Social Protection Package" defined by Social Security dept.	
2006	"Global Social Security Floor" term used within Social Security dept.	Townsend et al, meeting of key experts held in September 2006 in Geneva; defined the basic package
2007	Case articulated by Social Security dept for a new ILO convention on income security	Steps to build a coalition for a global social floor, with other un agencies and civil society organisations.
2008	Basic social security floor redefined as set of guaranteed outcomes not specific benefits	Coalition's campaign for a global social floor; presentations at the UN, Doha Conference on Financing for Development, and other meetings
2009 April		ILO DG ensures SPF becomes one of the nine UNCEB economic crisis response initiatives. SPF-I launched.
2009 June.		World Bank, ILO etc. annual "show and tell" event sets ILO's SPF-I against World Bank's safety net approach.

Year: month	SPF ILO internal process	SPF ILO external influence and context
2009 September	Tripartite meeting of experts agrees to two-pronged extension of social security strategy involving a horizontal SPF and a vertical social security staircase.	
2009 October.		UN SPF-I meeting in Turin of several UN agencies, World Bank and civil society organisations agree a strategic framework for promoting the SPF.
2010 June	ILC agrees social security will be discussed at 2011 conference	
2010 August		First meeting of SPF-I Advisory Board chaired by Bachelet, established by DG.
2010 November		UNCEB SPF-I second meeting and UNDP-ILO South–South development expo
2011 March		UNCEB SPF-I small workshop. Second meeting of SPF-I Advisory Board
2011 June	ILC agrees to discuss setting a new standard in 2012: it will be a Recommendation on social protection *floors*	Joint ILO-UNDP report on social protection, required by Seoul 2010 G20, produced for G20 Development Group. (calls for better inter-agency coordination for SPF-I points to the example of the High Level Task Force on Global Food Security).
2011 September	Social security dept publishes a draft Recommendation on SPFs in the form of a questionnaire to governments	First limited edition issue of Bachelet Report on SPF hurriedly published for G20 Labour Ministers meeting purpose. G20 Labour Ministers endorse call for SPFs
2011 October		Bachelet Report published. (inconsequential meeting of UNCEB) (side meeting agrees next SPF-I meeting to be convened by UNICEF in Feb 2012)

Year: month	SPF ILO internal process	SPF ILO external influence and context
2011 November	Deadline for responses to SPF Recommendation questionnaire	G20 Cannes endorses SPFs concept "adapted to the circumstances of each country" and calls on "international organizations, especially the UN, WTO, the ILO, the WB, the IMF and the OECD, to enhance their dialogue and cooperation, including on the social impact of economic policies, and to intensify their cooperation"
2011 December		An ILO-convened meeting with UN agencies and World Bank accepts a non-paper by Gabriele Kohler and agrees to consider a UN coordinating mechanism based on the format of the *High Level Task Force on Global Food Security* and a new Social Protection Knowledge Platform located at UNDP Centre in Brazil
2012 February	Summary of responses to questionnaire produced by Social Security dept and Draft Recommendation on SPFs published for consideration at ILC 2012	Fourth SPF-I inter-agency meeting takes place in New York hosted by UNICEF. Head of ILO Social Security Department addresses Civil Society Meeting on SPF on fringe of the Commission for Social Development
March 2012		World Bank new Social Protection and Labor Strategy published. It will support countries wishing to develop a SPF. UNICEF's Social Protection Strategic Framework published. It will support the SPF as a first step towards a SP system
April 2012		Launch of joint UNICEF-ILO etc SocialProtectionFloor-Gateway web site
May 2012		G20 Mexico Labour Ministers welcome SPF developments
May/June 2012	ILC 2012 agrees form of words of Recommendation on SPFs	G20 Mexico Summit continues to endorse the SPF.
June 2012		High level panel of experts report on social protection for food security is published.[1]
July 2012		First meeting of the Social Protection Inter-Agency Cooperation Board

Year: month	SPF ILO internal process	SPF ILO external influence and context
September 2012		FES seminar with civil society organizations to promote the SPF. Formation of the *Coalition for the Social Protection Floor*[2]
October 2012	Juan Somavia retires from position as DG of ILO, Guy Ryder takes over.	Second meeting of the Social Protection Inter Agency Cooperation Board (agenda makes no reference to SPFs)
October 2012		UN Human Rights Rapporteurs call for a Global Fund for Social Protection (GFSP)[3]
November 2012	ILO publishes its social security strategy for building social protection floors and social security systems	
December 2012.	Michael Cichon retires from ILO. Replacement appointment awaited	Michael Cichon takes up presidency of the ICSW

Notes

[1] Not strictly an instance of the ILO external influence, rather an example of an external actor potentially influencing the future of the SPF.

[2] As 1 above.

[3] As 1 above

TWO

The global economic and social policy context

Introduction

As we shall see in the next chapters, it was not until 2012 that the ILO agreed to recommend to countries that they establish SPFs. We shall also see that it was not until 2005 that the first real steps were taken inside the ILO to bring this about. The concept of some sort of global social floor was not formulated until 2000. However, the context that gave rise to the *need* for such a policy and the *opportunity* to get it agreed reaches back to the 1980s and 1990s. Only by understanding the impact of the neoliberal globalisation project both on the actuality of embryonic welfare states in Africa, Latin America and South Asia (as well as on post-Communist social policy) and on the global debates about desirable national social policy can we understand why, by 2000, a counter move had developed to repair the damage done to the idea of welfare states and to (re)establish the principle of universalism as a cornerstone of progressive global and national social policies. This chapter provides an overview of this recent history.

The chapter proceeds through six steps. First, it outlines the challenge that took place in the 1980s and 1990s to universal welfare states and to the universal social policy principles with which they were associated. Here we see the birth and subsequent dominance of the residual targeted safety-net policy of the World Bank, which challenged fundamentally the Bismarckian wage-related state social security policies that protected formal workers and with which the ILO had traditionally been associated. Second, we see the emergence of a counter project driven by global social reformists and social development experts seeking to re-establish the case for universal social policies within a development context. Third, we observe a significant fracture among the global forces seeking to defend these earlier social security achievements between those, mainly in the Global North, who were perceived by many in the Global South as social protectionists, wanting to conserve these largely northern country welfare states against competition from low-wage-cost economies in the Global South. Fourth, we observe the rebirth of a new form of social policy universalism from below within large parts of the Global South exemplified by the development both of conditional cash transfer programmes providing social transfers to families to encourage school and health clinic attendance and of universal categorical social pensions. These developments enabled a dialogue to be re-established across the North–South divide about the best way to work for the principle of universal social security coverage in the 21st century. Fifth, we shall see how this renewed debate about how to extend social security coverage globally became polarised between different ideas and fractions. There were those who argued that in developing countries new forms of non-state mutual insurance schemes would be needed to extend coverage to the informal sectors. There were those who argued that the days of defending state wage-related social security benefits were numbered in an automated and global economy, creating flexible and insecure labour such that a new citizen's income was needed. And there were those who argued that the new universalism from below represented by conditional cash transfers should be generalised to provide an SPF for all that could be combined with contributory wage-related social security for those still securely employed. Finally, we shall see that these debates entered the Social Security Department of the ILO itself between 2000 and 2005 until they were resolved by dint of reorganisation and promotions in 2005 effectively in favour of one of these approaches.

The era of targeted safety nets

The elections of Margaret Thatcher in the UK (1979) and Ronald Reagan (1981) in the US marked a trend towards the Right that was to impact on social policy thinking and practice across the countries of the Organisation for Economic Co-operation and Development (OECD) and beyond. The 'golden age of universal welfare states built across Europe and their embryonic counterparts in Latin America and the emerging post-colonial countries would come under challenge. Equally important was the onset of the debt crisis after 1982. The crisis started in Latin America when Mexico reneged on its debt repayments for previous loans, but was evident in many African countries as well. Rising interest rates, the second oil shock, and the slowdown in the global economy in the early 1980s reversed the large flow of private lending that had gone to developing countries in the 1970s. This scarcity of private capital flows increased the leverage of the IMF and World Bank over developing country policy.

A new orthodoxy emerged, dubbed the 'Washington Consensus'. This new approach argued that the debt crisis had been the result of inward-oriented, state-led development strategies of developing countries in the 1950s and 1960s. The problems of the developing countries were not shortage of capital, but policies that concentrated resources in the public sector, distorted incentives to the private sector and limited trade and foreign investment. A crucial innovation of the debt crisis period was the rapid growth of 'structural adjustment' lending by the World Bank and the IMF. Such lending was extended not in support of particular projects, but in support of policy reform. These reforms included macroeconomic policy adjustments – fiscal, monetary and exchange rate policy – and a variety of other measures as well, from privatisation to trade liberalisation and financial sector reform.

Over the 1980s, the scope of policy conditionality within these structural adjustment loans widened dramatically, and encompassed a number of social policy issues. This emphasis on policy conditionality continued well into the 1990s as the World Bank became deeply involved also in policy lending to Eastern Europe and the newly independent republics of the former Soviet Union. It was the perceived negative impact of this period of structural adjustment on the prospects for people living in poverty and for the sustainability of social services in developing countries that led to the beginnings of a challenge to such structural adjustment lending. This began with criticism by Cornia et al (1987) in a UNICEF report entitled *Adjustment with a Human Face*. Partly in consequence, the World Bank's report on poverty in 1990 (World Bank, 1990) began the period where the World Bank was to declare that its prime goal was actually that of poverty alleviation. In 1991 the policy paper *Assistance Strategies to Reduce Poverty* (World Bank, 1991) was published. This was followed in 1992 by the *Poverty Reduction Handbook* (World Bank, 1992). By 1993 the World Bank was able to claim in its annual report that the share of adjustment lending that addressed social issues climbed from 5% in fiscal 1984-86 to 50% in fiscal 1990-92. The World Bank thus became heavily involved in policy-based lending to try to reduce poverty in poor countries, and indeed in post-communist Eastern Europe after 1989. Of concern here is the *content* of that anti-poverty policy. The World Bank wanted to continue with its preferred approach of limiting public expenditure on what it regarded as at best premature or at worst undesirable public sector social protection systems while supporting people living in poverty. At issue was what to do with poor people who should be helped without jeopardising the economic requirements and constraints of adjustment.

Faced with this problem, the World Bank, the IMF and other external donors encouraged governments to protect poor people but urged them to stand firm against the demands of the labour unions and urban classes. In essence, a *social safety-net approach* to poverty alleviation was being constructed that had echoes of US residual social policy. As Carol Graham, who was then a visiting fellow at the World Bank in the Vice Presidency for Human Resources, put it on the dust-jacket of *Safety Nets, Politics and the Poor* (Graham, 1994):

> Rather than focus their efforts on organised interest groups – such as public sector unions – which have a great deal to lose in the process of reform, governments might better concentrate their efforts on poor groups that have rarely, if ever, received benefits from the state. The poor, meanwhile, may gain a new stake in the ongoing process of economic and public sector reform through organising to solicit the state for safety net benefits.

Against organised labour, against European corporatist social security policies that had been exported to Latin America, and for very poor people; that was the political strategy of the dominant anti-poverty thinking in the World Bank. An alliance was to be struck between the World Bank and INGOs such as Oxfam who have an interest in being involved in attempts to reach the poorest people living in poverty. One element of this focus on people living in poverty became the social funds that were championed by the World Bank 'as a mechanism for mitigating the social costs of structural adjustment' (Foli and Beland, forthcoming). These were established with donor money as semi-autonomous budgets set up to bypass government social security departments and to address directly the needs of people living in poverty. However, they were subsequently criticised (Hall and Midgeley, 2004: 274) on four counts:

- they often did not reach people living in poverty but instead proactive non-governmental organisations (NGOs);
- they were not mainstreamed into government anti-poverty policy;
- they became substitutes for government expenditure so that if a social fund was active in health provision, the equivalent government budget line might be cut;
- they were not linked to funding sources that were sustainable in the long term.

In terms of social policy in a development context I concluded (Deacon, 1997) that the opportunity created by the collapse of the communist project was grasped enthusiastically by the World Bank. In alliance with social development NGOs, a social safety-net future was being constructed. This approach I concluded 'was challenging powerfully those defenders of universal social security based welfare states to be found in the EU [European Union] and the ILO' (Deacon, 1997: 197). Thus, the World Bank's role in shaping and damaging national social policy in a development and transition context was very important in the 1980s and 1990s. Its insistence on user charges prevented access to education and health. Its beneficiary index demonstrating that public spending often benefited those other than people living in poverty was used in effect to undermine the embryonic welfare states of Africa, Latin America and South Asia. The losers would be the urban middle class who had depended on state universities and hospitals and pensions. One element of this development was of course the pension policy and practice of the World Bank. Orenstein (2008) has reported the way in which the World Bank's preference for private, defined contribution pensions was to lead to the partial replacement in many countries of Latin America and Eastern Europe of the state, public, defined-benefit pensions by such private schemes.

Voipio (2011: 104) argues that the structural adjustment drive

> was motivated not only by the World Bank and IMF economists' objective analysis about what would be best for the poor countries and their poor people, but also by a deliberate ideologically motivated effort to *re-frame* the idea of "aid-for-poverty reduction" into an instrument for promoting the *paradigm* of pro-market/anti-government neoliberalism and the political *programme* for privatisation, deregulation and liberalisation aimed at extending the "free global markets" to as many countries of the world as possible ... the smaller the governments would be in the various countries of the world, the better it would be for the transnational corporations.

But, as Voipio (2011: 105) also notes, '[b]y the turn of the new Millennium this "minimalist state ideal" had, however, become discredited'. It is to that challenge to the hegemony of the safety-net paradigm that we now turn.

The struggle to re-establish universalism

The intellectual and social movement opposition to the worst aspects of neoliberal globalisation and the associated structural adjustment policies took many forms and happened in many locations. It is beyond the scope of this section to review all of these developments. For those wanting a general account, Held's (2004) *Global Covenant: The Social Democratic Alternative to the Washington Consensus* might be referred to. Our focus here is on the emergence of oppositional ideas focused on social policy and social service provision, in particular on ideas about universal provision and universal coverage and the importance of state-not market-led social policies that were to re-emerge within social movements, within UN agencies, even to some extent within the World Bank, but never in the IMF during the late 1990s and early 2000s.

The UN social agencies such as the ILO, WHO, United Nations Educational, Scientific and Cultural Organization (UNESCO), UNICEF and to a far lesser extent UNDP did represent one locus of oppositional ideas to those being promulgated by the World Bank and IMF. This story was told in *Global Social Policy and Governance* (Deacon, 2007). In terms of the global dispute about pension policy, I showed there (2007: 170) that:

> the ILO fought long and hard to expose what it regarded as flaws in the dominant World Bank thinking on pensions by arguing that there was no demographic imperative leading to privatisation, that the European-type schemes are reformable and sustainable, and that the privatisation strategy is merely a cover to increase the share of private capital savings.

More generally, I drew attention (2007: 171) to:

> something approaching a 'war of position' between those agencies and actors within them who have argued for a more selective, residual role for the state together with a larger role for private actors in health, social protection and education provision and those who took the opposite view.... It does seem, in 2006, that the tide has turned against the targeting and privatising view, and the opportunity now exists for the UN working with sympathetic donors such as the Scandinavians and some other European countries

to begin to undo the damage wrought by the Bank over the past decades.

It was not to be as straight forward as this, however. On the one hand the UN system did seem to provide a counterbalance to the World Bank and IMF and this was symbolically represented by the 1995 UN Copenhagen Social Summit, chaired significantly in terms of the story in this book by Juan Somavia. That summit concluded with 10 commitments embracing poverty eradication, full employment and social integration. Most important was the commitment to 'promote and attain the goals of universal and equitable access to quality education, the highest attainable standard of physical and mental health and the access of all to primary health care' (United Nations, 1995: 18). However, five years later the same UN, but in the form of an announcement of a policy cooked up behind the curtains rather than deliberated on by a full conference, announced the instigation of the MDGs, which were to be met by 2015. These goals focused on alleviating poverty and were couched in such a way as to further encourage the perpetuation of social policies targeted on people living in poverty. In that sense they facilitated the continuation of what I have called 'the global politics of poverty alleviation' rather than 'the global politics of social solidarity' (Deacon and Cohen, 2011: 234). The struggle to secure the idea that social security and social services such as health and education should be provided by governments to all their citizens or residents could not just rely on the UN social agencies alone.

Within this context, several scholarly and civil society initiatives got under way, joining forces with sympathetic social development advisors in donor countries and with sympathetic international civil servants within UN agencies, to advance the case for a return to universalism of social provision within national and global social policy thinking. The Globalism and Social Policy Programme (GASPP) between 1997 and 2004 convened annual GASPP seminars, which brought together progressive social policy thinkers in academia and development agencies and international organisations. Individuals in the OECD Development Assistance Committee's Social Development Advisers' Network kept many outside that network informed of developments. A team of like-minded colleagues in the UN's Department of Economic and Social Affairs produced UN social policy advice to counter World Bank thinking (Ortiz, 2007). The campaigning work of the International Council on Social Welfare (ICSW) to shape the UN agenda on social issues was important. In 2006 in Kellokoski (Finland) an expert meeting entitled 'Social policies for development in a globalizing world' was held. This generated the document *New Consensus on Comprehensive Social Policies for Development* (Wimann et al, 2006: 12), which asserted: 'Universal policies, expanding coverage of social services, health insurance and social pensions are a crucial priority in efforts to achieve socially sustainable development.' The meeting was attended by experts from major donors (Canada, Finland, Germany, Norway, Sweden and the UK Department for International Development – DFID), several UN agencies (ILO, the International Social Security Association – ISSA, UNDESA, UNICEF, UNRISD and World Bank), representatives of global civil society (ICSW and HelpAge International) and several African governments. The campaign for a cash transfer approach to social protection and in particular for universal social pensions in Africa led by HelpAge International was a significant contribution to this shift in ideas and discourse. Somewhat separate from this network was the research work of UNRISD on social policy in a development context involving many scholars located in the Global South. Its first publication (Mkandawire, 2005) echoed the critique by others of structural adjustment–driven safety-net social policy.

Overlapping attendance at several of the above meetings, frequency of email communications, longstanding friendships and trust built up over several years of *flying into global policy spaces* and nurtured over time in saunas and restaurants on the fringes of UN and academic conferences define the network. Silent support with funding and other forms of backing from sympathetic governments helped to maintain the emerging network. Of special importance here is Finland and Sweden. Viopio, a member of many of these meetings, has analysed the wider contest of competing policy frames, paradigms and alternative social policy programmes within which this movement for universal social policies was situated. He argues (2011: 252) that:

> It is important to identify the key actors, to situate them correctly into 'schools-of-thought' or political or institutional 'camps', and to analyse their roles in generating, maintaining or changing the various theories, frames, programmes or public sentiments.... I have attempted to situate a number of key actors, real-life 'institutional entrepreneurs' in the policy struggles about global poverty reduction ... decision-makers, theorists, framers, constituents and brokers can be identified and named in Global Poverty Politics, and ... this analytic tool is a useful one.

The crystallisation out of from this broader progressive global social policy stream of the specific Global Policy Advocacy Coalition for a Global Social Floor can probably be dated to November 2007 when a bid was drafted for funds for a campaign to establish a Coalition for a Global Social Floor. Then it was envisaged that there would be 'an alliance of organisations united in the common pursuit of a fairer globalisation and the right to social security for all, driven by the conviction that a global social floor is achievable and essential to fast-track poverty reduction' (Coalition for a Global Social Floor, 2007: 2). We return to this story in later chapters (particularly Chapter Five) and find out how some of these ideas were subsequently brought inside the ILO and other UN agencies, leading to real global social policy change.

The North–South progressive impasse

It was to take until 2012 to achieve this significant global social policy change. Even though there was a movement around 2000 to advance these ideas as just described, nothing could be achieved at that point. Indeed, one such an attempt failed.[2] The-then UK Chancellor of the Exchequer, Gordon Brown, argued for a

> code of global best practice in social policy which will apply for every country, will set minimum standards and will ensure that when IMF and World Bank help a country in trouble the agreed programme of reform will preserve investments in the social, education, and employment programmes which are essential for growth. (Brown, 1999: 6)

Moreover, this code 'should not be seen in narrow terms as merely the creation of social safety nets. We should see it as creating opportunities for all by investing more not less in education, employment and vital public services' (1999: 1). Although initially referred to the World Bank, the World Bank agreed that further development of the principles of good practice in social policy was best pursued within the framework of the UN as part of the follow-up on the 1995 World Summit on Social Development.

The motive for this referral to the UN was concern on the part of some southern governments that the IMF and World Bank would use the new principles as a set of social conditions in the context of loans or debt relief. It was now for the UN and in particular the Preparatory Committee for the Copenhagen plus 5 meeting to be held in 2000 to do the technical work on this. The World Bank, in its initial deliberations, bequeathed a first draft to be built upon. It suggested that the principles should be based on:

- achieving universal and equitable access to basic social services, including access to quality basic education and health care;
- enabling all men and women to attain secure and sustainable livelihoods and decent working conditions;
- promoting systems of social protection;
- fostering social inclusion.

Interestingly, a background paper aimed at influencing these further deliberations was produced by staff of the DFID (Ferguson, 1999). Addressing the topic of global social policy and human rights, it argued that 'the global architecture of UN conventions, declarations, and world conference documents provide the most authoritative available source for the construction of these principles' (Ferguson, 1999: 3).

Alas, this seemingly (to Western social democratic eyes) fine initiative to help shift globalisation from a neoliberal project to one that respected a set of core social policy principles crashed to nothing in the back rooms of the UN Copenhagen plus 5 conference in 2000. A form of words that would have asked the UN to establish a working party to consider such a set of principles was rejected by a combination of poor and middle-income countries (Egypt, India, Indonesia and Pakistan among them) who argued that the West was being hypocritical in seeking to impose a set of principles on the South without being willing to fund the transfers of funds to enable them to be realised in practice. Furthermore, the South's experience of the Structural Adjustment Programmes of the 1980s had taught it that such principles would become a new conditionality in the context of either trade negotiations or debt relief. It was also argued that what might be regarded as desirable principles in one region or country might not be so regarded in another region or country. It marked a turning point in UN business. Progressive Northern thinking about a socially regulated globalisation was being rejected by the South in the name of the national sovereign right of countries to shape their own economic and social policies. At the time, I concluded:

> The impasse in the North–South debate about global social standards can only be overcome if the North is more committed to much greater North–South Transfers and if the South begins to own for itself a set of social policy

principles based on best practice appropriate to developing country conditions. (Deacon, 2000: 69)

Indeed we shall see in the next section that the second of these two requirements was indeed met between 2000 and the failed global social policy principles and 2012 when the SPF Recommendation was agreed. This development, described below, goes a long way to explaining how it was possible for Gordon Brown to fail in 2000 and for Michael Cichon to succeed in 2012. We shall also see, however, how the legacy and continuing reality of this North–South tension led to significant compromises on the way to securing the 2012 agreement.

New universalism from below within the Global South

Barrientos and Hulme (2008: 3) noted in 2008 that '[t]he concept and practice of social protection in developing countries have advanced at an astonishing pace over the last decade or so…. Social protection practice has also changed from a focus on short term social safety nets and social funds to a much broader armoury of policies and programmes.' This quiet revolution, as they term it, was the bottom-up rediscovery in the Global South of the importance of cash transfers, often distributed universally to categories of recipients, which were a necessary counterpart to the Northern-driven arguments for universal social protection that were described above. This process took place over several continents but of prime importance was the move within Latin America to establish conditional cash transfers encouraging school and clinic attendance and the move within Africa to establish social pensions, sometimes universally, which would serve also as a means of child support in an age where many grandchildren were cared for by grandparents because of the death from HIV and AIDS of parents.

The Latin American and Caribbean region was the starting point for this recent wave of cash transfer programmes. In relation to the rest of the developing world, the region has the most stable and long-running initiatives such as in the case of Brazil, Chile, Colombia and Mexico. Brazil's *Bolsa Família* is a conditional cash transfer programme designed to promote immediate poverty relief and to break the cycle of intergenerational poverty by providing subsidies to poor families who comply with health and education requirements. The programme started in 2004, encompassing the various federal conditional cash transfers, under one single database. Today it benefits 11 million families and is the largest in the world. In Mexico, *Oportunidades* is a federal conditional cash transfer programme designed to improve the development of individuals living in conditions of extreme poverty, with a special focus on the empowerment of women. Originally named *Progressa,* it provides support on health, nutrition, education and income through monthly grants directed to female heads of households. Is has three basic components, two of which are conditional (food support transfer conditional on attending training sessions on nutrition and health, as well as scholarships to children and young adults) and one is non-conditional (to older people).[3] This is not to say that there are no criticisms of the design and effectiveness of such schemes. There is a huge literature evaluating them, which is not the purpose of this short section to explore. The point in the context of this book is that historically, social protection in Latin America focused on workers in formal employment. The majority of the region's population was excluded from public social protection. The structural adjustment period described above resulted in rising poverty. The initial response to this was to introduce fragmented, often externally financed, safety nets and social funds. But by the mid-1990s, the new democratic governments had to engage with the strong popular demand for more universal forms of social protection.

Cash transfer programmes are now growing rapidly in Africa under broader social protection frameworks, most often with the support of donor organisations and multilateral agencies such as the UK's DFID, the Swedish International Development Cooperation Agency (SIDA), Germany's Organisation for Technical Cooperation (GTZ), UNICEF and the World Bank. Most of the programmes in Africa are in their early development stage. South Africa is an exception, with consolidated programmes that basically consist of cash transfers to different target groups (older people, orphans and so on). There are also the cases where there are longstanding cash transfer programmes in place, such as the *Programa de Subsídio de Alimentos* in Mozambique. Another highlight in the region is the case of non-contributory universal old-age pensions as in Lesotho. Within Africa we can observe the meeting of a Northern-driven Global Advocacy Coalition for Universal Social Pensions led by HelpAge International with these bottom-up home-grown initiatives of the Global South. In 2006, the African Union, in collaboration with the Government of Zambia and with the support of HelpAge International and the UK's DFID, organised the Livingstone Intergovernmental Conference on Social Protection where the main focus was on cash transfers. Several countries took part and compared their experiences.

Leutelt (2012) has shown how HelpAge International intervened in and helped to shape the agendas and outcomes of a series of Global and African Regional Meetings, culminating in the endorsement by the Africa Union in 2008 of its Social Policy Framework, which embodied the call to countries to establish universal forms of social pensions and other social protection developments. The stages led from the UN's 2002 Madrid International Plan of Action on Ageing, the 2002 African Union Policy Framework and Plan of Action on Ageing, the 2006 Livingstone Call for Action and the 2008 African Union Social Policy Framework for Africa agreed at the Africa Union's first ever meeting of social development ministers. Leutelt (2012: 31) concluded that:

> HAI's [HelpAge International] *slow and steady* engagement [enabled it] ... to influence the outcome of global conventions, to build up a large infrastructure of affiliates ... and to establish useful informal relationships to policy makers. In the end, to be influential on national policy-making spreading social pensions globally, HAI has to wait for appropriate *windows of opportunity* like favorable historical moments or political constellations. A long and steady engagement is necessary in order to *build a momentum* or to be prepared when windows of opportunity open.

The significance for us of the HelpAge International story is twofold. It reveals the emergence of a genuinely Global North–South and South–South process of social policy learning and transfer in the sphere of social pensions. It enabled those in the ILO seeking to advance the campaign for SPFs to counter any argument that this was another example of the imposition of Northern ideas on a reluctant South. It is also not without significance that HelpAge International was involved from the outset of the launch of the Global Policy Advocacy Coalition or Campaign for a Global Social Floor in 2007, to which we will return later.

ILO and visions for extending social security

The question that now follows is what was the ILO Social Security Department's response to these global developments? How did it envisage taking the opportunity to build on the challenge that was now being mounted to the earlier stage of safety-net structural adjustment? How would it respond to the emergence within the Global South of new forms of non-contributory cash transfers, which had no links to the contributory social security systems, covering only a small part of the population with which the ILO was historically associated? What new ideas for providing universal social protection coverage would be right in an age of globalisation?

Before beginning to answer these questions, perhaps a brief synopsis is needed of the role of the ILO historically in the global social policy-making process. The ILO derived its brief to set and keep common international labour and social standards from the social democratic climate of the period after the First World War when it was established. The ILO strategy has been to persuade governments by peer and moral pressure to sign up and ratify conventions of good practice in labour standards and social security. Only when governments ratify conventions has the ILO any power to seek an enforcement of them. Initially, the ILO conventions were concerned strictly with labour standards, although by 1934 Convention 44 required that those states ratifying the convention maintain a system of unemployment benefits or allowances. Just as the political climate of 1918-20 established the ILO, so did the next phase of social optimism in the wake of the Second World War provide greater scope for the work of the ILO. The Keynesian climate encouraged the ILO at its Philadelphia meeting in 1944 to declare the Convention on Freedom of Association and the Protection of the Right to Organise. The Declaration also asserted that lasting peace was only possible on the basis of social justice, and this required the right of human beings to economic security and equal opportunity. As a consequence, the ILO was to be responsible for 'examining and considering all international economic and financial policies and measures in the light of this fundamental objective' (Plant, 1994: 158). At the same time, the ILO was instrumental in enabling the UN to convert its 1948 Declaration of Human Rights into the 1966 Covenant on Economic, Social and Cultural Rights.

Throughout the 1950s, 1960s and 1970s, therefore, the ILO established a large number of conventions, which, if ratified, provided for a well-functioning system of social security. The conventions, nearly 200, cover employment policy, human resource development, social security, social policy, wage-fixing machinery, conditions of work, industrial relations, labour administration and the protection of women, children and indigenous peoples. An important emphasis in the internal workings of the ILO and in its policy prescriptions is tripartism, that good governance to secure social security requires the consensus of industry, workers and government. At that point the ILO could claim some success over the years of its existence. By 1994 the average number of ratifications per country had reached 41 (ILO, 1995: 115).

Alongside the obvious achievements of the ILO in laying down labour and social standards was the criticism levelled at it that the ILO remained essentially an organisation concerned to protect *workers* as distinct from *citizens or even residents*. The core social security standard of the ILO – Convention 102, which dealt with contributory social insurance schemes – still only applied to a small fraction of the world's workers. The low level of coverage in Latin America had been one of the reasons why the World Bank could challenge such contributory systems in the name of people living in poverty. However, while the so-called first-generation standards, those adopted before the Second World War, were only about social insurance, this had actually changed with the post-war adoption of Recommendations 67 and 69. These documents speak clearly about providing income security and medical care *to all*. The same can be said to apply to the so-called higher-level standards adopted later, covering specific areas of social security – health care, old-age, disability, survivorship, employment injury, unemployment and maternity. All these instruments it can be shown were aimed at all. The problem was perhaps not so much in the standards but in the way they were for decades interpreted and implemented – mainly as social insurance instruments – because those in the informal economy were not organised and not able to lobby for their rights. Indeed, it was the historical precedent of Recommendations 67 and 69 that was to form the basis of the case that the new 2012 SPF Recommendation should apply to *all residents and children*.

So how did the ILO respond to the challenge that was being mounted in the 1990s to the earlier stage of safety-net structural adjustment? In fact, the ILO response was complicated by a major organisational change at the ILO introduced in 2000 by the new director-general, Juan Somavia. Until 2001 the ILO had a *single* Social Security Department (headed since the beginning of the 1990s by Colin Gillion) with two branches: Social Security Policy and Development Branch (SOC/POL) and Social Security Financial, Actuarial and Statistical Branch (SOC/FAS). Questions of standards and legal issues were in SOC/POL where Ursula Kulke, who figures later in this story, was located. Michael Cichon was chief of SOC/FAS from 1995 when he returned from the ILO Budapest office. Emmanuel Reynaud became chief of SOC/POL in 1998.

However, in 2001 the two Social Security Department sections became a smaller part of a new larger division named, misleadingly, the Social Protection Division (Standing, 2008: 372). A former African minister was appointed as executive director in charge of social protection. It was a large and complex department with seven subdivisions, three of which are particularly relevant from the point of view of our analysis of what happened next. In effect, within this broad social protection sector there were now *three* new heads of sections, all having some stake in the future of ILO social security and social protection. Emmanuel Reynaud was head of SOC/POL or Policy and Development. Guy Standing arrived from heading the ILO's East European office in 1999 and was in charge of the new Socio-Economic Security work programme. Finally, Michael Cichon was head of SOC/FAS, which was concerned with actuarial and financing issues. As the text written in the context of the ILO Century Project noted: 'The Social Protection sector ... was at the time divided into different programmes, conducted by separate units, each with its own approach, which made it difficult to develop a unified approach' (Rodgers et al, 2009: 168).

Each of these three sub-departments articulated and introduced policies and practices that embodied alternative responses to the challenges posed by neoliberal globalisation to the ILO's existing social security policy. The problems perceived by each were not dissimilar. The ILO had been wedded to the idea that its standard setting policy, which had focused on Social Security Convention 102 dealing with wage-related contributory benefits of formal workers, would in time apply to more and more of the world's population. In fact, this was not happening. Not only were poorer countries not following this assumed modernisation path, the very idea of the tripartite-managed, wage-related social security system had come under severe pressure even in its heartlands of Europe and Latin America. In-formalisation and precariousness, rather then formalisation, were growing in the labour markets of the world. Poverty was not being eradicated although, as we have seen, innovative forms of cash transfer schemes were being put in place. Something needed to be done if the ILO was not going just to preside over a smaller and smaller section of the world's social protection system focused as it was on still seeking to get more countries to adopt Convention 102 and expand formal social security schemes. The three rather different approaches that emerged are described briefly below.

Extending social security to all

In 1999 the governing body of the ILO decided that the 2001 ILC should discuss social security policy. No such discussion had been held since 1993. It fell to Reynaud to lead the preparation for this conference. He contributed significantly to the World Labour Report of 2000, entitled *Income Security and Social Protection in a Changing World*

(ILO, 2000a). Many of the ideas of this report found expression in the report to the 2001 conference prepared in late 2000 (ILO, 2000b). Roger Beattie, who had co-authored an earlier paper challenging the World Bank's pension policy, also contributed but died suddenly in August 2001. The ideas also drew on an earlier book by van Ginneken (1999) entitled *Social Security for the Excluded Majority*, who wrote Chapters 7, 8, 9 and 10 of the World Labour Report. The focus of the report was how to extend social security to more people not already covered, including those in the informal economy. Four approaches were considered:

- extending social insurance schemes;
- encouraging micro insurance;
- introducing universal benefits or services financed from general state revenues;
- establishing means-tested benefits or services.

The report favoured the first approach where possible, spoke positively about the prospects for micro-insurance schemes particularly for health, instancing the Self-Employed Women's Movement (SEWA) in India as a frontrunner, favoured universal services and was very critical of means-tested benefits for all the standard reasons. The report was written before the subsequent explosion of conditional cash transfer policies in Latin America. Conference discussion of the report gave rise to the conclusion that '[a] major campaign should be launched in order to promote the extension of coverage of social security' (ILO, 2001: 5).

Only in June 2003 was such a campaign launched. The website from that time (www.ilo.org/coverage4all) stated that the first phase of the campaign would last until 2006. During this period the objective was to place, in as many countries as possible, the extension of social security at the top of the development agenda and to support national and international policy makers in developing strategies to extend coverage. Wouter van Ginneken, who was appointed campaign director, reported in 2004 (van Ginneken, 2004) that 'by end of 2003 eighteen papers had been published. Thirteen of them are country case-studies that show how various developing countries have been successful in the extension of social security in programmes, such as social health insurance and tax-financed pensions.'

A significant element of the extension campaign focused on the prospects for micro insurance and third sector innovative ways of extending coverage through mutual insurance associations. This aspect of the work drew on the already existing Strategies and Tools against

Social Inclusion and Poverty (STEP) programme within the ILO. This had its origins in work by colleagues in Africa, funded by Belgium and Portugal. According to an old ILO STEP website (www.ilo.org/public/english/protection/secsoc/areas/step.htm), among STEP's pioneering approaches, its work on the development of community-based social protection schemes (such as micro insurance, mutual health organisations and so on) has been 'hailed as a promising perspective for poor populations excluded from formal systems in particular in the least developed countries'. The 'official history' (Rodgers et al, 2009: 168) noted that the STEP programme, financed by Belgium and Portugal, was operating by then in over 40 countries. It actually and curiously had quite a lot in common with some of the micro credit and social funds used by the World Bank in the 1990s.

In 2005 there was another reorganisation of the Social Protection Division and Reynaud's and Cichon's sections were merged once more into a new all-embracing Social Security Department to which Cichon was appointed head. Had Reynaud taken the helm of the merged sections instead of Cichon, he said[4] he would have continued his work on extending social security by these means. Alas, his ideas only found expression in a special issue of the *Comparative Labor Law and Policy Journal* published after he was no longer at the helm (Reynaud, 2006). Here we find the articulation of the concept of Framework Agreements on the Extension of Social Protection, which would be drawn up between the ILO and individual countries. Such agreements would supplement the system of declarations, conventions and recommendations.

> We tried to design a legal mechanism likely to encourage member countries to draw up a national social security strategy. This strategy has to be rooted not only in the guiding principles of social security as set out in existing standards, but it also has to start from each country's particular situation. (Supiot, 2006: 120-1)

Or again, as the introduction to the special issue of the journal devoted to the subject put it (Javiliier et al, 2006: ix-x):

> The main idea is to have a contractual mechanism comprising a framework agreement drawn up by the ILO, and national agreements concluded between the ILO, the State concerned, and, where appropriate, other partners, with a view to developing and implementing a national

plan for extending social protection. The proposals combine the universal nature of standards with the definition of a common set of core values, principles, and objectives that everyone has to adopt, and a range of ways of implementing these in practice, depending on different national situations and choices. They thus bypass the conflict between hard law and soft law in that, by defining a method for developing national plans, they make soft law complement hard law and enable it to be applied effectively in very different realities and situations. These proposals mark a real advance in thinking about the role of law and standard-related activities at international level, and were welcomed by constituents of the ILO to which they were presented in March 2005.

Such plans would be drawn up in an inclusive way and involve representatives of mutual aid organisations. According to Supiot (2006), the framework agreements would have been couched within the guiding principles of dignity, solidarity, equality and participation.

Basic income as socioeconomic security

Guy Standing on the other hand arrived back[5] at ILO headquarters having been involved with Somavia's transition team, believing Somavia as the new ILO director-general to be a force for radical change within the ILO. The experience of chairing the Copenhagen Social Summit would mean that Somavia would open up a space for the involvement of newer civil society activists and new agendas focused on unpaid work and informal workers. His and other observers' hopes were to be a little dimmed as the tripartite structure of the ILO reigned in some of these aspirations with regard to civil society involvement, which will be discussed in Chapter Five (Baccaro and Mele, 2012). Nevertheless, Standing set up with much enthusiasm and hope the InFocus Programme on Socio-Economic Security (IFPSES), which was to reach out to the newer movements such as SEWA in India. He also reached out to women's groups more generally in support of the project to get labour replaced by work, including domestic work, in ILO parlance. The ILO use of the term 'decent work' and not decent labour he claims as one of his achievements.[6]

The IFPSES work programme had a broad brief concerning insecurities and how to address them. It formulated the concept of 'seven forms of security', which would be needed for decent work to be a reality:

- labour market security;
- employment security;
- work security;
- job security;

- skill reproduction security;
- income security;
- representation security.

During its lifetime, the programme undertook major surveys of the extent of these insecurities in a number of countries, convened a number of global conferences and produced quite an extensive set of publications. These included a book on South Africa and the basic income grant (Standing and Samson, 2003) and the 2002 Basic Income Earth Network (BIEN) Congress, which Somavia addressed. *Care Work: The Quest for Security* (Daly, 2002) became influential in later policy developments in the field of care workers. The programme's final flagship report *Economic Security for a Better World* (ILO, 2004a) argued for new forms of universalistic social protection such as categorical cash benefits. The report was sharply critical of several of the conventional schemes for attacking income insecurity, such as social funds, means-tested benefits, public works and micro credit of the kind Reynaud was associated with. It suggested on the basis of their already existing reality that there were a number of promising avenues to universal income security. Among these were (ILO, 2004a: 380-9):

- *Social pension*: 'If a pension were set at about 20 per cent of the average earned income, it is fiscally feasible and would cost about 1–2 per cent of GDP [gross domestic product].'
- *Minimum-income-with-schooling schemes*: 'The success of cash-for-schooling schemes in Brazil and Mexico suggests they could be copied elsewhere.'
- *Capital grants*: 'Some governments and some social scientists have been enthusiastic about new efforts to universalise access to capital such as the baby bond in the UK ... and the Alaskan Permanent Fund which allocates all citizens US$2,000 annually.'
- *Basic income as of right*: 'Finally there is a growing advocacy for policies that would provide a basic income for everybody – or at least for specific vulnerable groups gradually to be extended to all – as a right without conditions.'

I wrote at the time (Deacon, 2007: 67): 'It remains to be seen if this kind of policy advocacy becomes mainstreamed within the ILO or whether political resistance to such ideas inside the ILO will win out in favour of the far more conventional, and some would say far less convincing, campaigns to merely extend social security.'

This radical social protection agenda did not fly inside the ILO even as it became more supported outside. Guy Standing's strategy for the social security policy of the ILO was, in effect, not to extend social security or to promulgate new recommendations concerning social protection but to use a citizenship income approach to break with the work–income connection. He was reflecting the spirit of Karl Marx's *Grundisse* within which it had been argued that capitalism makes labour-time the only source of income even as it reduces the need for labour power. Socioeconomic security in a post Bismarckian, post male breadwinner, post globalisation era was to be provided by the guarantee of a basic income, which would provide an element of security on which recipients could then make life choices. Voice security, which meant extending the rights of those outside formal labour to participate in policy making, was the twin aspect of Standing's argument. While at the ILO he was a leading figure in developing BIEN,[7] where he advanced the notion of a universal unconditional basic income because globalisation was not going to allow full employment. Effective redistribution would require a basic income. He was to develop these arguments to their logical extreme much later after leaving the ILO by arguing that labour must indeed be completely commodified (Standing, 2011). This would have been anathema to ACTRAV of the organisation.

It was probably this policy, but also the extent to which Standing appeared to use his position to promulgate policies effectively in the name of the ILO without always having the house's agreement, that was to lead to an internal review and recommendation (ILO, 2005), proposing in effect the end of the programme and the incorporation of its agenda into the merged Social Security Department in 2005. The report also criticised the management arrangement that had set up the three independent sections within the Social Protection Department, all dealing with aspects of social security policy and the subsequent lack of oversight of these. The 'official history' comments on the work of Standing that 'substantial research was undertaken ... leading to conclusions at variance with the mainstream ILO approach ... when the programme came to an end in 2007 ... its influence on ILO policy had been limited' (Rodgers et al, 2009: 167-8). It is a debatable question as to whether the SPF Recommendation for a guaranteed access to a minimum income to be agreed in 2012 reflected the concerns with a universal citizen's income that Standing had argued tirelessly for or whether its premises were in fundamental contradiction to it. This point is returned to in the final chapter where the SPF Recommendation is assessed.

Promulgating a recommendation on a global social protection floor for citizens

At this time between 2000 and 2005, Michael Cichon, an actuary, as head of the section concerned with the financing of social protection, was not yet explicitly arguing for a third approach to social protection although he was involved, with others, in informal discussions about how to advance this concept.[8] At this time he invented the idea of the Global Social Trust[9] (ILO 2002a) whereby additional voluntary social security contributions made by workers in the richer countries would be transferred to support embryonic social security schemes in poorer countries. A meeting of experts organised by SOC/FAS in 2002 made recommendations to the ILO governing body to establish a trial of such a Global Trust Fund (ILO, 2002b). A pilot was established in Ghana with funds transferred from Luxembourg. Given this early interest in establishing a global fund it is significant that when his ideas for the SPF were being argued through the International Labour Conference, later Cichon should play down the importance of global funding. This will be explained in Chapter Four.

Cichon was to develop his 'third' approach to advancing social protection later when he took over the headship of the merged Social Security Department in 2005. His approach, in contrast to that of Standing and Reynaud, would be to argue that the ILO should extend its global standard-setting powers to the field of non-contributory social transfers, or social assistance. Whereas Reynaud wanted to extend social security to all through new forms of communal and mutual insurance and national framework agreements and Standing wanted to break with the work–income connection and win the ILO over to a basic income, Cichon wanted to use the mainstream practice of the ILO, that of promulgating standards, conventions and recommendations, and apply this practice not only to the 20% of the world's workers who were formal employees but also to 100% of the world's residents. In other words, he was to break somewhat with his own Bismarckian background and argue for a new ILO convention or recommendation for people. The concept of the SPF was to be born. The opportunity arose for Cichon to develop this approach when he took charge of the new department in 2005. He was to base his case that the ILO should develop an instrument concerned with the social protection of all residents on the pre-existing, but oft forgotten, 1944 ILO Recommendations 67 and 69, which were the Income Security Recommendation and the Medical Care Recommendation respectively, which addressed the needs of all people, not just workers.

He would come to argue as we will see that such an SPF was consistent with human rights, needed, affordable and doable.

However, his job would be made much easier because by 2005 the concept of the 'global social floor' on which the concept of the 'SPF' was to be built had already become mainstream within the ILO following on from Somavia's important ILO report (ILO, 2004b), which was produced by the World Commission on the Social Dimension of Globalization. How the concept of the 'SPF' was born and how it was subsequently to be advanced are discussed in the next chapter.

Thus, between 2000 and 2005, three competing visions of how the ILO might address its big problem – that its conventions on social security were not being made relevant to 80% of the world's population – were devised. One strategy involved the ILO sitting down with governments, the third sector and micro-insurance providers to develop county-specific national plans for extending coverage by a variety of means. A second strategy involved breaking the work–income connection altogether, arguing that governments provide a basic or citizen's income for all. A third would call on states to acknowledge their primary responsibility for the social protection of their citizens and residents through the mechanism of a new global standard – the SPF Recommendation – which would complement the existing social security standards.

THREE

The development of the SPF Recommendation

Introduction

This chapter tells the story of the development of the 'SPF' concept from initial conceptualisation in 2000 in the context of debates about the need for a global social floor through to its being accepted as ILO policy. It examines how en route to acceptance compromises had to be made and changes in thinking introduced. These changes included the shift of the SPF from being a defined *benefit package* to a set of *guarantees* to be ensured by governments in ways they see fit, the shift from the SPF being a *global social floor* to being a set of *national SPFs* and from it being a *global social contract* to something that would be essentially a *national responsibility*. The question as to whether the SPF would be primarily about *social transfers* or also *access to services* is also addressed.

From a benefit package to a set of guarantees

There is some uncertainty about by whom and where and in what context the concept of a 'global social floor' was first articulated. Interestingly, a member of Somavia's Cabinet,[10] when asked this question, was insistent in an email that 'Somavia's article [Somavia, 2000] published in Feb/2000 ... *for the very first time* [emphasis added] proposed the term "social floor".' The email continued:

> He said 'workers' rights aren't fringe benefits to be gained at a later date, or when the economic conditions are convenient, they constitute the "social floor" of the global economy below which no person should fall.' That came as a follow-up of the 1995 Summit. At this point, he was referring to a floor of social rights. Afterwards, ... he provided the guidance and requested the house to start to work in a more operational definition.

Certainly in terms of the work of Somavia as ILO director-general the concept of the 'global social floor' evolved within the context of the World Commission on the Social Dimension of Globalization (ILO 2004b), which called for a *global socioeconomic floor.* Those involved in the secretariat for the report all recall that this term was uncontentious and clearly had the support of the director-general. However, in terms of its subsequent transformation into the concept of a 'global social protection floor', it is interesting to note that as early as 2000, Wouter van Ginneken, then a member of the Social Security Department, expressed the following view (van Ginneken, 2000a: 7) at a DFID– Overseas Development Institute inter-agency seminar on social protection held in June 2000: 'The concept of a global social floor can be extended to include the guarantee of some basic entitlements with regard to education, health and social protection.' In the version of this paper subsequently published in the volume resulting from the conference, he wrote (van Ginneken, 2000b: 42):

> The ILO could therefore consider formulating new standards on the extension of social protection. Such standards could: reaffirm the right to social security as included in the UN International Covenant on Economic, Social and Cultural Rights; seek commitment from Governments and their social partners to elaborate and carry out strategies for extending basic social protection.

According to van Ginneken, an informal group consisting of himself, Rolph van der Hoeven (associated with the ILO World Commission), Michael Cichon and others interested in the social floor and the SPF floor kept the concept alive.[11] No real progress could be made until Cichon became head of social security in 2005. The precise definition of a global SPF took a while to evolve. In an early Issues in Social Protection Discussion Paper entitled *Can Low Income Countries Afford Basic Social Protection,* (Pal, Behrendt, Léger, Cichon and Hagemejer, K, 2005) along with his colleagues defined such a basic social protection package as: 'Access to basic health … a system of family benefits that permit children to attend school … a system of self-targeted basic social assistance (cash for work) for the able bodied and a system of basic universal pensions in old age, invalidity and survivorship that in effect support families' (as quoted in *Global Social Policy Digest* 6.3 from a 'Show and Tell' event in February 2006).

By 2006 this was expressed in a key Social Security Department consultation paper as a '*global social security floor*', which should consist of (ILO, 2006: 34):

- Access to basic healthcare through pluralistic national systems that consist of public tax-financed components, social and private insurance components and community-based components that are linked to a strong central system.
- A system of family benefits that permits children to attend school.
- A system of self-targeting basic social assistance (cash-for-work programmes) that helps to overcome abject poverty for those able to work.
- A system of basic universal pensions for old age, disability and survivorship that in effect supports whole families.

In 2007 the Campaign or Coalition for a Social Protection Floor was initiated at a meeting called by Michael Cichon in Turin (the ILO Training Centre). The 'core' of this coalition was the ILO, UNDESA, UNICEF and HelpAge International. It later expanded to many other UN agencies, and ultimately became the inter-agency group working for the UN SPF-I as is described in Chapter Five. The campaign strategy document *Building a Coalition for a Global Social Floor*, (Coalition for a Global Social Floor, 2007) formulated the global social floor in the following terms:

> The Global Social Floor consists of a basic and modest set of social security *benefits* [emphasis added] for all citizens:
>
> - Financing universal access to essential health care,
> - income security for all children through child benefits, some modest conditional support for poor people in active age, and
> - income security through basic tax financed pensions for older persons, persons with disabilities and those who lost the main breadwinner in a family.

It is significant that at this stage the floor was defined in terms of a set of specific *benefits* such as universal pensions or family benefits. Later this was to change into a set of outcomes that could be met by governments in whatever way they saw fit. The case for this benefit-based package was further articulated by Cichon and his senior colleague Hagemejer in ISSA's journal, *International Social Security Review* (Cichon and Hagemejer, 2007: 183, emphasis added):

> The time seems to be right to define a basic set of social protection *benefits* that should be achieved by all countries in the shortest possible time. This could be the minimum benefit package as part of a global socio-economic floor that was advocated by the World Commission on the Social Dimension of Globalization.

In this article the case is developed for this basic package to become defined in a new ILO Social Protection Standard agreed at ILC level. Seeking historical precedent for this the case is made that there were already much earlier ILO formulations that expressed aspects of this idea. The problem was that they had become dead letters. Thus (Cichon and Hagemejer, 2007: 183):

> In 1944 the ILO adopted two path-breaking recommendations on Income Security (Recommendation No. 67) and Medical Care (Recommendation No. 69). Recommendation No. 67 calls for universal income security through social insurance and as a fallback through social assistance for those who are not covered by social insurance. Recommendation No. 69 clearly expressed a preference for universal access to healthcare. If international labour Convention 102 (Minimum Standards) sets standards for social security benefits provided either through social insurance or through universal or means-tested programmes, however, it sets rather low minimum coverage thresholds and does not explicitly call for universal coverage. Universal access to at least minimum income security was never codified in a Convention.

Here the objective of a possible new convention on income security was set out (Cichon and Hagemejer, 2007: 193): 'Convention No. 102 could be complemented by a new international instrument stipulating universal access to a clearly defined social floor.' The convention idea never saw the light of day. A convention was not acceptable so another recommendation was all that could be achieved, albeit a recommendation that was more detailed in its focus on social protection than the 1944 ones. In this same article, Cichon and Hagemejer are critical of the alternative strategy of nationally negotiated extensions of social security contracts that had been associated with Reynaud. Thus (Cichon and Hagemejer, 2007: 183):

> Achieving success here requires that the concept of a social floor wins global credibility. It is not sufficient that a group of social security experts around the world agree more or less on the nature of a basic social security package. An explicit formal endorsement of basic social security rights that stems from the Universal Declaration of Human Rights is required.

The case was being built in this series of consultation papers and articles for a social floor on the grounds that:

- it would be based on existing *human rights* declarations;
- it would be *feasible* because some developing countries had been shown to have developed such a floor;
- it would be *affordable* even at low levels of development.

It is important that by 2008 the explicit endorsement of a particular set of *benefits* that might constitute the minimum social security package gave way to an emphasis on a set of social *outcomes* or *guarantees* that could be achieved in a variety of ways by each country:

> The Basic Social Security Floor, as defined here, consists of a basic and modest set of *social security guarantees* – implemented through social transfers in cash and in kind – for all citizens ensuring that ultimately:
>
> - All residents have access to basic/essential health care benefits through pluralistic delivery mechanisms where the State accepts the general responsibility for ensuring adequacy of the delivery system and its financing;
> - All children enjoy income security at least at the poverty level through various family/child benefits aimed at facilitating access to nutrition, education and care;
> - Some targeted income support is provided to the poor and the unemployed in the active age group;
> - All residents in old age or with disabilities enjoy income security at least at the poverty level through pensions

for old age, disability and survivors (ILO, 2008: XX, 2 emphasis added).

The consultation paper continues;

> The Basic Social Security Floor thus consists essentially of a guaranteed set of basic social transfers in cash or in kind to all. *It is formulated as a set of guarantees rather than a set of defined benefits. This leaves the option open to individual countries to realize these guarantees by way of means-tested, conditional or universal transfers.* (ILO 2008: 2), emphasis added)

The shift to the formulation of guarantees or entitlements was said by van Ginneken[12] to reflect a concern to link the concept as we saw above to that of social rights. Ursula Kulke, then in the Social Security Department undertook an exhaustive review of the implications of the various UN human rights conventions and covenants (Kulke, 2007), echoing the work of Ferguson (1999) undertaken years earlier for the failed 'social policy principles' concept. Her analysis of the extent to which existing ILO conventions and standards did not adequately reflect them provided a sound underpinning of the department's subsequent strategy to formulate the additional SPF Recommendation.

However, while leaving it open to countries to choose the mechanisms, it did not, at least as expressed in the formulations of 2007 and 2008, leave it open to countries to choose *whether* to provide a basic minimum. Kulke (2007: 135) was very clear in her conclusions of the way in which rights to social security had been interpreted by human rights lawyers faced with the argument that countries could only 'progressively realise' these rights once they had sufficient resources:

> Such a minimum social floor is not negotiable and should cover the basic needs in social protection. Moreover, it should not be questioned from an economic perspective. Besides, the implementation of this basic social floor shall not be postponed. Rather, it shall be given immediate effect by all States, irrespective of their economic or social development. This view is confirmed by the developing jurisprudence of the CESCR [Committee on Economic, Social and Cultural Rights], according to which resource scarcity does not relieve States of certain minimum obligations in respect of the implementation of the right to social security.

It is important to note that in this period, around late 2006, 2007, 2008 and into early 2009, the adjective 'global' was dropped from the publications of the Social Security Department. Only later, when the external attention given to the concept of an SPF became apparent and after the decision of UNCEB in April 2009 to argue for a SPF-I was made (see below) did the Social Security Department return to the use of this term.

There continued to be some contradiction in Social Security Department policy and thinking about this shift to guaranteed outcomes because whenever the department wanted to secure the case that a minimum social security package was *affordable* it had to revert to costing something specific and hence particular benefits packages. Thus, as late as 2009 we find Behrendt and Hagemejer (2009: 109) suggesting the affordability of:

> just one basic social protection package … [including]:
>
> - A basic universal old age and disability pension
> - A universal child benefit for all children up to the age of 14, and
> - Access to essential health care interventions as selected by the Commission on Macroeconomics and Health.

This paradox notwithstanding, the concept of 'outcomes' or 'guarantees' was to be the party line of the Social Security Department from then on. However, the definition of the global SPF was to become far more complicated by the UN SPF-I argued for by Somavia in the context of the global economic crisis. This is the subject of the next section.

Only cash transfers or access to services also

The campaign of Michael Cichon to pursue the strategy of winning the ILC over to agreeing a new SPF Recommendation became complicated by the ILO director-general's success in getting the UN to agree to an SPF-I as a part of its response to the global economic crisis of 2008. How this initiative came about is explained in detail in Chapter Five. Basically, UNCEB agreed at Somavia's behest to a set of Global Financial and Economic Crisis Joint Crisis Initiatives, including Initiative Six on social protection about which it said (UNCEB, 2009: 46):

No universally agreed definition exists at this time but a social protection floor could consist of two main elements that help to realise respective human rights:

- Essential Services: geographical and financial access to essential services (such as water and sanitation, adequate nutrition, health and education); and
- Social Transfers: a basic set of essential social transfers, in cash and in kind, paid to the poor and vulnerable to provide a minimum income security and access to essential health care.

But it also adopts the 'guarantees' concept (UNCEB, 2009: 47) while incidentally confusing the concepts of 'residents' and 'citizens':

The term 'guarantees' leaves open the question of whether all or some of these transfers are granted on a universal basis to all inhabitants of a country, if they are granted on compulsory contributory broad based insurance schemes or whether they are granted only in case of need or are tied to a number of behavioral conditions. The decisive point is that all citizens have access to essential health services and means of securing a minimum level of income. [But a footnote urges some 'at least' policies.]

The Social Security Department thus had a doubling of its work as a result of this initiative. On the one hand it continued to pursue through the proposed ILO Recommendation the second half, or social transfers half, of this new definition while at the same time taking leadership, nominally jointly with the WHO, of the inter-agency SPF-I with its broader definition. Within this context a series of meetings or workshops were convened to take the SPF-I forward, in November 2009, November 2010 and March 2011. A further meeting was convened by UNICEF in January 2012. Given the presence of a large number of agencies and interested parties at the initial Turin Workshop of 2009, it was not surprising that definitional issues arose. A modified definition was agreed based on the expanded version of the April UNCEB concept note:

Essential Services: geographical and financial access to essential services (such as water and sanitation, adequate nutrition, health and education, housing, and other essential services including life and asset saving information); and

Essential Social Transfers: i.e. social transfers, in cash and in kind, paid to the poor and vulnerable to provide a minimum income security and health security. (ILO, 2009: 2)

Thus, housing and life- and asset-saving information is added and health care becomes health security. However, Table 1 of that outcome document goes on to be rather more specific about transfers to ensure that there is in the economy effective demand from 'children, people in active age groups with insufficient income from work and older persons (ILO, 2009: 3). Clearly, the Social Security Department was going to have to be constantly vigilant in trying to keep everybody on message as regards the transfers being discussed and the guarantees being ensured. For some, the much wider definition of the SPF-I, which embraced access to water, education and sanitation, opened up the prospects of a broad campaign for investment in drains and sewers and much more besides, but no such wider vision was going to disrupt the narrower and precise focus of the ILO Social Security Department, which was now centred on the future ILO Recommendation involving only income guarantees and access to health.

The SPF-I of UNCEB was to be bolstered, as described in more detail in Chapter Five, by the appointment of an advisory board working out of the director's office and under the leadership of Michel Bachelet. In definitional terms, the Bachelet Report (ILO, 2011d) reflected the broader UNCEB definition and, in selecting quotations from the record and agreement of the 2011 ILC, it preferred extracts that reflected this wider approach:

The 2011 International Labour Conference undertook an extensive discussion of social protection, and in the process of defining its view of the social protection floor, concurred with a *unified approach to income security and access to essential goods and services* set out as follows: '....social protection floors, containing basic social security guarantees that ensure that over the life cycle all in need can afford and have access to essential health care and have income security at least at a nationally defined minimum level. Social protection floor policies should aim at facilitating effective access to essential goods and services, promote productive economic activity and be implemented in close coordination with other policies enhancing employability, reducing informality and precariousness, creating decent jobs and promoting entrepreneurship.' (ILO, 2011d: xxiii, emphasis added)

The involvement of other UN agencies through the mechanism of the SPF-I was to continue to muddy the definitional waters of the SPF. Bringing all UN agencies and the World Bank into the SPF as a UNCEB decision was strategic to have buy-in of the SPF, but the definition including services and transfers became more problematic. Many UN agencies saw their role as education or housing, for example. The final formulation in paragraph 4 of the draft Recommendation to the ILC of 2012 (ILO, 2012c: 10, emphasis added) attempted to bring together the transfers and services element:

> Members should put in place and complete as rapidly as possible, and maintain, their social protection floors comprising basic social security guarantees. The guarantees should ensure at a minimum that, over the life cycle, all in need have access to essential health care and to basic income security *which together secure effective access to goods and services* defined as necessary at the national level.

This, in my view, untidy and ambiguous formulation can only be explained by attempts to merge the two definitial strands.

The extent to which UNCEB's SPF-I really did weld the several UN agencies together into one concerted push for an SPF is discussed in Chapter Six.

From a global social floor to national SPFs

The struggle to win the ILC over to supporting a new recommendation meant, however, a narrower focus on the social transfer guarantees outlined earlier. So in September 2009 a Tripartite Meeting of Experts on the Extension of Social Security Coverage was convened in Geneva. This was eventually reported in 2010 as *Extending Social Security to All* (ILO, 2010a). The key document considered by the experts was drafted and presented by the Social Security Department and rehearsed the definition in the following terms:

> In the context of its campaign to extend social security to all, the ILO is *promoting the social transfer component of the social protection floor* [emphasis added], that is, the social security

floor, a basic and modest set of essential social guarantees realised through transfers in cash and in kind that could ensure a minimum level of income security and access to health care for all in need. The goal of such a basic set of guarantees is a situation in which, in all countries:

- all residents have the necessary financial protection in order to be able to afford and have access to a *nationally defined* [emphasis added] set of essential health-care services, whereby the State accepts the general responsibility for ensuring the adequacy of the (usually) pluralistic financing and delivery systems;
- all children have income security, at least at the *nationally defined* poverty level, through family or child benefits aimed at facilitating access to nutrition, education and care;
- all those in active age groups who are unable to earn sufficient income in the labour market should enjoy a minimum level of income security through social assistance or other social transfer schemes (such as transfer income schemes for women during the last weeks of pregnancy and the first weeks after delivery), combined with employment guarantees or other labour market policies;
- all residents in old age or with disabilities have income security, at least at the *nationally defined* poverty level, through pensions for old age and disability (ILO, 2010a: 20).

The 'four guarantees' as they were now known are clear but what is significant is the spelling out of the *national definition* of not only the means by which these guarantees might be secured but also the poverty level with which these guarantees might be associated. In a public lobbying position paper 'The UN SPF-I: turning the tide at the ILO Conference', Cichon, Behrendt and their newer colleague, Wodsak, repeated these words and argued:

What is important is that everyone who is in need of income transfers or health services can access these transfers in cash or in kind.... The four guarantees set minimum performance or outcome standards with respect to the access, scope, and level of income security and health in national social protection systems. (Cichon et al, 2011: 9)

The paper also emphasised that governments can choose between 'universal benefits' and 'social insurance schemes ... they may be conditional or unconditional', they may be 'social assistance schemes' or services in kind.

So the scene was set for the ILC in June 2011 to consider, not the question of the wording of a recommendation on the SPF, but simply agreeing that the subsequent 2012 ILC would formulate such a recommendation. The passage of this policy through the conferences is discussed in the next chapter. Continuing the focus of this section on definitional questions, the report prepared by the Social Security Department for consideration at the Committee for the Recurrent Discussion on Social Protection at the 2011 ILC (ILO, 2011a) repeated word for word (para 5.1.3) the paragraph prepared for the earlier 2009 Tripartite Meeting and merely added rather tentatively in its concluding section an invitation for conference input on it (ILO, 2011a, para 63):

> What is the role of ILO standards in further promoting the extension of social security coverage for all? What further measures should be taken to enhance the ratification and application of Convention No. 102 and other up-to-date ILO social security standards? What further instruments or other mechanisms (Conventions, Recommendations, guidelines, codes of practice, etc.) could be developed to guide the implementation of the SPF in the context of the two-dimensional strategy for the extension of social security for all?

The process of the discussion at the conference is reported and discussed in the next chapter. The 'Conclusions regarding the recurrent discussion on social protection' (ILO, 2011b) in 2011 were that the 2012 ILC should agree a new recommendation on social protection and paragraph 9 (emphasis added) asserted that:

> The horizontal dimension should aim at the rapid implementation of national Social Protection *Floors*, containing basic social security guarantees that ensure that over the life cycle all in need can afford and have access to essential health care and have income security at least at a nationally defined minimum level.

And paragraph 10 asserted that:

> As a one-size-fits-all approach is not appropriate, every member State should design and implement its Social Protection Floor guarantees according to national circumstances and priorities defined with the participation of social partners. While expected outcomes of these guarantees are of a universal nature, member States find different ways of implementing Social Protection Floor policies, which may include universal benefit schemes, social insurance, public employment programmes and employment support schemes, and social assistance schemes that provide benefits only to people with low income, or appropriate combinations of such measures.

Christina Behrendt, who was a joint author of the campaigning Friedrich Ebert Stiftung paper, (Cichon, Behrendt and Wodsak 2011) was a lead rapporteur of the committee. The common authorship of both is evident, revealing one of the means by which the Social Security Department staff continued to largely maintain control of the agenda.

The appendix to the conclusions of the 2011 ILC (ILO, 2011b) already contains 'elements of a possible recommendation' and paragraph 4 outlining its scope suggests in section A6:

> The horizontal dimension of the social security extension strategy should prioritize the implementation of a national Social Protection Floor, consisting of four basic social security guarantees, i.e. nationally defined minimum levels of income security during childhood, working age and old age, as well as affordable access to essential health care. These guarantees set the minimum levels of protection that all members of a society should be entitled to in case of need. Focusing on outcomes achieved, these guarantees do not prescribe specific forms of benefits, financing mechanisms or the organization of benefit delivery.

The line of reasoning and wording of the four guarantees is the same as had been articulated by the social security secretariat for at least three years. What had become now so obvious to all and pushed by particular country lobbies at the ILC (see the next chapter), the Social Security Department had moved from defending the concept of a global SPF to defending a range of national SPFs. This shift to the plural was very significant. It was no surprise therefore that the title of the Department's report in preparation of the all-important 2012 ILC was entitled *Social Protection Floors for Social Justice and a Fair Globalization* (ILO, 2011c).

Produced after the June 2011 ILC by the Social Security Department and prepared by July 2011, this report contained a questionnaire to countries inviting them to answer specific questions concerning the possible content of the new SPF. Turning the questions into positive statements indicates the kind of recommendation hoped for by the secretariat. *This Recommendation is formally based on the conclusions of the 2011 Conference but reflects the thinking in the Social Security Department since 2005 and the ideas of individuals since at least as far back as 2000* but is tempered by the pressures for (a) national variation and (b) continuing support for the wage-related social security Convention 102.

Thus, in paragraphs 6 and 7 of section IV of the questionnaire, the four guarantees reappear (ILO, 2011c). The questions are:

> Should the Recommendation provide that Members should establish and implement as rapidly as possible their social protection floor containing basic social security guarantees that ensure that over the life cycle all in need can afford and have access to essential health care and have income security at least at a nationally defined minimum level?

> Should the Recommendation provide that each Member should provide at least the following basic social security guarantees:

> a) all persons ordinarily resident in the country have the necessary financial protection to access a nationally defined set of essential health-care services, including maternal health care?
> b) all children enjoy income security, at least at a nationally defined minimum level, through family/child benefits in cash or in kind aimed at facilitating access to nutrition, education and care?
> c) all persons in active age groups ordinarily resident in the country who are unable to earn sufficient income enjoy minimum income security through social assistance, maternity benefits, disability benefits, other social transfers in cash or in kind, or public employment programmes?

d) all persons in old age ordinarily resident in the country enjoy income security, at least at a nationally defined minimum level, through benefits in cash or in kind?

The response to this questionnaire by countries and the Office analysis of them are discussed in Chapter Five. Here what is important to note is that the four guarantees remained intact in the draft SPF Recommendation produced by the secretariat in response to the governments' views. Thus, finally the formal draft published on the ILO's website on 1 March 2012 stated (ILO, 2012c, emphasis added):

The social protection floors referred to in paragraph 4 should comprise *at least the following basic social security guarantees*:

a) access to a nationally defined set of goods and services, constituting essential health care, including in the case of maternity;
b) basic income security for children, at least at a nationally defined minimum level, providing access to nutrition, education, care and any other necessary goods and services;
c) basic income security, at least at a nationally defined minimum level, for persons in active age who are unable to earn sufficient income, including in case of sickness, unemployment, maternity and disability; and
d) basic income security, at least at a nationally defined minimum level, for persons in old age.

From a global social contract to national responsibility?

In the early formulation of the global social floor linked to social protection by van Ginneken (2000a: 10), the question of some form of innovative international funding to pay for this was clearly part of the thinking: 'This floor will only be properly founded with fresh international financing sources, which – in addition to redirected national expenditure, debt relief and targeted donor contributions – would also come from better collected taxes on capital income. A new global contract is needed to achieve all this.' The publicity leaflet entitled 'A new deal for people in a global crisis: social security for all', prepared for a public presentation of the Campaign for a Global Social

Floor by representatives of the ILO, UNDESA, UNICEF and HelpAge International at a side event of the Doha Financing for Development Conference in December 2008, asserted that:

> The current global financial crisis is an opportunity to create a Global New Deal to deliver social protection in all countries through basic old age and disability pensions, child benefits, employment programs, and provision of social services.... Social security is a human right (Articles 22 and 25 of the Universal Declaration of Human Rights) and it is affordable, a basic package is estimated to cost from 2 to 5 percent of GDP as an average. *It is feasible if the international system commits to providing financial support for a Global New Deal to jump start an emergency response to the urgent social needs of our times* [emphasis added].

However, there was a tension between this call for international support and the campaign within the ILO predicated on the arguments and evidence that a basic social protection package was *affordable*. If countries could afford it then why, it could be asked, was there a need for international funding? A formulation was invented in 2008 or possibly earlier to reconcile this problem, which held out the possibility of some additional international funding for the poorest countries initially. This formulation has appeared quite regularly in the various articulations of the SPF policy outlined earlier. Thus, in one of the *Can Low-Income Countries Afford Basic Social Security?* papers produced in the context of the 2008 ILO Global Campaign on Social Security and Coverage for All (ILO, 2008: 3, emphasis added), we find:

> However, one has also to consider the international context with respect to the need to ensure that global competition does not drive countries and their populations below agreed minimum labour and social standards, and to *obtain international support in financing provisions of minimum basic social protection in low-income countries during the transitory period* until these countries have the necessary domestic fiscal capacity to do so themselves.

The report provided to the 2009 Tripartite Meeting of Experts on the Extension of Social Security Coverage suggested (ILO, 2010a) *Extending Social Security to All* in paragraph 2.4.2. that '[a] basic social protection package appears affordable, but in most cases on the condition that it is progressively implemented. In some cases, it may require a joint effort between low-income countries and the international donor community during a transition period.' Even though this is referring only to traditional donor support even this was clearly controversial during the meeting. The chair's conclusions reported in paragraph 4.2 (emphasis added) are that:

> The means for funding the schemes and programmes through which extension of coverage may be achieved, and in particular the mobilizing of appropriate fiscal space, *must be the responsibility of each country individually*, in the light of prevailing concerns, constraints and opportunities, and is expected everywhere to reflect a pluralistic approach.

At the 2011 ILC, employers and some countries continued to express some unease about global funding. However, the Social Security Department was able to write into its report to the conference (ILO, 2011b, para 258) that:

> While the cost of a basic social protection package appears to be within the reach of many low-income countries, in most cases the package will have to be implemented on a gradual basis. Some of these countries may require the international donor community to help them on a joint basis for a suitable transition period.

And in its conclusions (ILO, 2011b, para 18) it stated:

> While national Social Protection Floors should be financed from domestic sources of revenue to ensure their long-term sustainability, there may be cases where these resources are insufficient to extend the Social Protection Floor to all in a short time frame. International cooperation can play an important role in helping member States to initiate the process and build the national resource base with a view to ensuring sustainable financing mechanisms.

Continuing this now familiar line, the questionnaire to countries asked (ILO, 2011c): 'Should the Recommendation provide that the national social protection floor should, in principle, be financed by domestic resources, while noting that some low-income countries may need to have recourse to transitional international financial support?' The responses by governments to this questionnaire, which are examined in more detail in Chapter Five, enabled the Social Security Department to continue this approach to the next stage of the draft Recommendation published in March 2012, which stated: 'National social protection floors should be financed, in principle, by national resources. Members whose economic and fiscal capacities are insufficient to implement the entire set of guarantees may seek transitional international assistance' (ILO, 2012c, para 12).

In the parallel joint UN SPF-I, some discussion of donor support continued in a similar vein. Thus, the November 2009 SPF-I manual (ILO, 2009) suggested (3.6 Funding, para 2): 'relevant donors whose support will be key and will condition the establishment of the SPF especially in the poorest countries'. The November 2010 SPF-I workshop (ILO, 2010b) resolved that within the following three to five years there was need for a focus on '[d]eveloping a fundraising strategy for the SPF, for example through Multi Donor Trust Funds or bilateral and multi-lateral funds', but this was more concerned with fundraising for technical assistance projects.

It was in this context of the wish of the Social Security Department to downplay the importance of international funding that the *advance G20* copy of the Bachelet Report produced by the ILO directorate (ILO, 2011e: 86, emphasis added) contained the rather weak formulation in its recommendations to the G20 that:

> Innovative financing mechanisms *could* be designed to support low-income countries to start up the process. Some low-income countries, particularly in sub-Saharan Africa, need external support to help build social protection, and *would* benefit from additional international funding to accelerate construction of their social protection floor.

I suggest weak as the French President of the G20 in 2011 (as noted in Chapter Five) had already indicated in France's priorities for the G20 that '[i]nnovative sources of finance can and *should* be mobilized' (G20, 2011d, emphasis added). The G20 Bachelet Report did, however, make a call for an international trust fund to pay for the joint technical assistance envisaged between the ILO, UNICEF, World Bank, UNDP and so on in advising countries on the SPF and in mapping through a knowledge platform of country experiences. The public communiqué prepared jointly by the ILO and the OECD reporting the recommendations of the Bachelet Report to the G20 repeated all the recommendations *except the one concerning global funding* (ILO, 2011f).

In the event, despite this, the outcome of the G20 labour ministers' meeting was to '[r]ecommend that the international community suggest new ways of supplementing international solidarity arrangements in order to implement social protection floors throughout the world' (G20, 2011b). Vinicius Pinheiro, who had worked for a short time within Cichon's Department and had been picked by Somavia as the official working in the Cabinet of the director-general on the Bachelet Report, was a sherpa for the ILO at this meeting and played a major role in ensuring that these words were included in the outcome document (see more details in Chapter Five). So while the G20 version of the Bachelet Report was muted on global funding, the final version was far more forthcoming about the need for such funding. Thus, in addition to calling on donors to provide multi-year funding support to country social protection budgets (ILO, 2011d: xxxi), it argued (ILO, 2011d: xxxii):

> We strongly support the development and implementation of innovative financing mechanisms to raise additional funds to support the implementation of social floors. These could include a financial transaction tax, including on currency transactions; debt swap mechanisms; solidarity levies on airline tickets; and measures to facilitate remittances.

Furthermore, in Box 10 of the Bachelor Report (ILO, 2010b, p 74), each of these possible innovative sources of funding is explained in more detail.

This paradox that just at the moment when the global politics of the idea of a global financial transaction tax had never been so favourable[13] to its introduction, the concrete discussion of using it to create a global fund for paying for social protection in poor countries was in retreat certainly within the Social Security Department of the ILO if not within the ILO directorate and among those who wrote the Bachelet Report requires comment. What was going on was partly an assertion by poor countries that they wished to be out from under aid dependency, having suffered enough under structural adjustment, partly the coming together of a set of arguments that had showed how a certain kind of project-based funding had undermined government capacity, and partly an assertion by those supporting the idea of the SPF that governments of poorer countries had now to raise revenues from national resources, whether from mineral wealth or richer residents to prove their commitment to it. A joint ILO and Friedrich Ebert Stiftung seminar held in the immediate wake of the 2011 ILC to which Cichon was invited concluded the following (Liebert, 2011), which captures this new paradigm well:

> Finding national solutions and the mobilisation of domestic resources instead of a donor-driven process help to promote national ownership. It has been shown that basic social protection is affordable – provided governments are willing to collect taxes and create an environment that is conducive to job creation. Sole reliance on international aid, by contrast, not only stands in the way of national ownership, but also carries risks, such as dependence on changing development agendas and inadequate and fluctuating funds. This is not to say that international development cooperation is superfluous for rolling out national Social Protection Floors. It plays an important role by helping to build the necessary infrastructure and capacity.

Despite this caution among those who were focused on advocating for the SPF within the ILO, a policy brief arguing the case for a Global Fund for Social Protection was to emerge after the ILO had agreed to support the SPF Recommendation from the rapporteurs for the UN Human Rights Council. This surprising development is discussed in Chapter Seven.

These issues of definition:

- whether the SPF should be about *specific* benefits and their levels or about a *diverse* ways of ensuring a set of *guaranteed outcomes*;
- whether the SPF should primarily be about a set of *cash transfers* or also about *access to services* and not only health services;
- whether the SPF was to be defined *globally* or left up to countries to define their own *national* social protection floors; and finally
- whether the SPF should be funded within *national resources* or supported by *international finance*;

are returned to in the next chapter. What I am suggesting here is that because these definitional shifts had already taken place between 2005 and 2010, the passage of the SPF Recommendation through the ILCs of 2011 and 2012 would be that much more straightforward. Table 3.1 summarises the shifts and shows how the final agreed Recommendation of 2012 reflects the modified formulations that the Social Security Department was working with by about 2010. This reinforces my argument that I seek to illustrate in more detail in the next chapter that the secretariat of the ILO is a central and active player in the making of this global social policy.

Table 3.1: Shifting conceptualisation: from global social floor to national social protection floors

Timeline. Source	Concept	Meaning
2000 Somavia	Social floor of the global economy	"The social floor of the global economy below which no person should fall"
2000 van Ginneken	Global social floor	"Guarantee of some basic entitlements with regard to education, health and social protection"
2004 World Commission	Global socio-economic floor	"A certain minimum level of social protection needs to be accepted and undisputed as part of the socio-economic floor of the global economy"
2005 Cichon	Basic social protection package	"Access to basic health…a system of family benefits that permit children to attend school…a system of self-targeted basic social assistance (cash for work) for the able bodied and a system of basic universal pensions in old age, invalidity and survivorship"
2006 Cichon	Global social security floor	As above but the benefits elaborated in more detail
2007 Coalition for a Global Social Protection Floor	Global social floor	"The global social floor consists of a basic and modest set of social security benefits for all citizens: – financing universal access to essential health care, – income security for all children through child benefits, – some modest conditional support for the poor in active age, and – income security through basic tax financed pensions for older persons, persons with disabilities and those who lost the main breadwinner in a family"

Timeline. Source	Concept	Meaning
2008 ILO	Basic social security floor	"A basic and modest set of social security guarantees...ensuring that ultimately...all residents have access to basic/essential health care benefits...all children enjoy income security at least at the poverty level through various family/child benefits...some targeted income support is provided to the poor and the unemployed in the active age group...All residents in old age or with disabilities enjoy income security at least at the poverty level through pensions for old age, disability and survivors"
2009 UNCEB	Social protection floor	"Social protection floor could consist of two main elements that help to realise respective human rights: Essential Services: geographical and financial access to essential services (such as water and sanitation, adequate nutrition, health and education); and Social Transfers: a basic set of essential social transfers, in cash and in kind, paid to the poor and vulnerable to provide a minimum income security and access to essential health care"
2010 ILO (tripartite meeting of experts on social security 2009)	Social transfer component of the social protection floor, i.e., the social security floor	"A basic and modest set of essential social guarantees"....(the definition goes on to refer as usual to health, children, working age and elderly but each reference contains the phrase: e.g)... "all children have income security, at least at the *nationally defined* poverty level, through family or child benefits"

Timeline. Source	Concept	Meaning
2011 ILO (conference report)	National social protection floor	"Consisting of four basic social security guarantees, i.e. nationally defined minimum levels of income security during childhood, working age and old age, as well as affordable access to essential health care. These guarantees set the minimum levels of protection that all members of a society should be entitled to in case of need. Focusing on outcomes achieved, these guarantees do not prescribe specific forms of benefits, financing mechanisms or the organisation of benefit delivery"
2011 ILO (questionnaire to govts)	National social protection floor	"Their social protection floor containing basic social security guarantees that ensure that over the life cycle all in need can afford and have access to essential health care and have income security, at least at a nationally defined minimum level"
2012 ILO (draft recommendation)	National floors of social protection	"Social protection floors comprising basic social security guarantees. The guarantees should ensure at a minimum that, over the life cycle, all in need have access to essential health care and to basic income security which together secure effective access to goods and services defined as necessary at the national level"
2012 IL0 final text	National social protection floors	"For the purpose of this Recommendation, social protection floors are nationally defined sets of basic social security guarantees which secure protection aimed at preventing or alleviating poverty, vulnerability and social exclusion The guarantees should ensure at a minimum that, over the life cycle, all in need have access to essential health care and to basic income security which together secure effective access to goods and services defined as necessary at the national level"

FOUR

The SPF, social dialogue and tripartite global governance in practice

This chapter tells the story of the passage through the 2011 and 2012 ILCs of the SPF Recommendation idea. Having nurtured and refined the concept within the Social Security Department for several years, as we saw in the last chapter, how would the secretariat try to ensure its smooth passage through these events? The chapter starts with an initial discussion of why getting agreement of the ILO to the SPF might be a challenge in the context of the tripartite governance structure of the ILO. It then describes and analyses how the policy was steered through the 2011 and 2012 ILCs to final acceptance.

Challenging path dependency

The ILO governance arrangements, cast as they are in the mould of tripartite negotiations between government and representatives of organised formal labour and employers, were not initially designed to address policies concerning the welfare of citizens or residents. Social protection for all – cash transfers for children, access to affordable health for people living in poverty, income security for the 80% of the world's population who are in the informal and agricultural sectors and often outside any economy altogether – is generally seen as the concern of other actors: social movements, non-governmental organisations and global social policy campaigners. In Chapter Two we saw the role of such movements in advancing the cause of universal social protection and universal pensions during the first decade of this century. To what extent would the workers and employers side with the case for a SPF for all?

The governing institutions of the ILO – the ILC and the governing body – are composed not just of government representatives, but also of representatives of labour unions, mainly the International Trade Union Confederation (ITUC) and employer associations, the International Organisation of Employers (IOE). Unions and employers each hold a quarter of the seats in the ILC and governing body, while government representatives hold the remaining half. The activities of the ILO are supported by a large secretariat. Important for our analysis is the fact that, unlike governments, unions and employers have their own organisational structures within the International Labour Office – ACTRAV and ACTEMP – which enable them to engage in dialogue with the Office. The relationship between the ITUC (the International Confederation of Free Trade Unions – ICFTU – as it was) and the workers' group (ACTRAV) inside the ILO is intimate. A revolving door exists whereby a secretary-general of the ITUC or a director of the ITUC's Geneva office becomes the ACTRAV director or deputy director. Similar processes exist for the IOE.

However, the representative nature of the workers' and employers' groups has been questioned by some as has their ability to represent non-worker beneficiaries of a future SPF. Bhatt (1994: 44) has claimed that in the case of India the ILO did not represent over 90% of Indian workers and Standing (2008: 379) has argued that:

> [The employers] can no more claim to be the democratic representatives of 'employers' around the world than the unions can claim to represent the 'workers', but it has been a long-time convenience to presume they are the voice of employers and 'capital'. In fact, they are representatives of employers' federations in member countries, those belonging to the IOE.

Somavia took over the helm of the ILO in 1999 in large measure because of the respect he had earned chairing the very important UN Copenhagen Social Summit of 1995, which had been a defining moment in the world of global civil society and global institutions coming together to formulate policies for a fairer world. In his earlier addresses to the ILO, he spoke of the need to engage the world of civil society and broader social movements in the work of the ILO. As Baccaro and Mele (2010: 221) remind us, in his address to the 1999 ILC he said:

> The growth and dynamism of NGOs is a hallmark of our era. They are important counterparts in international cooperation programmes…. The ILO has to support ways in which its constituents can work more effectively in partnership with these groups to pursue shared objectives. Closer links with civil society, if well defined, can be a source of great strength for the ILO and its constituents.

This attempt by Somavia to broaden the constitutional basis of the ILO governing structures failed. As Baccaro and Mele (2012;12) explain, the workers' group and the employers' group were united in their opposition to any such move that might weaken their influence and took the pre-emptive step of submitting to the 2002 ILC a 'Resolution on tripartism and social dialogue' (ILO, 2002: 5-6), which asserted the central role of the tripartite constituents and among other things asked the secretariat to 'ensure that the tripartite constituents will be consulted as appropriate in the selection of and relationships with other civil society organisations with which the International Organization might work'. There was to be no significant participation of the new civil society movements at the ILC or governing body.

A further prefatory consideration is the significance to the workers' and employers' groups of Convention 102 – the Social Security (Minimum Standards) Convention, which was agreed in 1952 – since it has remained the ILO's primary convention on social protection for more than 50 years. It calls on governments to introduce benefits for nine 'contingencies', all linked to employment:

- medical care;
- sickness;
- unemployment;
- old age;
- employment injury;
- family;
- maternity;
- invalidity benefits;
- survivor benefits.

While the convention has been criticised for its language of (male) breadwinners, its further ratification is seen within the ILO as the best way of ensuring that formally employed workers are provided with an appropriate high level of social security benefits. Traditionally within the ILO, any campaign to extend social security has meant extending the membership of such formal schemes and of working to get more countries to ratify Convention 102.

The challenge therefore faced by the Social Security Department was to steer a recommendation concerning the social protection rights of citizens and residents through an institution concerned historically to primarily defend the rights of workers for whom Convention 102 remained paramount. At the same time, the challenge was to steer the recommendation through a process in which employers might object to the raising of revenues that would be needed for such an SPF. Also of course the challenge was to steer it either past or by winning the support of possible reluctant governments not wanting their sovereignty undermined.

This study therefore brings into focus in a way that is unusual the fourth partner in the governance structure of the ILO: the professional secretariat. As the representative of the employers' group who was the contact point for the Social Security Department revealingly suggested to me: this is not a tripartite organisation, it is a quadripartite organisation. As he pointed out, the layout of the historic governing body room classically reflects this – a triangular wedge of government seats, of employers' seats and of workers' seats all facing a high table of numerous members of the secretariat. The dialogue is not only between workers and employers and governments but between all three groups and the secretariat.

However, that is not to say that the workers as a group were opposed to the concept of an SPF, so long as it was linked to improving contributory social security. Indeed, the June 2010 congress of the ITUC agreed to the following wording, suggested indeed by the workers' group within the ILO, in paragraph 16 of its resolution on extending social protection (ITUC, 2010a: 3, emphasis added):

> Congress therefore supports the establishment and implementation of *a minimum benefit package for all those in need*, which would include: access to health care including maternity protection; family support to parents sending their children to school and regular medical checks; guaranteed old age pensions; income security for the disabled, as well as obstacle-free access to public services; and income support for particularly vulnerable groups for example through public employment guarantee schemes. *A universal social floor* would be financed mainly from public funds and would cover all men and women regardless of their employment situation.

The securing of this formulation and agreement in principle to a SPF, which would make the passage through the ILC much easier, had been hard fought within the ILO workers' group. It was thanks to the thinking of people such as Ibrahim Patel, now Minister for Economic Development in South Africa, Sharon Burrows, now general secretary of the ITUC, both of whom had been in turn the workers' spokesperson on the Economic and Social Policy Committee of the ILO's governing body, and Guy Ryder, former general secretary of the ICFTU, now at the ILO, that new progressive thinking prevailed.[14] Indeed, Guy Ryder, who would become the new ILO director-general with responsibility for carrying the policy forward, had argued as early as 2006 that: 'A system needs to provide universal basic social services and a basic income floor ... we are not talking about people resting in a social safety net, but a right for everybody to walk with dignity and respect on a basic social floor' (Ryder, 2006: 6).

Indeed, more opposition was likely to come from the employers. In an explanatory note prepared by the IOE in February 2011 it was stated that 'any new mechanism should remain general and flexible, leaving the issue to national debate and including a progressive implementation', adding that 'the SPF should not encourage people in the informal economy where they may receive benefits without paying taxes' (IOE, 2011: 5).

Steering the SPF through the ILCs

Perhaps it is useful to have a sense of the size and organisation of the Social Security Department of the ILO before explaining its role in steering this policy through the ILCs. It is small, with about 30 permanent staff in all, supplemented by a number of interns and a few young staff seconded by interested governments. Divided into four sections concerned with policy, country operations, finance and legal standards, it is the policy division of about six people that is central. The names were familiar to anybody who cared to read the internal and external publications on the SPF during the period 2006 to 2012, notably Christina Behrendt, Krzysztof Hagemejer and Veronika Wodsak, among others.

The story of steering the SPF Recommendation through the 2011 and 2012 ILCs began long before they took place. So, soon after Cichon took over the reigns of the Social Security Department and prepared the initial Department consultation paper on the topic, work began to advance the case through the decision-making processes of the 'house'. One strand of this activity was the series of tripartite regional meetings held in Latin America, the Arab States, Asia and the Pacific during 2007 and 2008 in which Ursula Kulke also played an important role. Of particular significance was the subsequent endorsement of the idea by the Africa region in the form of the Yaounde Tripartite Declaration of 2010. Africa was open to the idea of tax-based social cash transfers by this time (see Chapter Two). Winning over Africa meant that the winning over of the Latin Americans might be easier. Whereas the explosion of innovation in conditional cash transfer policies that was taking place in the Latin American region might suggest support by governments for the SPF, some in the trades union movement in the region saw the floor as a threat to wage-related Convention-102-style contributory benefits. The floor some feared might become a ceiling.

What made the idea of the SPF more acceptable to the sceptics among the workers was the formulation of the two-dimensional strategy for extending social security. The two dimensional strategy and the social security staircase was born so that the SPF would be only one part: the horizontal part of the strategy; the other part would be the vertical part, which would ensure improved benefits by improvements in the contributory system (see Figure 4.1). Indeed, the SPF was to become a *stepping stone* to Convention 102. The call for the SPF was to be always linked to the call to extend the coverage of social protection not only by means of the SPF but also by means of bringing more people into formal employment and hence the ambit of Convention 102. Countries would be urged to ratify the Convention if they had not already at the same time as building a floor. This formulation was best first expressed in the Social Security Department's report forming the basis of the discussion at the important Tripartite Meeting of Experts on the Extension of Social Security Coverage convened in November 2009:

> The metaphor that thus emerges for the extension of social security coverage is the image of a social security staircase. The floor level comprises a set of basic guarantees for all. For people with tax-paying or contributory capacity, a second level of benefits as a right (defined and protected regarding the minimum levels by law) can be introduced and, finally, for those with the need or wish for high levels of protection, a 'top floor' of voluntary private insurance arrangements can be organised (but should be subject to regulation and public supervision in the same way as all private insurance schemes). This metaphor is appropriate to countries at all stages of development, albeit that the number of people whose only protection consists of basic social guarantees is naturally larger in countries at lower levels of economic development. (ILO, 2010b: 19)

While the concerns of some in the workers' group were focused on the whether the floor might become a ceiling and the priority to be given to Convention 102, the concerns of the employers were about the cost implications. Perhaps surprisingly, the employers did not jump to and support the floor, seeing the chance of turning it into a ceiling and using its existence to challenge the case for the wage-related system, which of course cost them money too. Influenced by the contextual global discourse concerning activation programmes, they were more concerned to ensure that the floor did not undermine the encouragement of beneficiaries into formal employment. The focus on encouraging formal employment brought the two sides together to some extent.

Figure 4.1: Vertical and horizontal dimensions of the extension to social security strategy

Source: (ILO, 2010b, p 20)

The 2011 ILC: should a recommendation on an SPF be decided on in 2012?

Turning to the 2011 ILC, it fell primarily to its Committee for the Recurrent Discussion on Social Protection to consider the issue as to whether or not it would support the idea that in 2012 the committee would reconvene precisely to promulgate a new convention or recommendation on the SPF. At the end of Report VI: *Social Security for Social Justice and a Fair Globalization*, prepared for the consideration of the committee by Michael Cichon's team, there was the carefully understated formulation:

> What further measures should be taken to enhance the ratification and application of Convention No. 102 and other up-to-date ILO social security standards? What further instruments or other mechanisms (Conventions, Recommendations, guidelines, codes of practice, etc.) could be developed to guide the implementation of the SPF in the

> context of the two-dimensional strategy for the extension
> of social security for all? (ILO, 2011a, para 456e)

Before reviewing in detail how the committee came to agree that an SPF Recommendation should be designed, we need to draw attention to the Parallel Committee on the Application of Standards, which in turn was charged also to consider in the ILC 2011 the report of the Committee of Experts, part III of which was a general survey concerning social security (ILO, 2011l). When the 304th session of the governing body of the ILO decided in March 2009 that the 2011 ILC was to focus on social security, it also asked the Committee of Experts to review progress with implementing social security standards by covering the first and the last on the list of up-to-date social security conventions: the 1952 Convention 102 and the 1988 168 Convention. However, the Standards Department and the Social Security Department agreed that actually the report would start with the long forgotten 1944 Recommendations 67 and 69 that had been so important in Cichon's case that the mandate of the ILO extended beyond that of the social protection of workers.

In preparation for the work of the Committee of Experts, Egorov, the social security expert of the Standards Department, in collaboration with the Social Security Department, designed a questionnaire for governments and social partners not only asking them about their implementation of the 102 and 168 Conventions but also asking them in question nine: 'Does your country consider the establishment of a set of basic guarantees for income security and access to medical care for all, and if so, for what risks/contingencies' (ILO, 2011l: 278). The report noted progress along these lines in 40 countries (ILO 2011l: 126-30).

The report of the Committee of Experts (ILO, 2011l) was based on drafts written by Egorov and considered by a sub-committee of the Committee of Experts over five days. It includes a strong case for a human rights-based approach to a new recommendation on the SPF. Echoing the work of Kulke (2007) from the Social Security Department, which was reviewed in Chapter Three, the report sets out all the UN and regional conventions that build the case for social security being a human right (ILO, 2011l: 70-2). A new member of the Committee of Experts with a particular expertise in social security, Angelica Nusbergger, Judge at the European Court of Human Rights, was particularly supportive of the radical rights-based approach of the report.[15] The report of the Committee of Experts not only restated the case for the four guarantees being the basis of the SFP but also included a passionate defence of the need for such a new approach.

The report reviewed the earlier three generations of social security standard setting (1919-39, 1944-64 and 1965-88) and argued (ILO, 2011l: 13) that a new fourth generation was required:

> What needs to be clearly stated here, however, is that the current ILO mandate in social security, as reaffirmed and updated by the Declaration on Social Justice for a Fair Globalization of 2008, has largely outgrown the standards with which it has to be implemented. The available means are no more sufficient to meet the new ends. This is particularly evident as regards the objective of extending social security coverage to all, beyond the formal economy to the masses of population living in abject poverty and insecurity, which is placed at the heart of the ILO's mandate and mission. The Committee is certain that the task of globalizing social security requires the ILO to complement the current set of up-to-date standards with a new high-impact instrument embedding social security in a new development policy paradigm.

This report of the Committee of Experts was transmitted to the Committee on the Application of Standards where it received a very mixed reception. The vice-chair for the employers' group from the US argued (ILO, 2011m: 18, para 79) that the report 'went beyond the mandate of the Committee of Experts as ILO standards policy and the proposals of new standards were the prerogative of the tripartite bodies. However, in contrast, the workers' group welcomed the report although the Brazilian delegation articulated its usual concern that the floor would become a ceiling in the context of transnational corporations acting globally (para 130). A number of governments such as Argentina, Austria, France and Spain welcomed the report. Within the context of this disagreement it fell to Egorov to pen the conclusions, which were reluctantly accepted also by the employers.[16] They concluded (para 142) that 'the committee supports a social protection floor providing a time-based progressive approach is adopted'. Thus, support for the SPF from the Committee of Experts and the Committee on the Application of Standards was conveyed to the Committee for the Recurrent Discussion on Social Protection on the Friday (3 June) just before the last main session scheduled for Saturday 4 June. We return to this point below.

Turning to the Committee for the Recurrent Discussion on Social Protection, it met on 12 occasions. Its initial membership on 1 June 2011 consisted of 96 government members, 33 employer members and 69 workers with differential votes allocated respectively to each government, employer and worker representative to ensure a balance of power between the three groups according to the constitution. The record of the formal sessions of the committee proceedings are published (ILO, 2011b) but not those of the workings of the all-important drafting group empowered at its seventh meeting to draw up the conclusions for adoption by the committee. The proceedings of the worker and employer caucus meetings are not public either. The chair of the committee was a government member for Luxembourg working with two vice-chairs drawn from the workers and employers.

The significant role of the Social Security Department in the deliberations of the full Committee for the Recurrent Discussion on Social Protection is shown by the fact that each of the five discussion sections at the conference, as listed below, was introduced and summed up at some length by either a member of the Social Security Department (six times) or a senior member of another relevant department such as Social Dialogue or even the director's office (four times):

- the role of social security in social and economic development;
- policies extending social security coverage;
- affordability and financing of social security;
- governance of social security;
- the role of standards in social security and ILO follow-up.

They were also involved as the secretariat for the Drafting Committee.

In addition to the role of the secretariat it is important to note the role of the vice-chairs who summed up also after each discussion section. The role of the workers' vice-chair, Helen Kelly of New Zealand, was particularly noteworthy[17] for the frequent support she offered to the wording about the SPF put forward by the secretariat. As an example, in paragraph 38 of the report of proceedings (ILO, 2011b) it is reported that she said:

> The Office report suggested a number of additional principles for the efficient and timely implementation of a Social Protection Floor and provided useful guidance. Her group was also in agreement that outcomes mattered. Member States should only pursue and implement systems that could guarantee the desired outcome, including benefits and democratic governance. Concerning the horizontal extension, a growing consensus had emerged on a combination of essential services, provisions in kind

and cash transfers for those in need of protection. The report outlined a basic set of guaranteed transfers which complemented and facilitated the access to essential services such as water, sanitation, health and education, which should constitute the Social Protection Floor. The Worker members supported these.

She did of course continue by asserting the links between the horizontal and vertical extensions of social security:

> The Social Protection Floor should be considered as the ground from which the social partners and government could develop the vertical extension. Upholding collective bargaining rights was key. Convention No. 102 provided a framework for introducing progressive systems of social protection. It continued to be a landmark standard and its ratification by middle-income States showed that countries could extend their social protection. Ratification should be widely encouraged.

In contrast, the opinions of the employer vice-chair, Michel Barde of Switzerland, opened by noting that the Office report 'approached the topic with an often ideological and unilateral approach ... [and that] it remained influenced by European models ... [and was] concerned that the Committee's discussions were at risk of being solely focused on the establishment of a SPF' (ILO, 2011b, para 10). The employers' group were concerned with costs, reminded delegates of the benefits of private pension funds and wanted a policy that assisted workers to migrate to the formal economy. It is procedure at the ILC committees that the vice-chairs speak for their groups and all other interventions are normally government representatives. Additional persuasion to encourage the delegates to agree with what the secretariat wanted was provided by a representative of the Bachelet Report's SPF advisory group. Importantly, it was Ms Sudha Pillai, secretary of the Planning Committee of India, who spoke clearly about the fact that 'the Advisory Group ... looked to the ILC for a clear Recommendation, an international instrument supporting the concept of a Social Protection Floor' (ILO, 2011b, para 48).

An analysis of the reported debate of the committee reveals the important differences between governments who broadly supported the case for the idea of an SPF Recommendation, those whose reported contribution made no reference to it and those who expressed the view that there should not be a global or universal SPF but one adapted to the specific conditions of countries. Table 4.1 indicates these different alignments. While there is some uncertainty about where to allocate some countries as this is based on published shortened reported contributions, the membership of the third column is not in doubt.

Table: 4.1: Some country positions on the SPF concept at the 2011 ILC as reflected in the Official Report of the Committee for the Recurrent Discussion on Social Protection

Offered explicit support for SPF Recommendation without reservations	Made no effective reference to the SPF	Argued for social floors reflecting country circumstances
Brazil	Saudi Arabia	India
Hungary (for EU)	Turkey	France
Vietnam	Korea	Canada
Senegal	Egypt	China
South Africa	Pakistan	USA
Zimbabwe	Tunisia	UK
Namibia	Ethiopia	Algeria
Netherlands	Jamaica	Uruguay
Australia	Thailand	Singapore
Venezuela	Bangladesh	
Japan	Sri Lanka	
Indonesia	Kuwait	
Cameroon	Mexico	
Ghana		
Germany		
Papua New Guinea		
Argentina		

These all are reported as explicitly making the point about adaptation to country circumstances. Of note are the non-contributions of countries one might have expected to have views on this issue.

During the course of the committee's deliberations there was a hearing of other international organisations at which a considerable amount of support was expressed for the 'SPF' concept. Of course by 2011 many of these same agencies (WHO, UNICEF, UNDP) were part of the wider UN SPF-I that had been engineered into existence by Somavia's chairing of the High Level Committee on Programmes of UNCEB in April 2009 (see Chapter Six). Nonetheless, the views of Arup Banjeri, the new director of social protection and labour within the World Bank, were significant. He was reported as saying that '[i]ts [the World Bank's] work complemented the standard setting of the ILO. A new ILO Recommendation on Social Protection *Floors* would be a welcome complement to the Bank's work (ILO, 2011b, para 134, emphasis added). Even the IMF representative, Gilles Bauche, was pleased to note that the SPF was now high on the global agenda. Unfortunately, reflecting how flexible the concept of the 'SPF' is, which talks only of outcomes and guarantees rather than of specific universal benefit packages, he went on to argue for safety nets and for targeting (ILO, 2011b, para 133). It was he who finally galvanised individual worker representatives into taking the floor. Worker members from Portugal (under IMF scrutiny at the time) and Senegal (having suffered structural adjustment) critiqued the historic role of the IMF (ILO, 2011b, paras 139, 140).

Finally, at the session on Saturday 4 June the committee considered the aforementioned report from the Committee on the Application of Standards. However, the minutes of the Committee for the Recurrent Discussion on Social Protection (ILO, 2011b: 24) devote only five paragraphs to this discussion (150-5). These suggest that the employer and employee tension on the Committee on the Application of Standards was rehearsed again for the Recurrent Committee in their verbal reports to the Recurrent Committee and very little attention was devoted even by the worker vice-chair of the Committee on the Application of Standards to the SPF Recommendation. So, despite all the efforts of the secretary of the Committee of Experts (Egorov) to seek to align their work with that of the Social Security Department's Recommendation, this intervention, coming as it did at the end of several days of discussion where all the issues pertaining to the SPF had been exhaustively discussed, probably had little impact.

The final conclusions of the Recurrent Committee's deliberations (ILO, 2011b) clearly reflect exchanges at the conference but also, importantly for my argument about the role of the secretariat, the conclusions reflect the arguments and policy suggestions present in earlier Social Security Department formulations that were examined in Chapter Three. Thus, the case for social protection as a human right and that it is a social and economic necessity is rehearsed again (ILO, 2011b, paras 1-5). The two-dimensional strategy for the extension of social security is set out again. The concept of the 'guarantees' provided for by the future Recommendation that would cover all in need in terms of income support and access to affordable health care is repeated. Another Social Security Department formulation was retained concerning funding. While the SPF should be financed from domestic resources, 'there may be cases where these resources are insufficient to extend the SPF to all in a short time frame. International cooperation can play an important role in helping member States to initiate the process and build the national resource base with a view to ensuring sustainable financing mechanisms' (ILO, 2011b, para 18).

However, reflecting the will of the conference or of some of its active participants, the conclusions also state that:

- SPF policies should ... 'promote productive economic activity' (employers lobby) (para 9).
- A one-size-fits-all approach is not appropriate, every member state should design and implement its SFP guarantees according to national circumstances (lobby of some powerful countries) (para 10).
- Social security ... cannot stop at the ground floor of protection ... hence the vertical dimension (workers lobby) (para 11).

Essentially, so long as the plural s was added to the SPF the job of the secretariat was done and the ILO committee agreed to its case that the next ILC in 2012 should discuss and agree on the actual text of a recommendation on social protection *floors*.

Boosted by this progress, the Social Security Department felt able, in its subsequent report to the November 2011 ILO governing body setting out the Department's 'plan of action' for the period 2011-19, to include in it this grandiose ambition (ILO, 2011g: 2, para 6, emphasis added):

> The development of and discussion on a possible recommendation on social protection floors (SPFs) in 2012 and follow-up to its possible adoption will be one of the core standard-setting activities for the next eight years. *The aim is for the global community to send out a strong visible signal that 100 per cent of the global population should benefit at least from basic social security guarantees* and that, taking into account national priorities and circumstances, member States should aim to close the coverage gaps as soon as possible.

The Office draft of the SPFs Recommendation

Immediately after the June 2011 ILC, the Social Security Department set about in effect drafting the SPFs in the form of the questionnaire to governments. The initial work was carried out by the Social Security Department but the final shape of the text was developed by a formal group consisting of the Social Security, Standards and Legal Departments of the ILO. One had only to convert the questions into statements to understand what the Recommendation would look like if the Office version was accepted. Table 4.2, comparing the July 2011 questionnaire with the subsequent March 2012 draft and the final June 2012 text, and presented at the end of this chapter, reveals remarkable similarity over time.

An anxious period ensued waiting for the responses at the end of November. Once received, the small team of the policy section of the Social Security Department who had authored and supported the SPF to date locked themselves away for a couple of weeks in January 2012 to digest the responses. In the event there was no need for such anxiety as the vast majority of countries and indeed the separate responses received from national worker and national employer organisations were largely positive about most of the questions.

The Office commentary on the responses received states that '[a] large number of replies show a broad general consensus with respect to the possible content of the proposed Recommendation concerning national floors of social protection' (ILO, 2012b: 167). The 46 questions or sub-questions where a 'yes' answer indicated support for the draft generated support from over 70% of the 98 countries replying and often support from over 90% (ILO, 2012b: 167, Table 1). The level of support from employer organisations was often much less than from governments and, in general, support from worker organisations was often higher. It was later reported at the opening session of the Committee on Social Protection at the ILC on 29 May 29 2012 that the averaged level of positive replies to questions was 94% in the case of workers, 61% in the case of employers and 87% in the case of governments. In some cases the majority of employers did not support the draft. This was the case with regard to questions 8, 9, 13, 17, 18, 19, 20, 23, 24, 25 and 27. Thus, they were not in support of establishing a legal right to the SPF with an associated appeal procedure, nor in support of the suggested level of the income guarantees, nor in setting a timeframe by which countries with limited resources should plan to establish their SPF. This degree of reservation by some employers was not regarded as too worrying as they only represent 25% of the membership of the ILC.

These measures of the degree of overall consensus mask, however, significant dissent about key issues by some important and influential governments. Thus, broadly reflecting the list of countries we noted above who at the 2011 ILC had insisted on the *national* nature of any SPFs, we find the following countries most often expressing reservations about one or other aspect of the draft SPF implied by the questionnaire: China, India, the UK and to some extent the US. Sometimes the repeated appearance of these countries in the list of those who answered 'no' to a question simply reflects the detailed level of engagement of the country with the issues but generally it reflects the fact that those countries had a fairly critical attitude to the endeavour.

Significant was the position of the two most powerful emerging countries: China and India. Unlike their BRICS counterparts, Brazil, South Africa and to some extent Russia who were broadly supportive of the draft Recommendation implied by the questionnaire, China and India repeatedly expressed their opposition to clause after clause of the draft Recommendation implied by the questionnaire. Question 6, outlining the basic concept of the 'SPF' as a commitment to the four guarantees, met with this reported response[18] from China: 'Too ambitious requirement for many States, particularly developing countries, for a long time'; and from India: 'Establishing and implementing a SPF for all should be required, but without time frame. Developing countries face challenges of reaching out to vast populations with limited resources and infrastructure. States should decide when and how to ensure uniform coverage at a nationally defined minimum level.' Regarding question 7, the section concerning guarantees for children, India stated: 'Commitment to provide such vital services to "all children" should not be part of the Recommendation. States should decide whether to cover all children.' Similarly with regard to guarantees for those of working age, India stated: 'Provision of minimum income security, unemployment allowance, health-care and disability benefits for "all persons" in a country is not feasible.' Question 8, suggesting that the SPF should embody rights to be addressed through a complaints and appeals procedure, met with this response from China: 'Introducing complaint and appeal mechanisms would not support the realization of social protection's objective to promote social justice and harmony'; and from India: 'Countries with vast populations and facing poverty and unemployment challenges cannot afford to guarantee social security as a legally enforceable right.' With regard to setting time lines for implementation (question 17), India replied: 'Member States should not be required to lay down a definite time frame for the extension of the entire set of social security guarantees to all beneficiaries.' And in response to question 30 concerning monitoring, India noted: 'Strong monitoring mechanisms to be developed nationally, but no monitoring by external agencies.'

It is indeed ironic and a source of much perplexity for Northern-based progressively minded campaigners for a fairer world that when the ILO finally moves beyond its focus on social security benefits for privileged workers and addresses the needs of poor people in the developing world its most implacable opponents are the governments of the largest developing economies who will use their new-found global power to potentially scupper or at least hollow out the call for a global social floor. In that sense the North–South progressive impasse discussed in Chapter Two has not been entirely overcome. We shall see later, however, that two other of the BRICS – Brazil and South Africa – were key supporters of the Office draft.

Perhaps paramount among the consensus of responses was therefore the view that SPFs should be referred to in the plural and reflect various national circumstances. The Office commentary notes (ILO, 2012b: 168):

> One recurring comment from governments and employers' and workers' organizations, expressed in respect to almost all questions, is the importance and the need for the development of any extension strategy – as well as its implementation and monitoring – to be tailored to and consistent with national circumstances and priorities, and to take into account national capacities and available resources. In addition, a number of comments stress that national SPFs should consistently be referred to in the plural form.

There could be no way back to a globally defined floor.

An important issue to which we have given little attention so far was the definition of those who should be covered by the proposed SPF guarantees. From the outset the Social Security Department had always used the term *resident* rather than *citizen*, making the implicit point that entitlement to the SPF should be broad based. Precisely, the questionnaire had stated in question 7a, b, c and d concerning the four guarantees that these should be available to 'all persons ordinarily resident in the country', thus fudging somewhat the entitlement to social protection of unregistered or illegal migrants. In the case of children, however, question 7b asserted 'all children' should be entitled to income security without the ordinarily resident caveat. Some countries questioned the ordinarily resident formulation. The UK said 'replace "ordinarily resident" with "habitually resident"' (ILC, 2012b: 34). Cichon was really concerned that a protracted debate about issues of residency would put in jeopardy the whole Recommendation.[19] In response, the Social Security Department came up with the following formulation in the draft Recommendation to be submitted to the 2012 ILC, which would apply to all the guarantees (ILO, 2012c, para 6): 'Subject to their existing international obligations, Members should provide the basic social security guarantees referred to in this

Recommendation to at least all residents and children, as defined in national laws and regulations.' By way of explanation of this revised formulation using the term 'existing international obligations', the Office commentary on the responses argued (ILO, 2012b: 172):

> In this context, it may be noted that the General Comment No. 19 of the (UN) Committee on Economic, Social and Cultural Rights [CEACR] states, regarding the right to social security, that '[a]ll persons, irrespective of their nationality, residency or immigration status, are entitled to primary and emergency medical care'.[20] Furthermore, the CEACR, in reference to the scope of application of constitutional guarantees relating to social security, noted that, 'extending the right to social security, including the right to medical care, to non-citizens is a key challenge for many societies today. With regard to the non-citizens, even where they are in an irregular status on the territory of another State, such as undocumented workers, they should have access to basic benefits and particularly to emergency medical care.[21]

Whether this formulation and clarification would be enough to avoid a bruising debate in June 2012 would remain to be seen. China, for example, in response to the question about the guarantees, '[r]efers to the need to distinguish between citizens and migrants. The clause is acceptable if the scope of the prescribed basic social security guarantee is limited to citizens' (ILO, 2012b: 33).

Where the responses were found to be helpful was in enabling the Social Security Department to reformulate more precisely the principles that should underpin SPFs in all countries. Thus, the Office commentary made the point that (ILO, 2012b: 183):

> The proposed Recommendation spells out, in paragraph 3, a set of re-ordered and more precise principles. These seek to identify a common denominator of interests, as expressed by respondents in their replies. In line with the above suggestions, the list of principles now also explicitly mentions 'social solidarity', 'responsiveness to special needs', 'predictability of benefits', 'overall and primary responsibility of the State', and 'involvement of representative organizations of employers and workers

as well as consultation with representatives of other organizations and persons concerned'.

In terms of the diverse means by which the guarantees could be realised, the large majority of respondents agreed that member states may use different means and approaches to implement the basic social security guarantees of their SPFs, including universal benefit schemes, social insurance, public employment programmes and employment support schemes as well as social assistance schemes that provide benefits to people with low income, or appropriate combinations of such measures. Some governments suggested that the listing of possible options was not useful. Others suggested that such options should also include means and approaches provided by private actors and civil society. Most workers' organisations suggested that guidance should be provided as to which instruments are best suited to achieve universality of access and predictability of income security. In the event the opportunity was taken by the Office to specify in some detail a wide range of possible benefits and benefit packages to ensure the meeting of the minimum income guarantees. Paragraph 9 set these out in detail (see Box 4.1). Curiously, in addition, the Office decided also to include right at the beginning of the draft in paragraph 2 the formulation: 'Such guarantees may be achieved through contributory or non-contributory schemes, whether means-tested or not.' Quite why this was felt to be necessary is unclear.

Emerging from the Office review of the responses was the formal draft Recommendation to be discussed at the ILC in June 2012. In terms of the issues we have particularly focused on, the draft sets out:

- the way SPFs are to be *defined nationally* (paras 2 and 4);
- the *guiding principles* of both the SPF and the associated extension of the social security systems (para 3);
- the extent to which the obligations are *time-bound* (para 4);
- the content of the SPF *four guarantees* (para 5);
- the coverage of these guarantees *beyond citizens* (para 6);
- their existence as *rights appeal-able in law* (para 8);
- the *diverse means* by which the guarantees can be realised (para 9);
- the *fiscal means* by which revenues could be raised to pay for the benefits to meet the guarantees (para 11);
- the option of transitional funding with *international resources* (para 12);
- the procedures for their *monitoring* (para 19).

Box 4.1: Key paragraphs of the Office draft of the SPF Recommendation

2. For the purpose of this Recommendation, social protection floors are nationally defined sets of basic social security guarantees which secure protection aimed at preventing or alleviating poverty, vulnerability and social exclusion. Such guarantees may be achieved through contributory or non-contributory schemes, whether means-tested or not.

3. In giving effect to this Recommendation, Members should apply the following principles:

a) universality of protection, based on social solidarity;
b) entitlement to benefits prescribed by law;
c) non-discrimination, gender equality and responsiveness to special needs;
d) adequacy and predictability of benefits;
e) a fair balance between the interests of those who finance social security schemes and the interests of those who benefit from them;
f) coherence with social, economic and employment policies;
g) progressive realization;
h) diversity of methods and approaches, including of financing mechanisms and delivery systems;
i) transparent and sound financial management and administration;
j) financial, fiscal and economic sustainability;
k) involvement of representative organizations of employers and workers as well as consultation with representatives of other organizations and persons concerned; and
l) overall and primary responsibility of the State.

4. Members should put in place and complete as rapidly as possible, and maintain, their social protection floors comprising basic social security guarantees. The guarantees should ensure at a minimum that, over the life cycle, all in need have access to essential health care and to basic income security which together secure effective access to goods and services defined as necessary at the national level.

5. The social protection floors referred to in Paragraph 4 should comprise at least the following basic social security guarantees:

a) access to a nationally defined set of goods and services, constituting essential health care, including in the case of maternity;

b) basic income security for children, at least at a nationally defined minimum level, providing access to nutrition, education, care and any other necessary goods and services;

c) basic income security, at least at a nationally defined minimum level, for persons in active age who are unable to earn sufficient income, including in case of sickness, unemployment, maternity and disability; and ·

d) basic income security, at least at a nationally defined minimum level, for persons in old age.

6. Subject to their existing international obligations, Members should provide the basic social security guarantees referred to in this Recommendation to at least all residents and children, as defined in national laws and regulations.

8. Basic social security guarantees should be established by law. National laws and regulations should specify the range, qualifying conditions and levels of the benefits giving effect to these guarantees. Effective, simple, rapid, accessible and inexpensive complaint and appeals procedures should also be specified.

9. (1) In providing the basic social security guarantees, Members should consider different approaches as provided in paragraph 2 with a view to implementing the most effective and efficient combination of benefits and schemes in the national context. (2) Benefits may include child and family benefits, sickness and health care benefits, maternity benefits, disability benefits, old-age benefits, survivors' benefits, unemployment benefits and employment guarantees, employment injury benefits, as well as any other social benefits in cash or in kind. (3) Schemes providing such benefits may include universal benefit schemes, social insurance schemes, social assistance schemes, negative income tax schemes, public employment schemes, and employment support schemes. [NOTE paragraph 2 reads: Such guarantees may be achieved through contributory or non-contributory schemes, whether means-tested or not.]

11. Members should consider using different methods to mobilize the necessary resources to ensure financial, fiscal and economic sustainability of national social protection floors, taking into account the contributory capacities of different population groups. Such methods may include, individually or in combination, better enforcement of tax and contribution obligations, reprioritizing expenditure, or broadening the revenue base.

> 12. National social protection floors should be financed, in principle, by national resources. Members whose economic and fiscal capacities are insufficient to implement the entire set of guarantees may seek transitional international assistance.
>
> 19. Members should monitor progress in implementing social protection floors and achieving other objectives of national social security extension strategies, through appropriate nationally defined mechanisms involving representative organizations of employers and workers and, as appropriate, representatives of other organizations and persons concerned.

The 2012 ILC: final text of the SPFs Recommendation

Context

The scene was therefore set for the final hurdle. Would the Office draft of the SPF Recommendation be agreed largely unscathed at the 101st ILC in June 2012? In terms of the draft content almost all the compromises that needed to be made had already been made. These were to be national SPFs, not globally defined. The Recommendation would only specify outcomes, not one specific means of achieving them. The issue of international funding was relegated to a residual option. The level of international monitoring was scaled back. The possibility of regional variation within countries had been conceded presumably at the suggestion of China or India. Perhaps only the insistence on the floor as embodying rights and moreover rights of non-citizens might prove contentious. Possibly also the rather strengthened formulations concerning the primary responsibility of the state for social protection and the predictability of benefit levels would be objected to by employers. The extent of the involvement of civil society organisations other than trades unions and employers could prove tricky.

Michael Cichon as head of social security was by no means confident, believing that there had been temporary constellations of alliances in 2011, which had got the SPF this far. Others were clear that the ILC could not fail, having led the UN down this path and made so much publicity out of it. There were complicating factors. The leader of the employers' group who had been relatively helpful in 2011 had retired and was to be replaced by a Belgian. The focus of the delegates was going to be distracted by the election, a few days before the opening of the ILC, of the new director-general of the ILO replacing Somavia who, as reported in the next chapter, had been so instrumental in focusing global attention on the SPF. What would be the attitude of the new director-general, Guy Ryder, formally of the ICFTU and the nominee of the worker members of the governing body? The immediate impact was not clear.

However, the ILC opened with due ceremony on 30 May 2012 and the Committee for the Recurrent Discussion on Social Protection set about its work that same day. I was no longer an ILO visiting fellow, merely a visitor relegated to the public gallery and of course not privy to the work of the three caucuses or the back-stage drafting of the committee's proceedings and conclusions.

The significance of the decision that the conference was about to make was indeed drawn attention to by Somavia in his opening address to the ILC, by Diop as director of the broad Social Protection Division of the ILO opening the work of the committee and by Cichon himself, head of social security, in his opening remarks to the committee. Each interestingly drew on slightly different narratives to reinforce their point, reflecting their own particular involvement in the process and indeed the different strands of the story told in this book.

Somavia preferred to refer to a *four-year* build up to this day, mentioning its origins in the 2008 Global Justice Declaration and the 2008 global economic crisis, which triggered the UN SPF-I. He said that once the conference was over, while delegates would go back home to make the SPF work, he would take the message to the G20, to Rio plus 20 and to the UN Economic and Social Council (ECOSOC), drawing attention to his continued work on the global political and international organisation stage. He stressed the all-important symbolic difference between the SPF 'upon which people could stand and safety nets through which people could fall' (ILC, 101st session, provisional record, third sitting). Diop, reflecting his own 12-year headship of the Social Protection Division, more accurately referred back to the work from 2001 on extending social security and the technical work undertaken in the 2005 period on the affordability of social protection. Cichon allowed himself a brief expression of personal emotion, saying that he was at the same time full of "pride, joy and humility" as the committee assumed its "historic responsibility", which, if successful, would "influence global policies and debate on social protection for decades to come and impact positively on real lives". His pride was understandable and justified, his joy might be fleeting, his humility inappropriate.

The committee on the SPF

The committee room was set out in the time-honoured *quadripartite* format of the ILO: workers in the slice of chairs on the left, employers on the right, the doubly large size of the government delegation taking up the centre, with all of them facing the high table of the Office at which sat the Social Security Department staff. Also in keeping with ILO tradition was a very small space on the side for the small contingent of INGOs. The attendance was around 200-300. How on earth one wondered could such a large committee agree a text within two weeks?

Opening the real work, Cichon rehearsed all the steps to here and added two lists of possible issues for discussion, one drawn from replies to the questionnaire reported earlier and the other drawn from responses from UN agencies such as UN Women, the UN Human Rights Council (UNHRC) and INGOs. The first list included the issue of:

- specific benefits versus guarantees;
- global guidance versus national definition;
- progressive realisation over time;
- coverage beyond 'resident';
- timetables and targets.

The second included:

- greater emphasis on the human rights context;
- the additional principle of 'dignity' of recipients;
- the residency/coverage issue again;
- social protection for those having to do unpaid 'care work';
- involvement as distinct from consultation of social partners, including beneficiaries.

In making this second list, Cichon effectively drew attention to a list of proposed text changes lobbied for by his one-time colleague from the informal social-floor meeting days of 2000-05, Wouter van Ginneken. Van Ginneken now headed an INGO that had been instrumental, with the help of a Friedrich Ebert Stiftung seminar held on 29-30 March 2012 in Geneva, in attracting the signatures of 54 INGOs to a joint statement on the SPF. It so happened that van Ginneken had registered his INGO for the ILC and was fortuitously able to offer his services to present the statement to the committee.

From the point of view of someone trying to chronicle events, the next steps on this first opening day would be frustrating. This official meeting of the committee at which I was welcome lasted only one and a half hours. Next on the agenda for three or more hours were scheduled closed caucus meetings of the workers, the employers and several groups of governments such as the EU, Gulf states, Latin America and Africa. There was no way of accessing these meetings.

The Thursday session of the committee, continuing into Friday morning, would give some indication as to whether the Office was going to have an easy ride. It was an opportunity for general opening remarks by whoever chose to make them. The new vice-chair for the employers delivered a short speech, which suggested that either there was not an employer strategy or it was being kept hidden. In sharp contrast, the experienced vice-chair for the workers, Helen Kelly, delivered an inspired oration referring to the 300th anniversary of Rousseau that Geneva would be celebrating this year and referencing his work on the social contract. She reminded the committee of all that had already been agreed, warning against backsliding and nit-picking. She laid down a challenge to the new director-general to pick up and run with the SPF. She stressed the case for universalism and for state obligation. Now she argued, looking to the employers, was not the time to burden the SPF with concepts of activation into work. 'People must be enabled to decline the worst forms of work' and the SPF should help ensure this was the case.

Some 24 countries then spoke. The EU and the Gulf states were broadly supportive. No other group had yet got their act together. Of the several individual countries that made interventions most, as was the case in 2011 simply used the opportunity to report positive stories of their own country social protection policies without drawing out any implications for a SPF. Rather unsurprisingly, Canada, India and the US and stressed once again the case for flexible floors fashioned to country circumstances and resources. Bangladesh, Morocco and the Philippines were the countries to argue that migrant social protection should be equal to those of citizens. Significantly absent as speakers were three of the BRIC countries – China, Russia and South Africa – and also Japan. The session that carried over until Friday also saw the now familiar intervention by Somavia and provided, almost grudgingly, for a total 10-minute intervention by INGOs. Wouter van Ginneken, spoke on behalf of the 54 NGOs that supported his statement, which called for the *participation* of social floor beneficiaries in policy making, for the floor to be firmly based on a human rights (not political will) basis and for the guarantees of the floor to be extended to all people on the planet and hence all inhabitants regardless of status on a territory.

The draft SPF: preamble

Friday saw the first real work of the committee, deciding paragraph by paragraph on the preamble to the Recommendation. The session was not so much interesting for the outcome; the Office text was modified in a few mainly useful ways, but for what it revealed about procedure, the relevant influence of different players and something of the global politics of the issue. Some 20 amendments had been duly submitted and were considered in the three working languages of English, French and Spanish. The language issue perhaps offers a further reason for the singular non-intervention of China and Russia. In terms of the players it was clearly going to become a committee dominated in terms of active countries by the EU, a large group of Latin American states led by Brazil, India with its ally Bangladesh, the US when it could find a country to second any amendment, and perhaps a few African states with Zimbabwe speaking on behalf of Africa. Interestingly, the EU seemed to be tabling amendments stressing activation policies, anti-corruption policies and generally being regarded by some other countries as siding with or representing austerity against increased social spending. Indeed, the role of the passionate defenders of public spending on social security to stabilise the economy and create social peace fell not to the EU but to Latin America who proudly told its social protection success stories. Bangladesh, India and some African countries spoke up for the importance of social protection in informal contexts. Significant and worrying from the point of view of those who hoped to see the SPF usher in a new language of floors to challenge the language of safety nets was the way in which some countries, precisely Papua New Guinea, the Phillipines, Trinidad and Tobago and the US, referred to 'safety nets' favourably as an aspect of their or another country's social protection policy. The attempt to shift the discourse from safety nets to floors was not even universally achieved among the SPF supporters.

More powerful than any group of countries were and are the employer and worker groups who between them hold 50% of the votes. Time and time again on tabling an amendment for debate the chair turned first to either the worker spokesperson or the employer and then to the other and if both agreed it was more or less a done deal. Only when they disagreed did any serious attention have to be given to the division of opinion among the governments; in a few cases leading to a show of hands vote.

The influence of the secretariat resided in (a) the close attention being paid to the proceedings by the head of social security sitting next to the chair and advising him on how procedural matters might be handled and (b) the assumption adopted by the chair that if a paragraph of the Office draft had attracted no amendments then it was assumed to be accepted. However, Cichon was not called on to defend the Office version being officially regarded as a mere servant of governments and social partners.

The first two hours of Saturday were given over to finishing the preamble to the Recommendation. This saw another example of what was to become a quite familiar pattern. Brazil, speaking on behalf of the progressive alliance of also Argentina, Bolivia, Chile, Ecuador and Venezuela, wanted to insert a new paragraph into the preamble, which would have articulated a grand vision of a future for social protection beyond the floor, which read (D. 12):

> Considering that social protection floors are a first step in a process of advancing towards an integrated set of social policies aimed at universalizing and improving social protection in every country and ensuring income security and access to goods and services that guarantee social rights, in an integral, universal, equitable and irreversible manner, with special attention to vulnerable groups and to the empowerment of individuals as citizens….

The workers supported this but once the employers objected it fell to the now familiar list of Bangladesh, India, Trinidad and Tobago, the United Arab Emirates, Zimbabwe and the EU to ensure the Office draft was not amended to read more progressively. The contrast in line-up of forces with the failed attempt to get agreement in 2000 to a set of progressive social policy principles led then by the UK and Europe was telling. Latin America was now pushing the progressive agenda too far for the likes of many developing countries and the UK and Europe.

Draft SPF: objectives, scope and principles (Section I)

Next we saw the start of the debate about the real heart of the draft Recommendation: Section I dealing with the objectives, scope and principles that should underpin SPFs, and within this the important list in paragraph 3 of the 12 principles ranging from (a) universalism to (l) primary responsibility of the state (see paragraph 3 of the draft in Box 4.1). The pattern was repeated of attempts being made by the workers or by the Latin America group to seek to strengthen the Recommendation by urging more universalism, limiting means tests and stressing the need for complaints procedures. Of the 41 amendments tabled for this section, 16 were tabled by the workers, nine by the Latin America progressive alliance, five by employers, four by the US with Canada, three by the EU and two by Africa, with a single amendment from Iran and Turkey.

In the event, the Office list of principles remained largely intact, with the concept of the overall responsibility of the state 'elevated' to an opening phrase of the paragraph introducing the list: thus 'Recognizing the overall responsibility of the State should etc'. It could be argued that this actually shifted the concept of state responsibility as *provider* of services to the mere acknowledgement that governments had a *responsibility* to ensure that SPFs were provided by any provider. A number of new principles such as those ensuring that the guarantees aimed at 'social inclusion', and enabling access to 'high-quality public services' and allowing recipients 'accessible complaints procedures' were inserted largely at the behest of the workers' group as was the principle of setting a timeline to be met when the guarantees were 'progressively' developed by poorer countries. A new principle argued for by the workers but reflecting a campaigning point of the INGOs was that provisions should 'respect the dignity of people covered by the social security guarantees', and a new principle from the US asked for 'coherence across institutions responsible for delivery of social protection'. An attempt was made to extend the principle of gender equity to equity in relation to ethnic and other social groups by Brazil on behalf of the 'progressive' Latin America bloc but the listing of many groups was opposed and the amendment withdrawn. This section of the committee's work once again showed the progressive role of the workers caucus.

However, the other side of the face of the workers caucus was revealed next when its self-interest in the governance of social protection was up for discussion. One of the key issues both for the workers on the one hand and INGOs on the other was whether representatives of recipients of the SPF, in other words representative NGOs, have only the right to be *consulted* about policy or actually along with workers and employers be *involved* in policy making directly. Brazil and South Africa, responding to the INGO lobby, asked for 'consultation' to be changed to 'involvement' but straight away the issue became clouded by the US wishing to insert a further phrase that called for an open (consultation) process with 'special emphasis on the involvement of' such NGOs. This special emphasis on the NGOs was clearly going too far for the established trade union social partner. The Brazilian amended amendment was thus lost. There would be no call for the NGOs to be *involved* in decisions about the SPF. Just to reinforce this strangle-hold over the committee on this issue at two further points in the draft where the subject arose (draft, paras 7d and 19), the workers with the employers' support inserted the same formulation about tripartite discussions and merely *consultations* with others.

So once again, just as when Somavia had tried to talk up the role of NGOs in the ILO when he arrived at the ILO, so now, as he was retiring, the alliance of the workers and employers caucus rallied to their mutual defence and protected their command of the ILO decision-making process and sought to do this for the SPF processes as well. As van Ginneken commented afterwards: "They just could not do it ... invite NGOs to the table ... as it would undermine them and be an end to the ILO ... but of course tripartism-plus (involving NGOs) will be a reality in countries and is already."

Draft SPF: definition (Section II)

Attention then turned to the all-important Section II defining the content of the SPFs. At the outset a large coalition of 50 African countries wanted to qualify that SPFs should only be developed 'in accordance with national context and considering the level of national economic development' (Amendment D95). A similar amendment proposed by Bangladesh, India, Iran and Nepal would also have inserted reference to the fiscal resources of a country (D88). Helen Kelly, on behalf of the workers, argued convincingly against the main thrust of this, pointing out that countries at the same level of economic development had different levels of social protection and that the issue was political will, not level of development. In the event the reference to the level of economic development was not accepted.

In terms of the substantive content of the definition there was a serious challenge to one of the four guarantees. Bangladesh, India and Nepal, together with the US, aimed to delete the concept that children should be guaranteed basic income security (D87 and D89); India said that the concept of *child benefits* did not exist in India. This was deftly argued against by the workers representative pointing out that *family income* support such as that available under the Latin American conditional cash transfer schemes were forms of income support to children preventing them having to work. The four proposed guarantees were indeed endorsed and in the case of the guarantee of basic health care the clause was strengthened by the intervention of the workers.

Having clarified the definition of the four guarantees, the committee turned to the one issue that the secretariat had feared might derail the whole project: that of whether or not the guarantees should be available only to legally recognised residents or to all people on the planet including unregistered migrants and so on. Helen Kelly, for the workers, made a brave attempt to argue (a) that the *aim* should be to cover all people on the planet with a first step being coverage of legal residents and (b) that within the first step, coverage should be provided to at least all children (D71). She argued for a clause that would have said:

> As a priority step towards the realisation of the right of everyone to social security as stated in the Universal Declaration of Human Rights, the guarantees referred to in this Recommendation should apply to at least all children, and to all residents as defined in national laws and regulations and subject to their existing international obligations.

Kelly explained that the wording was an attempt to find a compromise between the worker members' view that everyone should have access to the basic rights referred to in the Recommendation, and the reluctance she expected from governments to grant universal coverage. The Universal Declaration of Human Rights covered everyone, regardless of status or nationality. The SPF should be universal, even for children who were illegally present in a country. The priority focus should be on children, as they were especially vulnerable, but governments should extend coverage to all residents. Shifting the comma and putting children before the caveat about national laws and regulations was crucial, she argued.

Kelly's argument pointed out that if indeed all countries introduced adequate SPFs, the push and pull of migrants in search of better protection might reduce. She argued 'we had to dream the dream that the SPF was intended to aspire to.' There was support for the coverage of all children from Brazil and other Latin American countries and even the US initially. The initial statement of the employers' representative suggested that he could accept the coverage of all children. The debate became complicated by the US wanting to insert reference to bilateral and regional agreements about social protection portability. A break between sessions allowed for private consultations, which had been seen as a way of incorporating (a) the aspiration to cover all eventually, (b) coverage of all children now and (c) the role of bilateral and regional agreements in social security portability. However, no complete deal was struck. On returning to the debate the workers' group proposed the following wording:

> As a priority step towards universal coverage, Members should provide the basic social security guarantees referred to in this Recommendation to at least all children, and to all residents as defined in national laws and regulations and subject to their existing international obligations including bilateral, regional and multilateral social security agreements.

Kelly argued that the ambition of universal coverage should be retained, the notion of the first step towards it would be acknowledged, and all children would be covered, even if not all governments seemed to agree on that. The employers retreated to a position of letting see what countries felt first before restating their views and making a commitment. Brazil, it seemed to me, supported the new wording and 'dared countries to argue against the commitment to all children'. However, led by the EU, countries fell into line with the original text simply by stating 'we support the original text' or adding 'the text is now getting too complicated' and thus seeming to defeat the effort to both build a future vision of universal coverage and of covering all children now. Indeed, the INGO report of the day (van Ginneken, 2012) noted that:

> There was quite a discussion on the residence concept (article 6). The workers' group had proposed a brilliant new text, saying that on the way to universal – planetary – coverage we could already accept coverage for all children – regardless of their legal status – and for 'all residents as defined in national laws and regulations and subject to their existing international obligations'. The amendment was spoiled by various sub-amendments, in particular by the United States, and the committee then adopted the originally proposed text. It is not clear to me whether this text extends coverage to at least all children.

However, it later transpired that the original wording of the Office document that said that the floor should be available to 'all residents and children, as defined in national laws and regulations' should be interpreted to read that the floor would indeed be available to all children subject only to national laws *about the age at which persons are regarded as children.*

The committee then turned to the discussion of points that countries should give consideration to in planning their SPFs. In general this process and indeed later sessions saw several attempts by either Latin America or the workers to strengthen formulations and commitments being knocked back by the alliance of Bangladesh, India, Nepal and a few other countries making a special plea for the realities of poor countries supported almost always by the EU. The US interestingly was often on the progressive side of the debate. However, the progressive voices did secure three significant improvements to the Office draft. The discussion about how to ensure that people accessing health care did not face financial hardship, led to the agreement that at least pre- and post-natal medical care should be free at the point of contact (D69). In terms of how countries should finance their SPFs, it was agreed that the suggested broadened tax base should be progressive (D105).

Of the three successes, the one that stimulated the most exciting and interesting and detailed debate so far in the committee was that concerning the mechanisms that should be put in place by countries to enable claimants to appeal against decisions of the bodies responsible for the SPF. The first suggested amendment to paragraph 8 concerning these procedures simply suggested the insertion of the qualifiers that the appeals process should be 'impartial and transparent' (D67). The employers did not agree, which therefore triggered the government debate. Again the EU opposed but it was outnumbered by the US, and a large number of other countries from Latin America, Africa and the Middle East. More significant was the proposal by the workers that access to such appeals procedures should be *free of cost* and not inexpensive as the Office draft had stated. For those interested in the bread and butter, basic issues of how to construct benefit appeals procedures the debate was well informed and dynamic.

Once again the EU was against the concept of cost-free access to an appeals procedure, leading many of the observers wondering what ever happened to the progressive position that the EU likes to think it adopts in global debates. A final show of hands suggested that bout 40 countries were in favour of a no-cost appeals process and about 30 against, which incidentally revealed how many countries were not engaged in the work of the committee. This conservatism of the EU was repeated often. It sought, against a majority, the deletion of the option of 'employment guarantees' as one of the different ways in which social protection could be provided (draft, para 9(1)) (D110). It found itself on the losing side of an argument against Latin America,

Africa and many others about whether the tax base for funding social protection should be 'progressive' or not as proposed in an amendment by the workers to draft paragraph 11 (D105). In a discussion about funding the SPF, it was suggested by the workers that there should be 'support for adequate wage levels and collective bargaining in order to increase the contributory capacity of workers' (for the SPF). Here the EU's opposition contrasted sharply with the US's support, reflecting the austerity versus spending-to-reinvigorate-the-economy transatlantic debate.

The last discussion within Section II of the draft addressed the issue of international financial support for the SPF. It had been a key point of the employers in many earlier discussions that funds for the SPF should come from national budgets. It had been one of the key arguments of the Social Security Department that SPFs were affordable even in poor countries. The broader international climate of opinion was increasingly favouring the case that poorer countries did have to get their houses in order with regard to raising revenues and dealing with corruption and excessive privilege of the few. Poor countries too wanted to be out from under paternalistic and conditional Northern aid funds. These funds were often being cut in the context of the economic crisis. It was some achievement then for those in the Social Security Department who did believe in the case for North–South or Rich–Poor transfers to have retained in the draft the formulation that: 'Members whose economic and fiscal capacities are insufficient to implement the entire set of guarantees may seek transitional international assistance.' Some of those countries who were defining themselves as poor for this purpose – Bangladesh, India and Nepal – were unhappy with the 'concept of transitional assistance'. In the event, thanks to an amendment by the workers (D99), the text was strengthened to remove 'transitional' and to suggest that what countries might seek was 'international cooperation and support that complements their own efforts'.

Draft SPF: country strategies for the extension of social security (Section III)

By Wednesday of the second week, the committee turned to address that part of the Recommendation dealing with the extension of social security vertically, ensuring both higher levels of contributory social security coverage and broader coverage of more residents within such schemes. The inclusion of this vertical extension was the deal struck with the workers to ensure their acceptance of the floor concept. So from the point of view of those interested primarily in the definitions and principles of the SPF, it was less important. In general, the session consisted of efforts by the workers or Brazil in alliance with the workers, sometimes successful, to make it even clearer that the SPF was not an alternative to decent wage-related social security as provided for within the ILO Convention 102. Thus, an amendment (D166) precisely ensured that when governments formulated their national social security extension strategies they were to be considered 'as a starting point for countries that do not have a minimum level of social security guarantees as a fundamental element of their national social security systems'.

On the other hand the session was characterised by some of the developing countries, often supported by the EU, wanting to lower expectations and obligations on countries both with regard to the level of the SPF and to the speed with which there would be further developments of the social security systems. Thus, Bangladesh and India in a failed sub-amendment did not even want the SPF to be regarded as a starting point. The starting point should be lower. In relation to the Office draft of paragraph 13b saying that countries should 'Seek to provide higher levels of protection to as many people as possible as soon as possible', the EU, supported by Africa, Bangladesh, India, Iran, Iraq and Tunisia, succeeded in inserting the caveat that the speed at which this higher level should be achieved must 'reflect economic and fiscal capacity' despite the objection of the workers that the speed was a matter of political will, not only the level of economic development.

In one such attempt where the focus was on the argument that the SPF should be structured in such a way that it would encourage people to be removed from informal employment so that they could access contributory social security, the gap between the preoccupations of securely employed formal workers and countries where most workers are informally employed was sharply revealed. In an amendment proposed by Latin American countries supported by both the workers and employers that the aim of the SPF was 'the reduction of informality' (D162), Zimbabwe on behalf of African countries pointed out that government loans were often geared precisely to the support of the establishment of forms of informal employment, which was a good thing as in time people empowered by this would become formally employed. It was argued that the whole idea of the SPF was that because coverage by ideal social security failed to meet the needs of the 80% uncovered by such schemes it would be better now to provide other forms of protection to those who were informally employed and likely to remain so for many years to come, as India also kept pointing out.

But, in general, the mantra of formal employment and the goal being Convention 102 for the formally employed was repeated and accepted.

And then China spoke! Where had they been? This was day seven of the deliberations. And what was their intervention? The workers were attempting to introduce a not very well-worded new paragraph (D147), which addressed the issue of policy coherence both at the national level and at the level of international agencies. This was an attempt to reflect some of the broader involvement of the ILO with the global dialogue on these issues. China wanted to see the deletion of the reference to the cooperation with international agencies, once again revealing the absence of any positive engagement by China with these issues at a global level.

Draft SPF: monitoring (Section IV)

The procedures to be adopted for monitoring and evaluating progress with the laying down of SPFs were the relatively uncontroversial issue to be agreed in the last section. It had already been agreed in 2011 that these would be low key, largely nationally based tasks. The draft was strengthened by the workers arguing successfully (D155) for an annual consultation process to assess progress of both the horizontal and vertical aspects of the Recommendation.

The committee did, however, get trapped into discussing for an hour a proposal from the workers that when countries collected and published data the data should be disaggregated by gender. This generated much controversy, with the US leading the way by insisting that the disaggregation should also be by other social groups. Bangladesh and India strongly objected, perhaps mindful of the caste debate in India. The United Arab Emirates did not like the emphasis on gender, arguing that there were equally important other issues. And so it went round the bloc several times, with many attempted amendments. Fearing this was going to derail the otherwise good progress, the chair unusually called the worker and employer vice-chairs to the podium and announced that as both accepted the final amendment attempt to say, 'disaggregate, in particular by gender', that we had agreement.

The committee then rapidly finished its SPF drafting business, a day early, with the chair asserting that "[t]he Committee had achieved an historical task", with Michael Cichon briefly indicating how proud he felt and with the delegates clapping themselves at length. The committee then quickly dispatched a Resolution submitted by Africa but almost certainly drafted by the Office calling on the governing body and the new director-general to implement measures to promote awareness of the Recommendation, to help in its implementation and to "intensify cooperation and coordination ... with other relevant international organizations ... as well as civil society, for the development of national social protection floors". Even at this last minute, the workers insisted on replacing civil society by "other relevant organizations of persons concerned".

Conclusion

And so the *Recommendation Concerning National Floors of Social Protection (Social Protection Floors Recommendation), 2012 (No. 202)*, (ILO 2012d, ILO 2012e) was agreed, subject to its formal adoption in the plenary of the conference in the following week. The fragile alliance between the workers and the employers held. While I have been critical above of the extent to which the two groups sometimes used their influence to defend their established roles within the ILO governance mechanisms and limit the potential role of other civil society actors, it is also the case that the two groups were broadly very supportive of the development of the Recommendation. The worker vice-chair spoke eloquently in its defence. The employer vice-chair was also clearly determined to ensure the passage of a recommendation that would improve the access to social security of people in developing countries and at no time used the opportunity to suggest that the floor could be a ceiling.

The strategy of the Social Security Department of linking the vertical and horizontal extensions of social security together worked and perhaps the workers' insistence on including the vertical extension in the Recommendation is not only about defending their existing interests, but also about maintaining a vision of a comprehensive social security system, while giving first priority to the horizontal extension as long as people have no protection at all. Perhaps the inclusion of both a horizontal and a vertical extension should not be regarded as a mere 'concession' to the workers, but an improvement of the concept? This point is returned to in Chapter Seven.

No government attempted seriously to rock the boat. The workers in Brazil and its allies in Latin America and sometimes Africa secured some improvements. India and its allies wanting to reduce expectations did not do much damage. The EU showed a conservative side to its interventions. The US was surprisingly radical. Several recently radicalised Arab states – Egypt, Iraq and Tunisia – made useful interventions. China and Russia played no significant part.

Table 4.2 reveals the extent to which the Social Security Department's ideas about the SPF(s) formulated between 2005 and

2010 and embodied in the 2011 questionnaire were maintained largely unchallenged and in places improved upon in 2012. This Office success was, however, as pointed out in Chapter Three, a consequence of its willingness to concede several points en route before 2011. Among these modifications in thinking before 2011 was that the SPF Recommendation:

- should not be about recommending *specific benefits and their levels* but about suggesting diverse ways of ensuring a set of *guaranteed outcomes*;
- should not be defined *globally* but left up to countries to define *national* SPFs; and finally
- should be funded primarily with *national resources* only in some limited cases supported by *international finance.*

Table 4.2: Shifting SPF formulations: from the consultation questionnaire following the 2011 ILC, through the draft presented to the 2012 ILC, to the version adopted at the 2012 ILC (significant changes indicated in italics)

ISSUE	Questionnaire August 2011[1]	Draft SPF March 2012	Final SPF June 2012
SPFs defined nationally	Minimum level of income security *should* correspond *at least to the* monetary value of a nationally defined basket of essential goods and services to ensure health and decency (para 9a) (or) correspond to agreed poverty lines, defined income thresholds for social assistance benefits or other income levels defined in national law (para 9b)	Nationally defined minimum levels of income *may* correspond to the monetary value of a set of necessary goods and services, national poverty lines, income thresholds for social assistance or other comparable thresholds established by national law or practice, *and may take into account regional differences*(para 7b)	Nationally defined minimum levels of income *may* correspond to the monetary value of a set of necessary goods and services, national poverty lines, income thresholds for social assistance or other comparable thresholds established by national law or practice, *and may take into account regional differences*; (para 8b)
Guiding principles	(a) universal coverage; (i) entitlement to benefits defined by law; (g) non-discrimination; (h) gender responsiveness and gender equality; (f) *adequacy of benefits and fair balance* of the interests of those who finance social security schemes and those who benefit from them; (c) coherence with macroeconomic, employment and other social policies; (b) progressive realisation; (e) diversity of means and approaches, including of financing mechanisms and delivery systems; (k) good governance, including sound financial management and administration (i) financial, fiscal and economic sustainability; l) involvement of employers' and workers' organisations through effective social dialogue mechanisms regarding design, governance and supervision; (d) general responsibility of the State; (para 29)	(a) *universality of protection, based on social solidarity*; (b) entitlement to benefits prescribed by law; (c) non-discrimination, gender equality and responsiveness to special needs; (d) *adequacy and predictability of benefits*; (e) a fair balance between the interests of those who finance social security schemes and the interests of those who benefit from them; (f) coherence with social, economic and employment policies; (g) progressive realisation; (h) diversity of methods and approaches, including of financing mechanisms and delivery systems; (i) transparent and sound financial management and administration; (i) financial, fiscal and economic sustainability; (k) involvement of representative organisations of employers and workers *as well as consultation with representatives of other organisations and persons concerned; and* (l) overall and primary responsibility of the State (para 3)	(a) *universality of protection, based on social solidarity*; (b) entitlement to benefits prescribed by national law; (d) non-discrimination, gender equality and responsiveness to special needs; (c) adequacy and predictability of benefits; (h) solidarity in financing while seeking to achieve an optimal balance between the responsibilities and interests among those who finance and benefit from social security schemes; (f) coherence with social, economic and employment policies; (g) progressive realisation, *including by setting targets and time frames*; (l) consideration of diversity of methods and approaches, including of financing mechanisms and delivery systems; (j) transparent, accountable and sound financial management and administration; (k) financial, fiscal and economic sustainability *with due regard to social justice and equity*; r) tripartite participation with representative organizations of employers and workers, as well as *consultation with other relevant and representative organisations of persons concerned* 3. Recognising the overall and primary responsibility of the State in giving effect to this Recommendation, members should apply the following[2] principles: (In Preamble) (e) *social inclusion, including of persons in the informal economy*; (f) *respect for the rights and dignity of people covered by the social security guarantees*; (m) *coherence across institutions responsible for delivery of social protection*; (n) *high-quality public services that enhance the delivery of social security systems*; (o) *efficiency and accessibility of complaint and appeal procedures*; (p) *regular monitoring of implementation, and periodic evaluation*; (q) *full respect for collective bargaining and freedom of association for all workers*;

ISSUE	Questionnaire August 2011[1]	Draft SPF March 2012	Final SPF June 2012
Time-bound obligation	Members should plan to improve existing social security coverage within a specific time frame? (para 24)	Members should put in place and complete as rapidly as possible, and *maintain,* their social protection floors (para 4)	Members should, *in accordance with national circumstances,* establish as quickly as possible and maintain their social protection floors (para 4)
Content of four guarantees	(a) all persons (ordinarily resident in the country) have the necessary financial protection to access a nationally defined set of essential health-care services, including maternal health care? (b) all children enjoy income security, at least at a nationally defined minimum level, through family/child benefits in cash or in kind aimed at facilitating access to nutrition, education and care? c) all persons in active age groups (ordinarily resident in the country) who are unable to earn sufficient income enjoy minimum income security through social assistance, maternity benefits, disability benefits, other social transfers in cash or in kind, or public employment programmes? d) all persons in old age ordinarily resident in the country enjoy income security, at least at a nationally defined minimum level, through benefits in cash or in kind? (para 7)	(a) access to a nationally defined set of goods and services, constituting essential health care, including in the case of maternity; (b) basic income security for children, at least at a nationally defined minimum level, providing access to nutrition, education, care and any other necessary goods and services; (c) basic income security, at least at a nationally defined minimum level, for persons in active age who are unable to earn sufficient income, in particular in cases of sickness, unemployment, maternity and disability; and (d) basic income security, at least at a nationally defined minimum level, for persons in old age (para 5) (NOTE: In this formulation reference to specific means is excluded and included instead in para 9 below)	(a) access to a nationally defined set of goods and services, constituting essential health care, including maternity care, *that meets the criteria of availability, accessibility, acceptability and quality;* (b) basic income security for children, at least at a nationally defined minimum level, providing access to nutrition, education, care and any other necessary goods and services; (c) basic income security, at least at a nationally defined minimum level, for persons in active age who are unable to earn sufficient income, in particular in cases of sickness, unemployment, maternity and disability; and (d) basic income security, at least at a nationally defined minimum level, for older persons (para 5)
Coverage beyond citizens	a) all persons ordinarily resident in the country have the necessary financial protection b) all children c) all persons in active age groups ordinarily resident in the country d) all persons in old age ordinarily resident in the country	*Subject to their existing international obligations,* members should provide the basic social security guarantees referred to in this Recommendation to at least *all residents and children, as defined in national laws and regulations* (para 6)	Subject to their existing international obligations, members should provide the basic social security guarantees referred to in this Recommendation to at least all residents and children, as defined in national laws and regulations (para 6)
Rights appealable in law	Basic social security guarantees should be legally recognised as a right that is enforceable through simple and rapid complaint and appeal procedures defined by national laws or regulations (para 8)	Basic social security guarantees should be established by law. *National laws and regulations should specify the range, qualifying conditions and levels of the benefits giving effect to these guarantees. Effective, simple, rapid, accessible and inexpensive complaint and appeals procedures should also be specified* (para 8)	Basic social security guarantees should be established by law. National laws and regulations should specify the range, qualifying conditions and levels of the benefits giving effect to these guarantees. *Impartial, transparent, effective, simple, rapid, accessible and inexpensive complaint and appeal procedures should also be specified. Access to complaint and appeal procedures should be free of charge to the applicant. Systems should be in place that enhance compliance with national legal frameworks (para 7)*
Diverse means to realise the guarantees	Members may use different means and approaches to implement the basic social security guarantees of their social protection floor, including universal benefit schemes, social insurance, public employment programmes and employment support schemes as well as social assistance schemes that provide benefits to people with low income, or appropriate combinations of such measures? (para 11)	Benefits may include child and family benefits, sickness and health care benefits, maternity benefits, disability benefits, old-age benefits, survivors' benefits, unemployment benefits and employment injury benefits, as well as any other social benefits in cash or in kind. Schemes providing such benefits may include universal benefit schemes, social insurance schemes, social assistance schemes, negative income tax schemes, public employment schemes, and employment support schemes. (para 9) Such guarantees may be achieved through contributory or non-contributory schemes, *whether means-tested or not.* (para 2)	Benefits may include child and family benefits, sickness and health-care benefits, maternity benefits, disability benefits, old-age benefits, survivors' benefits, unemployment benefits and employment injury benefits as well as any other social benefits in cash or in kind. Schemes providing such benefits may include universal benefit schemes, social insurance schemes, social assistance schemes, negative income tax schemes, public employment schemes and employment support schemes (para 9)

ISSUE	Questionnaire August 2011[1]	Draft SPF March 2012	Final SPF June 2012
Fiscal means to pay for benefits	Members may choose different options to mobilise the necessary resources to ensure financial and fiscal sustainability of their social protection floor, taking into account the contributory capacities of different population groups? These options may include better enforcement of tax and contribution obligations, reprioritising expenditure, and broadening the revenue base? (para 13)	Members should consider using different methods to mobilise the necessary resources to ensure financial, fiscal and economic sustainability of national social protection floors, taking into account the contributory capacities of different population groups. Such methods may include, individually or in combination, better enforcement of tax and contribution obligations, reprioritising expenditure, or broadening the revenue base (para 11)	Members should consider using a variety of different methods to mobilise the necessary resources to ensure financial, fiscal and economic sustainability of national social protection floors, taking into account the contributory capacities of different population groups. Such methods may include, individually or in combination, effective enforcement of tax and contribution obligations, reprioritising expenditure, or a broader and sufficiently progressive revenue base. In applying such methods, members should consider the need to implement measures to prevent fraud, tax evasion and non-payment of contributions (para 11)
International funding option	National social protection floor should, in principle, be financed by domestic resources, while noting that some low-income countries may need to have recourse to transitional international financial support? (para 14)	National social protection floors should be financed, in principle, by national resources. Members whose economic and fiscal capacities are insufficient to implement the entire set of guarantees may seek transitional international assistance (para 12)	National social protection floors should be financed by national resources. Members whose economic and fiscal capacities are insufficient to implement the guarantees may seek international cooperation and support that complement their own efforts (para 12)
Monitoring procedures	Members monitor, through appropriate mechanisms, the extension of social security, including the implementation of their social protection floor and progress towards achieving universal coverage as well as higher levels of protection? (para 30)	Members should monitor progress in implementing social protection floors and achieving other objectives of national social security extension strategies, through appropriate nationally defined mechanisms involving representative organisations of employers and workers and, as appropriate, representatives of other organizations and persons concerned (para 19)	Members should monitor progress in implementing social protection floors and achieving other objectives of national social security extension strategies through appropriate nationally defined mechanisms, including tripartite participation with representative organisations of employers and workers, as well as consultation with other relevant and representative organizations of persons concerned (para 19)

Notes

[1] The questionnaire version has been converted into a statement version to ease comparison.

[2] The list from (e) below is in addition to the list from (a) above and represents the additional principles agreed upon in the Committee that had not been in the original Office draft.

FIVE

The SPF and the struggle for global social policy synergy

Introduction

This chapter looks outwards from the ILO and asks and demonstrates how the SPF became a rallying point for the struggle for global social policy synergy, that is, for the struggle to try to ensure that all UN agencies, including the World Bank and the IMF, sung from the same songbook and lined up behind tackling the shortcomings of market-driven globalisation with a plan to construct a social floor under the global economy. It shows how the ILO influenced the UN initially through UNCEB; how it influenced the G8 and then the G20 under the French presidency of 2011; and how as a consequence it came to be able to try to influence the World Bank and the IMF. It ends by explaining how the ILO was able to play a major role, alongside UNICEF and the UNDP, in 'almost' bringing it all together in the form of a new UN Social Protection Inter-Agency Cooperation Board (SPIAC-B).

In the period of intense activity *inside* the ILO, described in the last chapter, between June 2011 after the ILC had decided that the ILO would promulgate an SPF Recommendation and the appearance of the first draft formulation of the SPF as a Recommendation to the ILC sent out in March 2012, the ILO was also busily selling the idea of the SPF *outside* to the world in the form of the Bachelet Report published in July 2011 (ILO, 2011d) and in interventions in the G20 in the run-up to the Cannes summit of November 2011. A division of labour in effect emerged between Michael Cichon, head of social security, who had all the eyes of his Department focused on drafting the Recommendation and subsequently on how countries were responding to the draft, and Vinicius Pinheiro, the social security advisor in the director-generals Cabinet who, reflecting the preoccupations of the director-general, had all his eyes looking out to the UN, to an upcoming meeting of UNCEB and to Cannes and the G20 process.

The story of the development of the SPF is, as I suggested earlier, at least two stories each with many stages. One is the work to persuade the ILO to adopt the SPF Recommendation. The other is the work to sell the idea externally. This chapter is concerned with this second story. We have already noted how Somavia as director-general was keen to turn the ILO into a major global voice, arguing in effect for a reformed globalisation, one that took the social dimension seriously. This was most evident in his launching of and his secretariat's steering of the World Commission on the Social Dimension of Globalization. Policy synergy between different international players had also been an important theme of Somavia's interventions at the ILO. In addition to the regular activities of the working party on the social dimension of globalisation was the work of the Policy Integration Department. For the ILO, 'the aim of policy coherence is to develop and strengthen mutually reinforcing economic and social policies ... policy coherence is one means to strengthen the social dimension (of globalisation) by ensuring that policies for economic growth also promote growth in productive employment, expand social protection and enhance social cohesion' (ILO, 2011h). The vision had been to try to ensure that the ILO policies to expand decent work and social security were not hampered but indeed supported by the activities of the WTO, the international financial institutions and the other UN agencies. This aspect of the ILO's work was strongly supported by the workers' group. For example, this is the ITUC's (2011b, para 6) resolution of June 2010 on the role of the ILO:

> Congress supports ILO leadership in the promotion of international policy coherence ... [and] calls for greater cooperation between the ILO and the International Financial Institutions to encourage common action to promote decent work.... Congress supports the enhancement of the ILO's role within emerging new global governance structures and encourages the ILO to take a prominent position within the G20/G8 process and within the UN structures, in its capacity as the principal centre for global social dialogue. Congress welcomes the ILO's participation in the UN High-Level Task Force on the Global Food Security Crisis, as a means to promote decent jobs in agriculture.

This decision is significant not only for its ringing endorsement of working through the G20 but also for its holding up of the UN High Level Task Force on Global Food Security Crisis as a possible model for collaboration in the social protection field. This was to be important in the discussions on policy synergy outlined below. However, while the ITUC might have supported ILO leadership in this inter-agency synergy work, the Bureau for Workers' Activities (ACTRAV) of the ILO continued to be worried about what this might mean for collaboration in practice with the INGO world.[18]

In an ILO Policy Integration Department Working Paper, Kohler (2011: 1) suggests that:

> [P]olicy coherence – the notion that different programmes and agencies could act on the basis of a common policy stance, or at least not undermine each other – is associated with the ambitious approach of – Delivering as One (DaO). The two are not identical, but certainly closely related, since a genuinely harmonised UN programme delivery would need to build on common policy stances.

She further suggests that social protection policy is one policy field that might lend itself to greater inter-agency policy coherence because:

> Social protection, in the form of cash transfers, has become – en vogue among bi- and multilateral agencies in a big way since 2005 (circa). The policy fault line is not on the need for social protection as an intervention, but – merely on how best to design and deliver, suggesting that policy divergence for this topic occurs at the operational, not the policy, level. (Kohler, 2011: 149)

This distinction between policy issues and technical issue (Kohler, 2011: 15, footnote 30) might be disputed. Kohler notes as *technical issues* disputes as to (a) whether social protection is caste in terms of a safety net or a right and (b) whether social protection is targeted or universal. Obviously, if all that each agency needs to sign up is that there should be social protection never mind these, in my view, major policy choice issues, then of course inter-agency synergy is likely. We can all agree to like apple pie.

How then did the ILO pursue its struggle for global policy synergy in the context of the development of the SPF? How did the ILO sell the idea to the world? And what did it achieve? In sum, as we shall see, it sold it by dint of a combination of the determined hard work of international civil servants, some political scheming and a good measure of fortuitous contingency or luck. We trace the campaign under the four headings of the UN, the G8 and G20, the World Bank and IMF and finally SPIAC-B.

Working with the UN

Attempts to win over a range of international organisations and international civil society organisations to the concept of a 'global social floor' or 'SPF' got under way as early as 2007 before the SPF was ILO policy. Cichon convened a meeting in the ILO Turin Training Centre of people from UNDESA, UNICEF, HelpAge International and others under the banner of 'Building a coalition for a global social floor'. The founding document (Coalition for a Global Social Floor, 2007) asserted that the 'Coalition for a Global Social Floor aims to become an alliance of organisations united in the common pursuit of a more fair globalisation and the right to social security for all, driven by the conviction that a global social floor is achievable and essential to fast-track poverty reduction.'

The core groups of the coalition should, the document argued, consist of:

• international organisations: UNDESA, UNDP POVERTY CENTRE, ILO, UNICEF, the United Nations Poverty Fund (UNFPA), WHO (?)
• bilateral aid agencies: GTZ, DFID, SIDA
• social partners: ITUC, IOE (?)
• NGOs: HelpAge International, Save the Children, ICSW (?)

Initially, it suggested (Coalition for a Global Social Floor, 2007):

> The coalition can operate without formal contractual arrangements. It would simply have a Steering Committee that would be hosted by the UN, ILO, UNICEF or other UN agency, in the spirit of One-UN. The ILO would be willing to invite the core group for a constituting first meeting to Geneva in January 2008; alternatively a meeting could be planned in New York in February, hosted by UN DESA, ideally at the time of the 46th Session of the UN Commission for Social Development (7-15 Feb. 2008) where a presentation can be made at a side event.

The 2007 meeting accepted this idea and there were side meetings held at the Doha Financing for Development Conference in 2008, at

UN Commission on Social Development events and so on. Another leg of the strategy to win over the UN and other actors to the concept of the 'SPF' was to seek to get the SPF into the UN General Assembly documents and hence accepted as policy by the majority of UN members. The UN Commission for Social Development did indeed acknowledge the work on the SPF idea thanks to the engagement of the-then ILO director in New York, Jane Stewart, and her team (Amber Barth and Griet Cattaert).

However, events were to unfold in a slightly different way to that envisaged when the twin strategy of establishing the Coalition for the Global Social Floor and influencing the UN General Assembly was conceived by Michael Cichon. In effect, while events unfolded differently and rapidly they were to unfold in ways that meant that Cichon and his Social Security Department was not always so directly in charge of them. The ILO's struggle for global policy synergy became complicated by there being more than one ILO official stirring the synergy broth. It was the global economic crisis of 2008 combined with the fortuitous circumstance of the ILO happening to hold the rotating chair of the High Level Panel on Programmes of UNCEB that triggered this. Hitherto UNCEB had been a rather bland and bureaucratic body charged with the task of coordinating the work of the many UN agencies. It consists of the heads of these agencies. Its profile would change in 2009 as is explained in the subsequent paragraphs.

In terms of the first coordinated world response to the 2008 economic crisis, it fell not to the UN, not to the World Bank, not to the IMF, but to the meeting of the G20 at heads of state level at the 2 April 2009 G20 London summit to fashion a global policy response on the hoof. As noted in a later section, the ILO was invited and may have had some influence on its outcome. The G20 committed US$1.1 trillion to support countries in crisis, as follows: US$750 billion to an unreformed IMF, US$250 billion for trade facilitation and only US$100 billion for development purposes (including social development), through unreformed multilateral development banks. The UN was only given a marginal role, to monitor the crisis, with no additional resources. This fore-fronting of the G20 and the IMF as *the* global agencies to address the crisis annoyed many in the UN system. By coincidence, a meeting of the UNCEB was to be held in Paris later in April 2009, which considered the UNCEB (2009a) Issue Paper, *The Global Financial Crisis and its Impact on the Work of the UN System* which drew on an earlier draft report (UNCEB, 2009b) considered in February 2009 by the UNCEB's High Level Committee on Programmes that Somavia had happened to chair and influence. The report, drafted by key members of Somavia's Cabinet and the ILO's Policy Integration Department, called for coordinated action across the UN system in eight key policy fields:

1. finance;
2. trade;
3. employment and production;
4. environment;
5. food security;
6. social services, empowerment and protection of people;
7. humanitarian, security and social stability;
8. international cooperation for development.

In terms of specific policies, the ILO would lead on a Global Jobs Pact and 'to help developing countries cope with the crisis, a counter-cyclical global jobs fund could be established' (UNCEB, 2009a:14).

Most important from this chapter's point of view was initiative (6), which was to work toward a global SPF that ensures 'a minimum income security and access to essential services including health care' (UNCEB, 2009a: 20). The ILO and WHO would lead on this policy, supported by a host of other agencies, including UNICEF and UNDESA. The global social floor had become UN policy, at least in terms of UNCEB. This initiative of Somavia came as a surprise to Cichon and the Campaign for a Coalition for a Global Social Floor. In effect the campaign goals suddenly became formal UN policy and so the informal coalition meetings that had been envisaged became formal inter-agency meetings led by the ILO and WHO starting with one in Turin (again) in October 2009.

The definitional complexity introduced by this new initiative was noted in the last chapter. In Chapter Seven we address the question of what this innovative multi-agency effort might eventually mean for greater UN system-wide coherence or global policy synergy. Here we trace some of the work initiated by the SPF-Initiative (SPF-I), as it was to become known, and examine how closely the UN agencies and other actors who became involved in it did indeed work together.

Between October 2009 and January 2012, four meetings of the SPF-I took place, the first three convened by the ILO, the last by UNICEF. In the first flush of enthusiasm for this innovative joint initiative, the attendance and the work achieved at the first meeting held in the ILO's Training Centre in Turin was truly impressive. Among those attending were: the ILO, UNICEF, WHO, UNDESA, UNESCO, UNFPA, World Bank, World Food Programme (WFP), Asian Development Bank,

German Federal Ministry for Economic Development Cooperation (BMZ), DFID, Finland's Ministry of Foreign Affairs, German Technical Cooperation (GTZ), HelpAge International, Save the Children and, via video link, UNDP, UN Habitat, IMF and UNCEB. It created and approved a draft manual and strategic framework for joint UN country operations, which was later refined and published in November (ILO, 2009). The UN resident coordinator would play a key role in launching a UN country team working with governments and other actors and 'insist on the inclusion of the SPF in the UN Development Assistance Framework' (ILO, 2009: 15). Such teams would:

- raise awareness;
- take stock of current policies;
- through national dialogue elaborate a first approach to building an SPF;
- evaluate the cost and identify fiscal space;
- help to implement and monitor and evaluate.

It was also agreed that at the global level a Global Technical Advisory Network (in effect the SPF-I meetings) would be set up and a knowledge-sharing platform developed, which was to be initially the Global Extension of Social Security (GESS) Network website of the ILO. There would be training for countries based in the ILO Turin Centre.

The second meeting took place in Geneva, November 2010. Many although not all of the same participants were present and they were joined by the European Commission, the OECD, Education Solidarity Network and the ICSW. Key decisions were to further support joint country operations where they existed, mainstream the SPF-I into the UN, work on a joint database and develop a fundraising strategy through possibly a multi-donor trust fund. To further support global advocacy in addition to the ILO's GESS website, a separate SFP website would be developed under UNICEF's leadership (ILO, 2010b). It was agreed that a smaller focused workshop would take place in early 2011 to refine the SPF Communication Strategy. This took place in March 2011 and developed an impressive Communication Strategy with key messages about what the SPF is, why governments should implement it and how they could. The UNICEF–ILO joint SPF website would be built, promotional material would be developed and a film would be made. At the same meeting the discussion about a possible multi-donor trust fund rather limped along but there was the suggestion that:

if members of the coalition reach agreement that this idea should be taken forward, a committee could be set up to develop a first proposal of the terms of reference and rules and regulations for such a fund. Ideally the fund would be installed by September (2011) so that in case that the G20 meeting stirs interest among donors, they have an 'address' that they can turn to if they are interested to provide funds. (ILO, 2011n: 8)

So by March 2011 a large agenda of activities had been driven forward by the SPF-I. Soon the gap between aspiration and reality would kick in and a serious stock-take would be needed of how far such a large agenda could be driven effectively by a few dedicated international civil servants and their interns in, essentially, the ILO's Social Security Department, the ILO New York office and the Economic and Social Policy Division of UNICEF, all working with little day-to-day practical input from many of the other agencies including the World Bank, with no real new funding but with inspiring support from several INGOs. For example, the suggested September 2011 deadline for a committee to develop a SPF trust fund committee passed with no steps taken. In January 2012, the logo for the joint UNICEF–ILO SPF-I website was still being decided on by a small UNICEF–ILO technical group.

This stock-take was to take place and priorities honed at the next SPF meeting in New York in late January 2012. We review progress at that meeting in a later section addressing whether the UN could be won over to mainstreaming the SPF. This discussion is postponed until then because we need to take account of the other factors that were beginning to affect (a) how much *priority* the ILO core staff and the head of social security could give to the UN initiative and (b) how much more *complicated* the inter-agency politics of this would become.

These factors were:

- the agreement of the ILC in June 2011 to consider a Recommendation on the SPF at the ILC in June 2012 (discussed in the last chapter), which was the absolute priority of the head of social security. In turn this would lead to a focusing down on the core social transfer elements of the Recommendation and a careful side-stepping of calls for global funding, which might put at risk agreement on the 'affordable' SPF floors within countries.
- the independent initiative of Somavia to win support for the SPF through setting up an international advisory board for SPF under Michael Bachelet;

- the role taken by Somavia's Cabinet's sherpa, Vinicius Piheiro in winning support from the G20 for the SPF-I;
- the question of whether the World Bank really would cooperate in practice with the SPF.

The last three points are considered in turn below.

The ILO's leadership of the UN's SPF-I provided Somavia with the opportunity to make more global impact for the SPF idea and for the ILO by establishing in August 2010 a social protection advisory group under the chair of Michelle Bachelet, President of Chile 2006-10 and now under-secretary general at the UN and first executive director of UN Women. The advisory group had a membership of eight internationally known figures including, of significance for the next stage of our story, Martin Hirsch, president of the French Civic Service Agency. Appointed to the position of executive secretary was Vinicius Pinheiro, the member of Somavia's Cabinet responsible for social protection. Its report was published as *Social Protection Floor for a Fair and inclusive Globalization* (ILO, 2011d). Some of its definitions of social protection and its recommendations were examined in Chapter Four. These, as was suggested there and addressed in more detail below, were to be instrumental in advancing the case of the SPF through the G20 process.

The 2009 UNCEB initiative to establish the inter-agency collaboration on the SPF also strengthened the arm of the ILO in making a case for more and more effective inter-agency coordination more generally. Thus, in the Bachelet Report (ILO, 2011d: 75) itself we find the following, which is celebrating the fragile beginnings of the inter-agency collaboration that UNCEB set in train and had until then been managed from within the small ILO Social Security Department, often in practice by short-term appointees financed by donor countries:

> Coordination is often lacking, for example between ministries, NGOs and UN agencies, between international financial institutions and UN agencies, and even between UN agencies themselves. Since its launch in 2009, however, the Social Protection Floor Initiative has made significant progress in this regard, forming a coalition of 19 UN bodies, international financial institutions and 14 development partners, including bilateral donors, development banks and international NGOs that cooperate and coordinate their activities at national, regional and global levels.

So the recommendation for the future is a radical call for an inter-agency mechanism to bring together the various actors:

> We recommend the establishment of a mechanism for collaboration and coordination that includes experts of the relevant UN agencies, programmes, funds, regional commissions and international financial institutions involved in social protection-related issues. The aim of this ad hoc inter-agency mechanism would be to ensure mainstream comprehensive, coordinated and collaborative action in response to immediate and longer-term social protection challenges, with emphasis on the social protection floor at global, regional and national levels. (ILO, 2011d: 94)

Moreover, this new body should set up a multi-donor trust fund to provide technical support to countries and it should develop a common knowledge platform for sharing experiences. We return to the realisation in practice of these proposals in a later section.

Working with the G8 and G20

Influencing the UN and persuading it to adopt a SPF-I is one thing. But power was shifting from the UN to the G20, largely influenced by an unreconstructed IMF. How would the ILO seek to influence the G20 and how would it be that the Cannes communiqué of 2011 concluded that '[w]e recognize the importance of social protection floors in each of our countries' (G20, 2011b, para 6)? There are two elements to the question: how did the ILO earn a place at the G20 table and how did it use its place in the 2011 G20 process to inject those words into the final communiqué?

The story starts, before the G20 became the focus of global club governance, in the work the ILO did to influence G8 policy in an earlier phase. At this point around 2007 the German sherpa for the G8 was Susane Hoffman, now of the ILO, who was clearly influenced by ILO thinking. The Dresden meeting of the G8 ministers of labour in 2007 concluded with the chair's summary under the heading (G8, 2007): 'Broadening and strengthening social protection in the developing countries and emerging economies'. The summary:

> recognize[d] that social protection is very important, and many aspects are even crucial in combating poverty and promoting economic and social development. It is therefore

part and parcel of the social dimension of globalisation. We note the findings of the ILO and the World Bank that adequate social protection is only available to roughly 20% of the world's population, whereas some 80% of all people have insufficient social protection [para 14]....

Our bilateral and multilateral development cooperation policies already contribute to promoting social protection. We need to build on this and intensify our efforts, in conjunction with national governments, to facilitate broader coverage of social protection which includes benefits and services aimed at improving *effective health coverage, child benefit, old-age pensions and employment* [para 17, emphasis added].

... we will work with international organisations in their commitment to pursue their joint efforts to strengthen and broaden social protection as part of the Decent Work Agenda. We encourage greater cooperation and coherence between international organizations. (para19)

Cichon has commented[18] that "we could not get the word floor in but that the elements of it were there." One year later in 2008 the Japan G8 labour minister's meeting concluded (G8, 2008): 'We confirm the agreements in Dresden and Heiligendamm on broadening and strengthening social protection and we take note of the ILO initiatives to promote basic social security systems in developing countries and emerging economies.' Similar sentiments were expressed in Italy's G8 in 2009. However much the G8 may have reached a consensus on this issue, the task would now become that of winning over the increasingly important G20 to the same agenda. Cichon's close link with and following of the G8 process around 2007 was to loosen somewhat when it came to the G20 because he was more focused then on the ILC process and the director-general's Cabinet advisor on social protection became the key interlocutor between the ILO and G20, as we shall see below.

Although there had been a hurriedly convened meeting of the G20 at heads of state level, rather than as hitherto at only finance ministers level, in Washington in late 2008 after the collapse of the Leman Brother's Bank the G20 only really took off as the new global centre of governance at the April 2009 summit convened by Gordon Brown for the UK. The ILO's first engagement with the G20 was that time but only in the form of an invitation by Brown to Somavia.[20] The outcome of that summit, with its paradoxical decision to urge a fiscal stimulus but at the same time to entrust the IMF to this job in a development context, was described in the previous section. The ILO only really came of age in the G20 at the subsequent Pittsburgh summit, still under UK official convenorship but hosted by President Obama for the US. President Lula of Brazil requested the ILO's formal membership at the table and Obama, who had some trades union sympathies, agreed (Kirton, 2011). The all-important role of sherpa for the ILO in the preparation for that summit was Maria Duce, the chief of Somavia's Cabinet. The summit urged an advance in the social dimension of globalisation reflecting the ILO's involvement in the sherpa negotiations.

Unfortunately, little progress on this was made at the 2010 G20 meeting in Toronto convened by the right-leaning Canadian government, which ushered in the age of austerity and fiscal retrenchment, overturning all the progress of the London 2009 summit. There had been a path-setting meeting of labour ministers in April 2010 but Somavia was only present on video because of the Iceland volcano crisis preventing flights. The recommendations of the labour ministers were largely ignored. Subsequently, the 2010 Seoul G20 summit under the Korean leadership took the issue of longer-term development rather than short-term crisis seriously and concluded with the creation of the 'Seoul Development Consensus'. This Consensus was accompanied by a nine-point detailed action plan – the development 'pillars' – including work on job creation, domestic resource mobilisation, infrastructure investment and so on, one of which (the sixth) was to be become an important vehicle to influence social protection policy.

By now the ILO sherpa was Vinicius Pinheiro. Responsibility for implementing this G20 development action plan, with tasks to be completed – many by the time of the subsequent November 2011 French summit or earlier – was shared out among countries and international organisations. The ILO had a role in for example human resource development (pillar 2) and job creation (pillar 4). There was, however, a fight over who was to lead the significant knowledge-sharing (ninth) pillar. The UK, which at this time had been highly critical of the ILO in its internal review of international agencies, argued against the ILO's leadership of this and insisted it go to the UNDP. Of most direct relevance to our story was the joint responsibility given by the G20 in 2010 in Seoul to the UNDP and ILO under Action 1 of the sixth pillar entitled 'resilient growth'(overseen by Australia, Indonesia and Italy) for the production by June 2011 of a report "identifying lessons learned from use of social protection mechanisms in developing countries (and) prepare best practice guidelines". How this responsibility was carried out is discussed shortly.

The scene was therefore set for the ILO to play a significant part in the 2011 French G20. A combination of the experience already gained of the G20 process by the former ILO sherpa, the resolve of the French President to table the issue of social protection, the opportunity provided by the upcoming Bachelet Report on the subject and, as we will see good, partly fortuitous and partly well-planned connections between the ILO and the French government were to secure a significance advance. Apparently,[21] the suggestion was put to the French government in the context of the April 2010 Asia–Europe Meeting (ASEM) summit that it include further discussion on the issue of social protection at its upcoming G20 summit. For this reason and probably because President Sarkozy, even though pursuing policies at home that were criticised by workers, was keen to present the European model of socially inclusive economic policies to the world put social protection firmly on the agenda. Indeed, the French government's public statement of priorities introduced by Sarkozy at a press conference in February 2011 stated:

> 'France would like to promote a "social protection floor" at an international level, whose goal would be to (a) ensure universal access to essential social services such as education and training, as well as health care and employment, (b) provide citizens with essential social transfers to give them income and livelihood security for accessing essential services. The floor would include social benefits for children, working age individuals who do not have a minimum income, seniors and those with disabilities.'

Clearly, already at this stage somebody within the Social Security Department of the ILO had the ear of the French government. The choice of words was too much to be coincidental. In fact there were parallel connections. Christian Jacquier, a French national within Cichon's Department, worked closely with the representative of the French Ministry of Labour in the French consulate in Geneva. Jacquier was about to retire but was asked to stay on until at least the end of the G20 labour ministers' conference held in September 2011. At the same time, Martin Hirsch, already an active member of the Social Protection Advisory Committee, had the ear of the French President. Hirsch was himself to publish in France a book on the SPF (Hirsch, 2011). Vinicius Pinheiro with Christian Jacquier was ILO sherpa at the G20 labour ministers' conference and it all worked like clockwork. An advance copy of the Bachelet Report (ILO, 2011e) was rushed out in limited numbers for delegates with an additional section, not included precisely in that form in the finally published version, listing a number of recommendations addressed to the G20. Among these were the recommendations not only to establish SPFs but also that innovative international funding could be designed to support low-income countries and that a coordination mechanism be established to include the ILO, UNDP, UNICEF, WHO, UNESCO, World Bank, regional banks and the IMF, building on the SPF-I to enhance global policy coherence. As if this was not enough, the director-general of the ILO together with the OECD secretary general issued a joint report (ILO, 2011f) and a joint press statement expressing concern about the global jobs crisis and stressing the importance of social protection.

The conclusions of the G20 labour ministers' conference therefore predictably recommended (G20, 2011a, para 15) that the G20 help '[d]evelop nationally defined social protection floors with a view to achieving strong, sustainable and balanced economic growth and social cohesion'. It went on to say that the floors should include 'access to health care, income security for the elderly and persons with disabilities, child benefits and income security for the unemployed and working poor' as well as echoing the points about innovative funding, global policy coherence and so on.

It was one thing to get the ILO's views through the labour ministers' conference. Would it be so easy to keep them in the final summit communiqué after Cannes in November particularly as by then the EU and hence Sarkozy was embroiled in the Euro currency and sovereign debt crisis. Indeed, the attempts by the G20 to address this financial crisis did take up about 15 paragraphs of 32 of Cannes' conclusions, and caught the press attention. However, once again, in part due to the work of the ILO sherpa, much of the labour ministers' conclusions were endorsed by the Heads of State. Para 6, significantly near the beginning of the communiqué, restated 'we recognize the importance of social protection floors in each of our countries, adapted to national situations' (G20 2011b). Of equal importance was paragraph 31 calling on 'international organisations, especially the UN, WTO, the ILO, the WB [World Bank], the IMF and the OECD, to enhance their dialogue and cooperation, including on the social impact of economic policies, and to intensify their cooperation'. Finally, it should be noted that the Bill Gates' (2011) report to the G20 argued the case for forms of innovative taxation to fund development although it did not mention social protection in this context. The G20 communiqué, however, merely noted it and noted that some countries were experimenting, agreeing only that 'over time new resources of funding need to be found to address development needs and climate change' (G20, 2011b, para 28).

Parallel to the G20 labour ministers' meeting were meetings of the G20 development group, which had been established in Seoul in 2010. At Seoul, as we have seen, a very large multi-annual development agenda had been set in train consisting of nine pillars of activity (G20 2010a, G20 2010b).[22] Pillar 6 – resilient growth – was the responsibility of Australia, Indonesia and Italy working through UN agencies. One aspect of this was 'developing social protection', with the UNDP and ILO given the responsibility. Pillar 9 was about knowledge sharing and the responsibility of Korea and Mexico. On 23 September 2011, in the shadow of the World Bank's annual meeting, the G20 development ministers met together with the finance ministers and 'welcomed proposals to implement and expand national social protection floors defined by countries themselves according to their individual circumstances'.[23] The ILO's main contribution to the development working group of the G20, which was given less publicity at the time but of great significance subsequently, was the joint report produced with the UNDP entitled *Inclusive and Resilient Development: The Role of Social Protection* (ILO–UNDP, 2011). Produced in mimeo version only in June 2011, it was significant for its conclusions and recommendations to the G20 regarding the need for a future knowledge exchange network to be 'hosted by a specific agency and owned by a broad initiative of agencies' (ILO–UNDP, 2011: 2, para 78) and a the call to establish a coordinating mechanism between agencies to advance social protection systems. The use of the word 'systems' rather than 'floor' was to create a problem later when this recommendation was indeed acted upon resulting in a social protection coordination mechanism not focused specifically on the SPF. Precisely, the report (ILO–UNDP: 41, para 78.1) recommended:

> 3. The G20 could call on international organizations, including the IMF, ILO, UNDP, UNICEF, the World Bank, the WFP, the WHO and the regional development banks, that provide technical advisory services in social protection, to establish a mechanism to improve their coordination and policy coherence towards supporting countries in designing and implementing f [sic] national social protection systems. The organizations could consider the example of the High

Level Task Force on Global Food Security or other well-functioning coordinating bodies.

This was reflected in slightly different terms in the subsequent report of the development working group to the Cannes summit[24] (G20, 2011c, para 55):

> We recommend that the World Bank and the ILO, in consultation with other relevant international organisations that provide social protection financing and technical advisory services to developing countries, develop before the Mexico Summit a mechanism to improve inter-agency coordination in support of country-led social protection measures, taking into account existing institutional and cross-institutional policy frameworks and coordination arrangements.

All of this intense and successful ILO work led to a point after the Cannes meeting where some might have felt that the ILO had been too successful in that it generated a large agenda with an important role for the ILO, raising the question of whether it could deliver on all of it. A presentation within the ILO after Cannes by the ILO sherpa (ILO, 2011i)[25] noted many future activities flowing from Cannes and the previous Seoul development working group, some of which were:

- report to finance ministers on job creation (IMF, OECD, ILO, World Bank);
- report to employment ministers on Task Force on Youth Unemployment and several related issues connecting employment, social protection and growth (ILO, OECD, IMF);
- report for the development working group on skills development (ILO lead, OECD, World Bank, UNESCO);
- report for the development working group on private investment and job creation (United Nations Conference on Trade and Development – UNCTAD – lead, ILO, UNDP, World Bank, OECD).

In terms of our focus on social protection, the ILO was now centrally involved in two separate streams of activities, one for the labour ministers and one for the development group. For the labour ministers, work on the SPFs included:

- "strengthening policy coherence and coordination";
- "supporting countries to develop indicators to map progress towards the implementation of social floors";
- "suggesting new ways of supplementing international solidarity arrangements with innovative financing";
- "supporting countries to define fiscal policies and enhance fiscal space to implement social floors". (ILO, 2011i)

All of this was to be done in collaboration with the IMF, World Bank and others. For the development group, the tasks were to develop a:

- "knowledge sharing platform"; and to facilitate an
- "inter-agency coordination mechanism" with ILO leading with UNDP and the World Bank involvement. (ILO, 2011i)

Some of this work such as working in countries with the IMF to find fiscal space and of developing indictors of progress and sharing of knowledge was of course a continuation of the ongoing work of the Social Security Department of the ILO. The UNCEB SPF-I had already enhanced the agenda of inter-agency cooperation too and plans were already being laid between the ILO and UNICEF for a social protection knowledge platform. Whether the World Bank would come on board was less clear and Cannes might enable this point to be pushed. The issue of innovative funding Michael Cichon had wanted to put on the back burner until after he had secured agreement in June 2012 of the ILC to the SPF Recommendation. The question will emerge later, when the emergence of the new SPIAC-B is described, as to whether the rush by the director-general's advisor and sherpa to get the G20 to recommend such collaboration would complement or contradict the inter-agency coordination already being pursued by Cichon through the SPF-I.

All of this leads us therefore in the next section to a more detailed examination of the *background* to and *history* of ILO, World Bank and IMF collaboration and policy coherence in the field of social protection before we pick up the story of further collaboration in the context of the possible G20 recommended High Level Task Force or Inter-agency Coordination Mechanism.

The G20 process, however, continued with Mexico's presidency in 2012. The priorities of this presidency were different from those of France and Korea before it. However, it did commit to continue the work programme already agreed in 2012 by both the labour ministers and the development working group. Keeping the ILO issues on the agenda fell once again to the indefatigable ILO sherpas, including Vinicius Pinheiro. Through his efforts the following paragraph appears in the conclusions of the G20 labour and employment ministers' meeting held in Guadalajara, Mexico, 17-18 May 2012:

> Social protection systems play an important role as automatic stabilisers in the crisis. At the meeting in Paris, we agreed to develop nationally defined social protection floors with a view to achieving strong, sustainable and balanced economic growth and social cohesion.... We will also encourage better cooperation with the G20 Development Working Group to assist developing countries in capacity building for implementing nationally determined social protection floors.... In consequence of our recommendations made in Paris, we welcome the cooperation that has taken place between ILO and IMF, in collaboration with other international organisations, on sustainability of social protection floors and encourage its continuation. We look forward to the possible adoption of an ILO recommendation on social protection floors during the upcoming ILC in June 2012. (G20, 2012a, para 12)

In parallel to this the ILO (Pinheiro) was also active in continuing to shape the sixth pillar – growth with resilience – and the ninth pillar – knowledge sharing of the G20 development working group. Two reports on the coordination mechanism and on a shared knowledge platform were presented to it by the ILO (G20, 2012b, 2012c). Finally, the 2012 report of the development working group (G20, 2012e) was used to report the plans to establish an inter-agency coordination mechanism and knowledge-sharing platform:

> To that end, we reaffirm our 2011 Cannes commitment to support the implementation or expansion of national social protection floors in LICs [low-income countries], on a demand-driven basis, including through coordinated North–South, South–South and Triangular cooperation, and we welcome the IOs' [international organisation's] efforts to progress this initiative [para 54].... The DWG welcomes the ILO, WB [World Bank] and UNDP's implementation of the 2011 social protection commitments – both the social protection gateway designed to assist LICs to develop effective, innovative and fiscally-sustainable social protection

programs and a board to improve high-level multilateral coordination on social protection assistance.... [we shall make] ... all efforts to ensure its work complements, rather than duplicates existing efforts. We request the board to report progress in two years' time [para 55].

It is important to note the slippage from paragraph 54, which continues to endorse the SPF, and paragraph 55, which sees the projected UNDP gateway and the board concerned with social protection policy more generally reflecting, as we shall see later, the terms under which the World Bank was willing to be associated with such a board. The note about not duplicating effort acknowledges the extra complexity that is now being ushered into existence. We were about to see the co-existence of the SPF-I on the one hand focused on the SPF and the new Inter-Agency Board with a more general brief on the other, and also the co-existence of the recently launched SPF-I gateway website on the one hand and the projected UNDP-based knowledge-sharing gateway on 'effective social protection approaches' on the other. How this story unfolds is picked up in a later section.

The final communiqué of the Mexico G20 summit, agreed on 19 June 2012 after the ILC decision on 14 June to recommend SPFs did continue to endorse the need to build SPFs, but of course with the obligatory caveat that these should be country specific, and the wish that international organisations should work more closely together:

> We recognize the importance of establishing nationally determined social protection floors. We will continue to foster inter-agency and international policy coherence, coordination, cooperation and knowledge sharing to assist low-income countries in capacity building for implementing nationally determined social protection floors. We ask international organizations to identify policy options with low-income countries on how to develop effective sustainable protection floors. (G20, 2012e, para 22)

Working with the World Bank and the IMF

Is it conceivable that the ILO and the World Bank and the IMF can share a common perspective on the subject of the SPF at a global level and then work together in countries to try to help the countries achieve their common goal? In the case of the ILO and World Bank, the answer is maybe. In the case of the IMF, it is not so sure until there is a sea change in the IMF's approach or unless the IMF regards developing SPFs focused on people living in poverty as yet one more way of enabling it to say it does protect social spending for the most vulnerable when cutting government budgets. We consider first the World Bank and second the IMF.

World Bank

Until quite recently the notion that the Social Security Department of the ILO would see eye to eye with the Social Protection and Labour Division of the World Bank would have been seen as absurd. The story of the fundamental clash of approaches, ideologies and policies between the two entities in the fields of pension policy, of safety net versus universal cash benefits policies, of even the definitions and purposes of social protection has been told many times (Deacon, 2007; Orenstein, 2008; Voipio, 2011). Professionals within the ILO itself had written papers critical of the World Bank's risk management approach to social protection and its privatising approach to pensions. This was not surprising as the World Bank's Social Protection Section, under Robert Holzmann, probably did more than any other player to undermine all over the world the legacy of the ILO's work in the 1960s and 1970s in building up Pay As You Go (PAYG) public defined-benefit pension schemes (Orenstein, 2008). Two things had now changed. One was the evident shortcoming of the World Bank's approach to pensions reflected in a pleasing mia-culpa by Holzmann, Robalino and Takayama (2009) in which he argues that the crisis in the private pension system caused by the stock market collapse need not worry us too much as (a) most citizens also still have access to public defined benefits as part of their pension portfolio (!) and (b) there could be some short-term public subsidy to inadequate private pensions. This has weakened the World Bank's standing in the field of social protection. The other is that Holzman has left the Washington headquarters of the World Bank and has been replaced there by a seemingly more cooperative Arup Banjeri.

Banjeri immediately started his own consultations towards the drafting of a new Social Protection and Labor Strategy for 2012-22. The proposed strategy (World Bank, 2011) then argued for an approach to social protection made up of prevention (insurance), protection (assistance) and promotion (human capital formation through conditional cash transfers, employment creation, public works). It even mentioned the ILO's/UN's SPF policy in a footnote although fell short of formally endorsing it. Banjeri wanted to turn social protection projects into systems, to focus on low- and middle-income countries, to emphasise the promotion aspects and, of course, emphasise the World Bank as a knowledge resource in this matter. It had little in its first version to say about pensions! Wide consultations took place and a report (World Bank, 2012c) of a consultation with global trades unions and others is available on the World Bank's website. The first round of consultations was completed and a new draft in the form of a PowerPoint appeared in September 2011. Banjeri's own Social Protection and Labor Strategy advisory group (not given as much global publicity as the Bachelet advisory group) also held its first meeting (World Bank, 2011c) in Paris, on 27-28 April 2011.

Commenting on the first draft, the social security policy team within the ILO – Cichon, Hagemejer and Behrendt – concluded that:

> After decades of ... controversial discourse and debate on pensions and safety net policies, this Note embodies a welcome departure from the ways of the past. It embodies a major turning point and a bold change of direction in the World Bank's social protection strategy, even if it does not explicitly advertise it ... regrettably the concept note does not explicitly acknowledge its conceptual proximity to the positions of UN agencies .... however, the new policy may give rise to the optimistic expectation that the Bank would now be in a position to become a much more active partner in the UN Social Protection Floor initiative. (ILO, 2011k: 2)

Irritatingly, the first indications of the second draft of the new policy were loaded onto the website in the form of a PowerPoint, which did not make the thinking any clearer. The SPF was this time not mentioned. The summary of the responses to the first round of consultation pointed out, however, that one of the often mentioned issues was that of the need for more inter-agency cooperation.

During this period from late 2011 to early 2012, the issue of closer cooperation between the ILO and the World Bank on social protection policy was being pursued actively at different levels and in different modes. On the one hand Cichon and his close colleagues held regular working meetings with Banjeri in Washington and on the other hand at the ILO director-general level the final version of the Bachelet Report launched in New York on 27 October 2011 contained the exhortation: 'We recommend that the social protection floor approach be fully integrated into the World Bank Social Protection Strategy 2012–2020 as well as in the social protection technical assistance programmes implemented by the regional development banks' (ILO, 2011d: 95). This exhortation did seem to have an impact as we will see below.

The final draft of the new World Bank Social Protection and Labor Strategy was circulated in full for final observations on 16 March 2012 (World Bank, 2012a) and was officially launched at the time of the World Bank and IMF spring meetings in April 2012 (World Bank, 2012b). Its main messages and slogans had shifted from the earlier three Ps formulation of prevention (social insurance), protection (social assistance) and promotion (access to work, human capital development) to the less alliterative formulation of R, E and O: resilience was still associated with insurance, equity with assistance and opportunity with work and human capital development. It advanced a life-cycle approach with interventions in the field of opportunity focused on childhood youth and working life, those in the field of resilience focused on working life, old age and disability, and those in the field of equity such as social pensions focused on all stages of the life cycle. Students of global social policy would now have challenging essay questions set in which they would be asked to try to distinguish between the ILO's four guarantees, which would secure over a lifecourse access to a minimum income and services to secure decent livelihoods and the World Bank's REO life-cycle approach.

In the field of pension policy, where the World Bank in the past had been strongly criticised by the ILO and others for advocating for privately managed defined contribution schemes, the new social protection and labour policy retreats to a much more cautious pragmatic approach within which the case for tax-based social pensions is given more prominence. Thus, we read (World Bank, 2012a: 32):

> The World Bank's advice will be pragmatic and context-specific, focused on balancing coverage and adequacy of pensions with financial viability, closely guided by the country's demographic/aging profile, its social contract, its fiscal capabilities and regulatory/administrative capacity. The right 'portfolio' of pensions programs will depend very much on these country-specific conditions.

The Background Paper on pensions by Dorfman and Palacios (2012), only finished in March 2012, stresses the issues of coverage, adequacy and sustainability. Echoing the pragmatic approach of the broader social protection strategy it now acknowledges that the urgency of the coverage question cannot wait for new contributory pension schemes to mature. Dorfman and Palacios (2012: 20) conclude:

> Even if labor force coverage rates were to increase dramatically in the short run, this would not address the needs of those that do not have sufficient time to accumulate enough to generate adequate pensions. ... social assistance, through general safety net programs or categorical targeting is an increasingly popular response to the coverage gap. For older workers that do not have enough time to accumulate pensions in contributory programs, this is the only option available.

Most significantly from the point of view of this book's main story, the advice of many commentators (World Bank, 2012c) on both the first and second drafts of the policy, that more inter-agency collaboration was needed appeared to have been acted upon. In a new section of the policy document entitled 'A global challenge: an emerging consensus' in which the growing international concern to centre-stage social protection and labour pollcy was acknowledged it noted that:

> This emerging global consensus is manifested in numerous country actions and global initiatives, including the prominent One-UN Social Protection Floor initiative (SPF-I), adopted by the United Nations Chief Executives Board in April 2009 [Box 3.1]. The SPL [Social Protection and Labor] strategy and engagement is consistent with these core principles of the SPF-I, particularly through the strategy's emphasis on building inclusive, productive, responsive SPL programs and systems tailored to country circumstances. The World Bank has been a strategic partner in the One-UN Social Protection Floor initiative (SPF-I), and has an important role to play both in helping countries who sign on to the SPF-I to operationalize it and in knowledge sharing. (World Bank, 2012b: 11)[27]

In terms of the actual REO World Bank policy, however, there are still a number of distinctions that could be made between it and the emerging ILO's SPF. There is more use within the World Bank document of the 'safety-net' concept rather than the 'SPF' concept. In particular, Annex One addresses the regional application of the policy and in each region the focus of the World Bank's work is broken down into four distinct policy fields: 'Labor Market Policy, Social Insurance/Pension Policy, SPL [Social Protection and Labor] Systems (of which more below) and *Safety Nets*' (emphasis added).

There is also a more ready acknowledgement of the role of non-state actors as providers of welfare and a continuing case made for social funds and micro credit. As one of the ILO's social security team commented to me:

> It is still very weak on the side of the necessary legislative framework which needs to define entitlements of beneficiaries on the one side and financing sources on the other. From our point of view it treats too lightly the issue of coverage as an objective … it treats coverage narrowly (as measured by actual numbers of beneficiaries) and even says somewhere that more effective systems can reduce numbers of beneficiaries.[28]

The notion that there is a human rights foundation to the case for the SPF, which is fundamental to the ILO's approach, is only acknowledged in Annex Six of the report where the approaches of other actors are reviewed and compared. The World Bank's own SPL strategy is not predicated upon a human rights argument.

A further distinction is the World Bank's use of the term 'social protection system', which it says it wants to see developed out of the patchwork of inadequate and fragmented coverage often found in countries. This concept does suggest an approach that is seeking comprehensive coverage and a goal that goes beyond a minimal SPF. Indeed, the ILO's main ally in the struggle for the SPF – UNICEF – published almost simultaneously with the World Bank on 15 March 2012, its Social Protection Strategic Framework entitled *Integrated Social Protection Systems* (UNICEF, 2012) in which, in its executive summary, it states: 'UNICEF promotes the development and strengthening of *integrated social protection systems* as a highly effective approach for addressing the multiple and compounding vulnerabilities faced by children and their families' (UNICEF, 2012: 6, emphasis added), adding: 'UNICEF supports countries considering putting in place a national Social Protection Floor – guaranteeing access to essential services and social transfers – *as an initial step*' (UNICEF, 2012: 8, emphasis added). Of course the ILO's SPF is part of a two-pronged ILO strategy to extend social security both horizontally (the floor) and vertically (wage-related social security) so the World Bank's and UNICEF's use of the term 'social security system' could be seen as the other agencies catching up with the ILO. In this context it is significant that the final ILO document published in November 2012 about the SPF reviewed in the last chapter (ILO, 2012g) uses for the first time in its title the concept of a 'social protection *system*'.

The UNICEF policy was officially launched in New York on 10 May 2012 and given a second outing alongside the World Bank's Social Protection and Labor Strategy at a meeting called by the EU Parliament on 6 June 2012 in the context of the European Commission developing its own communication entitled *Social Protection in EU Development Cooperation*.[29] The EU meeting was interestingly entitled 'Social protection in development cooperation: towards inclusive growth and resilience', echoing the G20's development pillar 6 – resilience and growth – and the World Bank's newly minted strategy, which talked in terms of resilience, equity and opportunity.

The question of how, in the light of this new World Bank social protection and labour policy, the World Bank might *collaborate in practice* rather than in word with both the ILO and the UN-SPF-I policies was already becoming quite fraught in the early months of 2012 even as the ink was drying on the new policy. This story is picked up again in the next section. As an ILO Social Security team member[30] noted:

> I would say that it is rather weak in potentially convincing WB [World Bank] staff to cooperate with the others – ILO, UNICEF, wider UN etc. Too often it presents the WB social protection team as to a large extent self sufficient in implementing its social protection strategy. In this sense it is not responding to the call from G20 for more cooperation between WB, ILO, UNICEF and other agencies in this area.

Indeed, the World Bank document, unlike the ILO's social protection and labour policy draft, is directed not to the world (in case of the ILO to all member countries represented by governments, unions and employers) and not even necessarily to World Bank 'clients' (that is, mainly some Ministries of Finance) but mainly to World Bank staff – this is a strategy of the World Bank as an institution for its lending and other programmes –aimed mainly at country directors. Thus, the difference between the ILO and UNICEF on the one hand and that of the World Bank on the other is their modes of intervention within countries regarding the SPF. For UNICEF and the ILO, an important element of the ongoing and future work (see below) would be to work with the IMF to help countries create fiscal space to be able to afford to put in place a permanent SPF. The advocacy, campaigning and standard-setting roles of the ILO and UNICEF linked to convincing governments that they should raise more revenues are quite different from the World Bank seeking business within countries by means of encouraging them to take out loans where it could support government policy making and social protection project implementation within which the projects would come to an end and there would be a bank exit strategy.

IMF

We turn now to the prospects for closer working of the ILO with the IMF. The likelihood of the ILO Social Security Department agreeing with the IMF on the *nature and content of actual social protection policy* in general and the SPF in particular was still slim. The IMF's explicit social protection policy is one geared to supporting only the most vulnerable while the ILO would see the SPF having a more universal approach. On the other hand agreement that the IMF should try to help countries find a fiscal space for some kinds of social protection expenditures was more likely. In terms of the first point, remember that UNCEB launched the idea of the SPF-I in April 2009 partly to counter the uncritical funding of the IMF by the 2009 G20 meeting. This concern, that the IMF might not pay due attention to maintaining social spending as it helped countries in the crisis, was not unfounded. The Center for Economic Policy Research (2009) has found that nine agreements that the IMF has negotiated since September 2008, including Eastern European countries, El Salvador and Pakistan – contain some elements of contractionary or pro-cyclical policies with a potentially negative impact on poor people. These include fiscal (budget) tightening, interest rate increases, wage freezes for public employees, and other measures that would reduce aggregate demand or prevent economic stimulus programmes in the current downturn. A 2011 UNICEF publication *A Recovery for All* (Ortiz and Cummins, 2012), echoing the 1987 *Adjustment with a Human Face* (Cornia et al, 1987), reviews 158 IMF country reports, revealing that governments are considering three main reforms:

- cutting or capping wage bills, which can impact the salaries of public sector workers that provide essential services to the population (in 73 countries);
- reducing or removing subsidies, including on food and fuel products, at a time when food prices are at unprecedented highs in many places (in another 73 countries);

- targeting and rationalising social protection programmes, that is, reducing social protection coverage at a time when governments should be considering scaling up a social protection (in 55 countries).

Developing an SPF that aims to guarantee income security across the lifetime is made more difficult in this context. The IMF continues to resist these arguments, seeking instead to prove that on the basis of a longer *pre-crisis* timeframe (1985-2008), low-income countries with IMF programmes have been associated with increased social spending (Clements et al, 2011).

If the ILO and IMF may not be able to agree on the specifics of what an SPF might mean, is there a basis for looking forward to cooperation to ensure that the IMF does what its defenders say it now does, which is to seek to protect social spending even in the age of fiscal austerity and create a fiscal space for enlarging social spending at least, using IMF terms, to protect the most vulnerable poor people in low- and middle-income countries. The 2010 IMF–ILO meeting is instructive. The historic first IMF–ILO conference was convened in September 2010 in Oslo 'in order to stimulate an active discussion of how international cooperation and policy innovation can address the urgent need to improve the capacity of economies to generate enough good jobs – decent work – to meet societies' "needs"' (IMF–ILO, 2010: 1). This was at a time when Dominic Strauss-Kahn was leading the IMF and seen by some as being willing to inject a greater social concern into the IMF's activities. Certainly, under his brief leadership the IMF webpage[31] proclaimed:

> The IMF tries to ensure that economic adjustments taken to combat the impact of the crisis also take account of the needs of the most vulnerable by developing or enhancing social safety nets. Social spending is being preserved or increased wherever possible.... About a third of programs in low-income countries include floors on social and other priority spending.

The IMF and ILO agreed at the conference to work together on policy development in two specific areas, one of which was indeed 'to explore the concept of a social protection floor for people living in poverty and in vulnerable situations, within the context of a medium- to long-term framework of sustainable macroeconomic policies and strategies for development' (IMF, 2010c: 1). Strauss-Kahn himself was, of course, given his resignation from the IMF, not able to follow this up despite his initial acceptance of an invitation to attend the 2011 ILC. Contact was continued, however, at a more practical level in relation to specific countries. On 3 December 2011 a meeting was convened at the Brookings Centre with the facilitation of Kermal Dervis between the ILO and IMF, focused on El Salvador, Vietnam and Mozambique, three countries where close IMF–ILO collaboration was being pursued. In the case of Mozambique, UNICEF was also involved. Indeed, by the time of the G20 labour ministers' meeting in Mexico in May 2012, the ILO was able to publish jointly with the IMF the first draft of a paper (primarily authored by Cichon and van Parys of the ILO) on the successful IMF–ILO collaboration in these three countries. Setting out how the IMF had worked alongside the ILO to create fiscal space, it explains how the SPF-I Rapid Assessment Protocol (RAP) had been used to cost the coverage gap in each case and gives this example of the value of the ILO–IMF collaboration (ILO–IMF, 2012: 17):

> A consolidated One-UN or a joint ILO–IMF assessment with regard to the feasibility of national social protection floor policies increases the viability and credibility of country based policy recommendations. For example in Mozambique, the results of the SPF study conducted were useful both from a technical as well as political perspective in building arguments that the Ministry of Women and Social Affairs (MMAS) used in negotiations with other ministries, including the Prime Minister Office and the Ministry of Finance. The MMAS specifically observed that having a one UN–IMF message supporting their arguments strengthened their position considerably when discussing budget allocations. The result was the decision to increase social protection expenditure by about 40 per cent.

In terms of engaging with the IMF to work out how to create fiscal space for SPF spending, UNICEF social and economic policy analysts have also been very active. They started a dialogue with the IMF in 2009, with several high-level meetings held in Washington and New York. UNICEF engaged also with the IMF in 11 pilot countries, and the dialogue proved productive. In Burkina Faso, for example, pioneering analysis of the crisis impact on children in terms of poverty, school attendance and access to health services, led to scaling-up social protection and an increase of the deficit ceiling to accommodate increased social spending in the IMF-supported economic programme.

However, the actual working relationship between the IMF and UNICEF was at times very fraught, with UNICEF being, in effect, told not to publish some its criticisms of IMF-supported austerity policies. Isabel Ortiz, at the time of writing director of UNICEF Social and Economic Policy Division in New York, moved to UNICEF in 2009 after a productive period at UNDESA where she had authored the *Social Policy Guidance Notes* (Ortiz, 2007), which were widely regarded as the UN's antidote to the World Bank residual approach to social policy, as well as being a strong supporter of the SPF. Despite useful dialogue between the IMF and UNICEF, relationships took a turn for the worse after February 2010, when the IMF published *Exiting from Crisis Intervention Policies* (IMF, 2010a) and *Strategies for Fiscal Consolidation in the Post-Crisis World* (IMF, 2010b). Based on UNICEF's mandate to promote the rights of all children, it called instead for a *Recovery for All* (UNICEF, 2010a, 2012). Concerned with the insufficiency of only having 11 country pilots at a time of global crisis, Ortiz's team started producing analytical work covering the largest possible number of countries. Subsequently in April 2010 UNICEF completed *Prioritizing Expenditures for a Recovery with a Human Face: Results from a Rapid Desk Review of 86 Recent IMF Country Reports* (UNICEF, 2010b) in time for the IMF–World Bank spring meetings. It was published by UNICEF as a brief and distributed through different channels, including the Recovery with a Human Face Network, a UNICEF-led e-discussion where practitioners and personalities such as Nobel Laureate Paul Krugman, former UN under-secretary general Jose Antonio Ocampo, Sir Richard Jolly and many others discussed a socially responsive crisis recovery. In May 2010, the IMF complained to UNICEF. UNICEF removed the paper from the UNICEF website, and all printed copies were disposed of. Ortiz was instructed not to work on this topic.

Nevertheless, UNICEF staff within the Policy Division continued to work on the topic in their personal time and updated the paper, which now covered 126 countries. As a protective strategy the paper was circulated for official comments to UNDESA, the ILO, the UNDP, academia and civil society. Official comments came back praising the paper and these positive comments were presented to UNICEF; after internal discussion, UNICEF approved the paper entitled *Prioritizing Expenditures for a Recovery for All: A Rapid Review of Public Expenditures in 126 Developing Countries* (UNICEF, 2010c). In 2011, fiscal consolidation/austerity swept across developing countries and the risks of worsened social outcomes increased. The paper was picked by the press at the annual meetings of the IMF and the World Bank and became an important source of information with which to challenge the IMF pro-cyclical economic policy advice being reported by the UK's *Guardian* newspaper, the Bretton Woods Project, the Third World Network, Social Watch and other social movements, as well as by the UN.[32]

The struggle of the small UNICEF social and economic policy team to continue their critical work continued against internal UNICEF opposition into 2012. In order to defend their position within UNICEF the team set up an economic and social policy advisory board, which attracted high-level international scholars who supported their work. I, as one, submitted advice, which read:

> Recent UNICEF papers pointing to the negative social impacts of current post-crisis IMF interventions in countries are very valuable. My point is that there is now a need for the social agencies to engage directly with the economic to refashion overall economic and social policy that works in tandem. For the sake of the children the job of economics can be left to the economists. The social agencies have to gear themselves up to be able to address the economic (Deacon, 2011b). Building on this the Pratolina conference entitled 'Consultation on Social Policy, Equity, Rights and Development' was convened in March 2012 to assess the work of the UNICEF economic and social policy team. The gathering of previous UNICEF scholars such as Sir Richard Jolly, directors of Save the Children, Oxfam, UNRISD, the ILO, the World Bank, academics and senior staff from UNICEF country and regional offices and headquarters concluded with a resounding message of support for continued economic and social policy analysis by UNICEF. However, despite this outside endorsement, the budget and support for this area of UNICEF's work was reduced.

What it is important about this 'UNICEF' digression are two things. First, it shows the determination it sometimes requires for dedicated international civil servants to put their head above the parapet and argue the case for tax and expenditure policies in the interests of social protection when orthodox economists who dominate the World Bank and IMF are preaching retrenchment. Second, it suggests that while the G20 calls for IMF and World Bank collaboration with the UN social agencies, the change of practice by these agencies might be very limited. The ILO, UNICEF and the IMF might be discussing collaboration in a few pilot countries, but in the meantime most governments are contracting public expenditures with implicit IMF endorsement. If the IMF was serious about the social impacts of the global economic crisis, about an SPF and even the MDGs, it would engage with UNICEF and the ILO to warn governments not to undertake fiscal austerity in the current terms.[33]

Up to this point in the story we can say that in terms of trying to secure a wider global support for the concept of the 'SPF' and in terms of winning other international organisations and global governance actors over it, the ILO has been in general remarkably successful. The director-general with the support of his Cabinet and sherpas, through the device of the Bachelet Report and in part by the accident of holding the chair of UNCEB at the time of its response to the 2008 economic crisis, and the good fortune of there being a strong French connection between the ILO and Paris to draw on has secured this support. The UN is lined up behind the SPF; the G20 is entrusting the ILO to advance work on it. The World Bank is tentatively stealing itself to work with the concept in practice. The IMF at least in terms of a formal communiqué is committed to giving it thought despite the problems identified by the UNICEF work. How further policy synergy and more concretely practical inter-agency collaboration, both in terms of global knowledge sharing and within country practice, would evolve is discussed in the next section and in the final chapter. As far as the ILO was concerned in November 2011 at its governing body meeting it agreed to ask the director-general to report on further steps to be taken to enhance policy synergy (ILO, 2011h). A future issue will be if the new ILO director-general will attach as much importance to the effort to put the ILO at the centre of the campaign for global policy synergy.

The new UN SPIAC-B

It has been suggested in the foregoing that while the head of the ILO's Social Security Department was primarily focused on ensuring that the SPF Recommendation would get adopted by the 2012 conference, some in the director-general's Cabinet, perhaps mindful of Somavia's upcoming resignation, which would have direct implications for their continuing role, were busy planning a wider agenda of carrying the SPF beyond Geneva to the ILO office in New York to ensure that it gained wider acceptance in the UN community perhaps in the form of a UN secretariat for social protection similar to the UN secretariat for food.

More particularly we have noted how the same message repeated in the Recommendations to the G20 via the Bachelet Report and in the ILO–UNDP development working group report, both of which were primarily director-general Cabinet outputs, focused on the establishment of both an inter-agency coordination mechanism and a shared knowledge platform for social protection, which went beyond the SPF-I coordination efforts hitherto driven by the ILO's Social Security Department. Indicative of the thought given to the strategy of how to achieve these goals was the way a meeting was conducted in Washington by the ILO on 2 December 2011 with UNICEF, the World Bank, the UNDP, the Pan American Health Organization (PAHO) (in lieu of the WHO) and a few others to take forward the call of the G20 to enhance inter-agency coordination.

It seems as if both the Social Security Department and the director-general's office had given some thought to this meeting. The Social Security Department commissioned a non-paper (ILO, 2011j) from an ex-UNICEF consultant, a co-patriot of the head of social security, to make recommendations on both (a) the knowledge platform and (b) the inter-agency coordination mechanism. The knowledge platform proposals ranged widely over the content of an inter-agency website and over several scenarios for its location. The ILO was suggested as an obvious choice, UNICEF was an option as was possibly the UNDP but the UNDP had little track record in the field. The World Bank option was dismissed as it was partial and might be seen to be drumming up lending business. A joint ILO–UNICEF option built on the SPF-I existing plans[34] was a possibility. Outsourcing was also an option.

In terms of the coordinating mechanism the idea that it might reside at UNCEB level and be a task force chaired by the UN secretary-general was dismissed as too top-down managerial. *Instead the view that it should be given to the already existing SPF-I process was preferred* (my emphasis). In terms of how it could work, the existing practices of the SPF-I were noted. Earlier 'show and tell' processes, which had been run over several years where each multilateral agency and many bilateral agencies convened just to share information about practice and policy but not necessarily change them, was critically commented on. The case for a small secretariat with funds was made.

The preparation by the director-general's office for this meeting was less transparent but is possibly revealed in how the meeting proceeded on 2 December. In the meeting, discussion about the coordinating mechanism was marked by the World Bank offering merely the traditional show-and-tell seminars and the Social Security Department of the ILO suggested building on the SPF-I annual meetings that had been held since 2009, the next one of which was due to be convened by UNICEF on 30 January 2012. Breaking the disagreement between these two approaches was the suggestion then made by the UNDP that a UN high-level inter-agency secretariat and board be set up with a new secretariat to operate at UN level, but probably located on a rotating basis within an agency. The parallel of the UN food security secretariat was suggested as a model.[35] The ILO Cabinet member present played a quiet role allowing the UNDP to speak but then added support to this idea setting out in some detail how it would work. This idea had as we saw been articulated by the Cabinet official responsible for social security and had already been encapsulated in the joint June 2011 ILO–UNDP report to the G20, which had had minimal publicity. The Social Security Department questioned whether such a development was needed, preferring the SPF-I mechanism.

The two tracks of the ILO activity – (a) work on the SPF Recommendation and the SPF-I on the one hand being managed by the Social Security Department and (b) work of the director-general's Cabinet on selling the idea of global policy synergy and the possible establishment of an umbrella UN social protection secretariat on the other – were beginning to throw up contending options. It seems that the Social Security Department did subsequently support the new secretariat, which would have a responsibility for social protection generally while the SPF-I might still continue for the SPF. It was assumed that the ILO would have the secretariat initially. The World Bank was unhappy at this outcome and sought in subsequent exchanges to call for a three-level mechanism with a council including bilateral agencies, meaning its friends in the UK DFID who were hostile to the ILO, a board and a secretariat. Arguments existed over who would chair the meetings of the new entity: the ILO or World Bank or joint?

In terms of the knowledge-sharing platform, despite the already existing plans for UNICEF to work with the ILO on this, it was agreed to let the UNDP's Inclusive Growth Centre in Brazil take the lead while the ILO and UNICEF would continue in some linked way. The significance of a Latin American centre taking leadership was consistent not only with the shift to the Global South of much new work on social protection but also with the nationalities of the soon-to-resign ILO director-general and his Cabinet officer responsible for social protection. The head of social security went along with this while continuing to encourage colleagues back in Geneva to work on the already proposed ILO–UNICEF portal and the still-existing GESS site. One ILO colleague working on the design of the ILO–UNICEF portal suggested that the difference between the UNDP's portal and the ILO–UNICEF one would be that the UNDP one would provide best practice models of social protection for developing countries to learn from each other and from middle-income countries, whereas the ILO–UNICEF one would provide more for an exchange of information on what each global agency, including INGOs, was doing in the SPF field.

This story of the development of the new social protection secretariat and the new knowledge platform is picked up again after the report below of the January 2012 SPF-I meeting in New York. We left this story off after the 2011 SPF-I meeting (see the first section of this chapter). Because of the implications of the G20 activities (see the second section) the UN SPF-I joint meeting in New York on 31 January 2012 met in rather changed circumstances. One of the issues was to become whether these changed circumstances and manoeuvrings between the ILO, UNDP and World Bank at a higher level would impact on the meeting. Another issue would be how far the need of the ILO to keep a low profile on global funding for the SPF would effect discussion about the possible SPF trust fund. Equally problematic from the standpoint of the ILO's ACTRAV might be the SPF-I engagement with a broad range of and, in the eyes of some of the ILO workers, unrepresentative INGOs. The meeting gathered a large number of attendees, including 12 UN agencies, six INGOs and representatives of Finland and France (ILO, 2012a). The holding of the event in New York the week the Commission for Social Development was scheduled to meet ensured that it would benefit from the annual gathering of the 'great and the good and committed' in the UN world of social development. Missing was the World Bank. Apparently, attendance on that day at a European Commission meeting consulting about the Commission's upcoming communication on social protection took priority. This meant that the elephant in the room was hardly referred to even though its new social protection and labour policy was shortly to be unveiled and even though it was, as noted above, behind closed doors, locked in a disagreement with the ILO (and UNDP and so on) about the form that would be taken by the inter-agency coordinating mechanism that the G20 had called for.

The meeting took stock of the SPF achievements and shortcomings to date. Among the achievements were:

- the global advocacy impacting on the G20;
- the solid inter-agency work in several countries to advance the SPF;
- the rapid assessments using the SPF costing tools in 30 countries;
- the training sessions in Turin;

- the refining of its communication strategy
- work on the imminent joint website.

Shortcomings were:

- ongoing failures to engage UN resident coordinators in the SPF;
- no progress with working with the World Bank, IMF, OECD and others on shared data;
- no progress on possible global funding.

Behind these shortcomings was a concern that UN agencies had not yet been won over to give the SPF priority over their own agendas. The SPF message had to be converted into messages for each agency. Significant given the forgoing account of the high-level negotiations concerning a new inter-agency coordination mechanism was the absence of serious discussion of this issue, partly because the meeting was not informed in any detail about it even by those engaged in the discussions. It was noted in the minutes (ILO, 2012a) only that '[w]e have to integrate the SPF Initiative into the G20 mandate, without losing the coalition (UN agencies, NGOs, Governments,…), and without duplicating mechanisms'. It is reported later how this complex issue was to be resolved.

How would the two other issues – global funding and a global civil society campaign – be taken forward? These would be difficult for the head of the ILO's Social Security Department to be too closely associated with during the last stages of the delicate negotiations leading up to the passage of the SPF Recommendation through the ILC in June 2012. It was the WHO joint lead agency representative who was pushing for work on a trust fund at this meeting, not the ILO. It was HelpAge International that was leading the calls for more campaigning at the national level. The neat resolution of this was to ask the governments present (Finland and France) to address the first issue of funding and the civil society members present (ICSW and HelpAge International) to pursue the second. In terms of the much-postponed and debated global funding, it was agreed (ILO, 2012a) that there was a '[n]eed for a real analysis of the funding options, which is not driven by institutional interest or power games. This funding strategy will be written by some donor countries (Finland and France), supported by the SPF secretariat'.

The other thread in the meeting was the concern that the SPF idea had to be injected into the other ongoing UN policy-making processes, which were now becoming more dominant: the post-2015 revised

MDG policy and the post-Rio plus 20 environmental policies. These issues are taken up in the last chapter. The SPF inter-agency technical meeting would reconvene in July 2012 immediately after the ILC and Rio plus 20 meetings.[36] Then it was felt, with the ILC decision made and perhaps the G20 recommended inter-agency coordination mechanism becoming clearer, the work could be pursued with even more vigour.

Returning to the G20 social protection inter-agency mechanism, the discussions on the possibility of a UN social protection secretariat were indeed doggedly pursued by the same ILO director-general Cabinet member, acting as ILO sherpa in the context of the Mexican presidency of the G20. By the time of the G20 development working group meeting of 19-20 March 2012, the initial idea of his that a high-profile, high-level UN secretariat on social protection be created similar to the high-level UN food security secretariat had been cautioned against by the World Bank and so a note was tabled to the development working group meeting jointly by the ILO and World Bank suggesting a rather less ambitious technical Social Protection Inter-agency Board (SPIB), which would be (G20, 2012b, para 11):

> A light, lean and agile interagency coordination mechanism – composed of representatives of relevant international organizations, partner agencies and bilateral institutions engaged in international technical cooperation on social protection. The main objectives of the Board would be to enhance global coordination and advocacy on social protection issues and to coordinate cooperation in country demand-driven actions.

Concretely, the board (G20, 2012b, para 12, emphasis added):

> would be chaired by the *ILO and the World Bank* and include representatives of IMF, UN–DESA, UNDP, UNICEF, WHO, Regional Development Banks, Regional Economic Commissions, other relevant international organisations and, *as appropriate*, bilateral institutions from G20 and non G20 countries working internationally at country level on social protection advocacy, financing and/or technical advice. Social partners and other organisations, including large NGOs with a major work program in social protection, *could* have observer status.

It would meet at least once a year and have a small secretariat initially located for two years at the ILO building on the work undertaken for the UN SPF-I. Subsequent exchanges took place between the agencies in April 2012 and the final meeting of the G20 development working group on 3-5 May. Nothing fundamentally changed and the June 2012 report of the G20 development working group continued to look forward to this increased international cooperation, as reported in the second section of this chapter.

In terms of the projected UNDP's knowledge-sharing platform and the UNICEF–ILO-based UN SPF-I web portal, both continued to be developed independently of each other in a similar and confusing manner. The SPF-I joint web portal was indeed launched in April 2012.[37] Introducing it to SPF-I colleagues, Isabel Ortiz said:

> This is a project that UNICEF has been working on since late 2011 and which other Coalition members, in particular the ILO and HelpAge International, contributed to through brainstorming, planning and review … the intent behind the website was to provide users with an agency-neutral, unified voice on the SPF and to serve as a resource for users not necessarily familiar with the concept.[38]

The site itself asserted that 'the Social Protection Floor (SPF) is a *first step* toward the implementation of comprehensive social protection *systems* worldwide. By establishing a nationally defined and context-specific Social Protection Floor, countries help realize the universal right to basic social security and essential social services while enabling and promoting future socio-economic development' (emphasis added). UNICEF's hand in this is perhaps reflected in the 'first step' and 'system' references. The site provided a comprehensive range of updates concerning the development of the floor in a range of countries as well as providing a platform for the SPF Coalition supporting the SPF-I. Initially, however, the new gateway was heavily dependent on the original ILO GESS website[39] to which readers were referred for detailed historical documents.

Despite this launch, work continued within the G20 development working group on the suggested UNDP-based knowledge-sharing platform. The note prepared for the G20 development working group meeting of 19-20 March was little changed from the ideas reported earlier in this section. Concretely, it proposed (G20, 2012c) that the UNDP, through its International Policy Centre for Inclusive Growth's (IPC-IG) Gateway on South–South Learning on Social Protection, could provide the vehicles for operationalising this knowledge-sharing mechanism in coordination with the ILO's GESS (GESS) and other partner organisations. The platform could sit administratively in the UNDP and be guided by a joint group of experts (including the ILO, UNDP, the World Bank and others) in alignment with the activities of the proposed SPIB. No reference was made to the UNICEF–ILO-based new SPF gateway launched in April. The puzzle remained concerning the relationship between the two seemingly overlapping gateways. Basically, the UNDP gateway is initially focused[40] on social protection as a whole rather than the SPF.

So it was that the SPIAC-B[41] was about to be born and possibly complicate further rather than simplify the global governance of social protection. It was not to be as grand as the ambitious UN food security secretariat. It would be more than a show and tell (and do nothing) series of meetings. It would work confusingly in parallel to the SPF-I because the World Bank did not want it to be constrained by the SPF. However, the ILO planned to attend the first meeting of SPIAC-B in New York in July 2012 armed with an offer to act as the secretariat of SPIAC-B back in Geneva. The ILO Social Security Department staff would be both SPIAC-B and UNSPF-I technicians. Meantime the initial advocate and prime mover of the higher-level UN secretariat, Vinicius Pinheiro, became deputy director of the ILO office in New York.

The first meeting of the SPIAC-B charged with progressing both inter-agency cooperation on social protection generally and the UNDP gateway on social protection, took place on 2-3 July 2012 in New York. Several, but not all, INGOs that had been involved in the SPF-I meetings were invited as, according to the constitution, observers. These included the ICSW, HelpAge International and Save the Children. Many UN agencies such as the UNDP, Food and Agriculture Organization (FAO), UNICEF and WHO were present. Significantly, Michael Cichon (ILO) who would have been joint chair with Arup Banjeri (World Bank) and who had strong views about how the coordination might play out was unable to attend due to illness and so it was Somavia's social protection advisor, the G20 sherpa, Vinicius Piheiro, recently promoted to the New York ILO office, who jointly chaired the meeting. Predictably, the first day generated the discussion about the overlap between the SPIAC-B and the SPF-I. More significantly, the INGO members, who were actually allowed to participate and not just observe, fired up by the implications of the recent adoption by the ILC in June 2012 of the SPF Recommendation a few days earlier, expected to discuss it but found the World Bank steering discussion towards what it perceived as a wider social protection agenda. The meeting did, however, ensure that the board might act rather than just compare notes and changed its name from the Social Protection Inter-Agency Board to the Social Protection Inter-Agency Cooperation Board and foresaw future regional meetings. The minutes of the meeting report the discussion on the link between the SPIAC-B and the SPF-I. The clarification was offered in the following terms (ILO, 2012f):

> Social Protection Floors are part of comprehensive social protection systems (e.g. as in ILO two-dimensional strategy for the extension of social security); while the SPF-I addresses the horizontal dimension (basic levels of social protection), the SPIAC-B provides a broader and more inclusive mechanism for sharing of information and coordination between partners, addressing social protection systems as a whole (including the vertical dimension); the shared secretariat hosted by ILO will ensure coherence and consistency in the coordination process; existing SPF-I work will continue as planned under CEB mandate (UN-Initiative), and its activities would be strengthened within a broader SPIAC-B perspective; SPIAC-B work could build on the experience accumulated in the SPF-I, especially at the country level.

By the summer of 2012 the concept of the 'SPF' had not only been transposed into formal ILO policy (Chapter Five) but had also become UN policy (2009), G20 policy (2011) and an element of World Bank policy (2012), and was being given fiscal space by the IMF in some country operations (2012). Serious steps had been taken to increase global policy synergy and to advance coordination between global agencies with a social protection mandate. Those engaged from 2007 in the Coalition for a Global Social Floor would have much reason to be satisfied about in 2012.

The results of the efforts at inter-agency coordination were, however, confusing to an observer. There was the co-existence of the ILO–WHO-led UN SPF-I on the one hand, which had held four meetings between 2009 and 2012 and developed many policy guidelines for country operations, and the new SPIAC-B, which had one meeting focused on trying to explain how it would complement the SPF-I. There was the even more confusing co-existence of the ILO's GESS social protection website (www.social-protection.org), the SPIAC-B linked website (www.socialprotection.org) and the UNICEF-inspired

SPF-I joint website (www.socialprotectionfloor-gateway.org), not to mention the go-it-alone World Bank social protection and labour website.[42] This reflected in part the existence of too many cooks within the ILO stirring the broth of inter-agency coordination and continued resistance by the World Bank Social Protection and Labour Section not to be constrained by UN leadership. How the complexity of inter-agency coordination might be handled by those who drove the initial Coalition for a Global Social Floor is returned to again in the final chapter as is the continued relative silence and lack of activity around the concept of 'global funding' to support SPFs. The next chapter changes gear to offer an explanation of all the developments we have observed in Chapters Two, Three, Four and Five.

SIX

Implications for understanding global social policy change

Recapitulation and explanation

At the outset of the book it was suggested that the decision by the ILO to agree a Recommendation on SPFs required explanation. There were indeed several aspects of the development of the policy on SPFs that demanded an explanation. An earlier attempt by the UK's Gordon Brown in 2000 to get the UN to agree to a set of universal social policy principles was unacceptable to much of the Global South. What shifted in the global political context between 2000 and 2012 to overcome, in effect, the objection of many in the Global South to a set of global social policy principles perceived earlier as emerging from and reflecting only the interests of the Global North? Furthermore, these new principles for an SPF for all residents and children of all countries went far beyond the traditional concern of the ILO to fashion standards only for the 20% of the world's population; workers covered by contributory social security systems. Why especially given that the ILO governance arrangements still give a large say to organised trade unionists? Who had influence inside the ILO and how was it used in order to win the institution over to promulgating the SPF Recommendation for all residents? Moreover, how did such a policy become endorsed by the UN normally resistant to acting as one and by the G20 not hitherto known for its concern with social protection? The World Bank's endorsement of the SPF also needed explaining given the history of ILO–World Bank contestation on issues of social protection. Finally, the willingness of the ILO and the World Bank to jointly chair a new SPIAC-B would need explaining against the backcloth of ILO–World Bank antagonisms. Who were the players and what were the means by which to some extent the ILO did succeed in generating greater policy synergy between international organisations in the UN around the concept of the 'SPF'?

Each of the foregoing chapters has addressed aspects of these questions. Chapter Two suggested that answers to some of the questions would be found before the issue of the SPF became an agenda item within the ILO. In an attempt to counter the safety-net social policy of the World Bank, itself a product of the structural adjustment years, a counter-hegemonic project was initiated in the late 1990s to win back the case for universalism within the global social policy discourse. It was in this context that the specific global policy Coalition for a Global Social Floor was to be built. Juan Somavia was to take over the helm at the ILO influenced by these debates. Chapter Two also suggested that it was only after there had been a significant development of new, more universalistic cash transfer policies within many countries of the Global South that a renewed debate about global social policy principles could begin. Despite this overcoming of the resistance of the Global South to the concept of 'global policies', Chapter Three detailed how the general call for a social floor had to be reframed not as specific benefits but as a set of guarantees to be fashioned by countries according to their circumstances to ensure final acceptance. It also described the importance of linking the (horizontal) social floor recommendation to the equally important concern of the ILO workers' group that the (vertical) wage-related contributory social security benefits be further improved. Here we also began to see the importance in the unfolding story of the role of individuals within the Social Security Department who were determined to make this happen. Chapter Four continued to emphasise the importance of the preparatory work of the Office, the unacknowledged fourth pillar of the 'quadripartite' ILO governance structure, to ensuring the smooth passage of the Recommendation through two ILCs. This smooth passage would not have been so smooth had it not been for the fact that the workers caucus within the ILO had already aligned itself behind the idea of the SPF and that support was readily available from the employers' group too. Chapter Five drew attention to several factors that go towards explaining the adoption by the wider UN community, the G20 and the World Bank of the 'SPF' concept. Among these were:

- the earlier campaign for a global social floor, which had cemented some inter-agency links;
- the circumstance of the 2008 economic crisis, which propelled the issue up the UN and G20 agendas;
- the contingencies of the French presidency of the G20;
- the replacement of an old ILO adversary from the leadership of the World Bank's Social Protection Division by a new more cooperative leader.

Chapter Five also revealed how, once the issue of the SPF hit the wider global social governance agenda, not all went smoothly. Key players within the ILO did not always work in synchronicity with each other, leading to the confusing co-existence of the older SPF-I governance structure and the new SPIAC-B governance structure.

The argument of this chapter is that the SPF resulted from the intersection of the *biographies* and careers of three individuals – the head of the Social Security Department at the ILO, the director-general of the ILO and his social protection advisor in his Cabinet (obviously supported by others in their teams and also outside the ILO) – with the *idea* that the world needed a global social floor, which had for some time been advanced by a policy advocacy coalition. This was, essentially, an idea whose time had come with the new *circumstances* of the 2008 global economic crisis, which provided the opportunity for UNCEB to act, an idea that could find an unlikely home inside the *institution* of the ILO, which was open to a degree of policy change because of the de facto *circumstance* of the development of forms of social protection in Latin America and Africa. This institutional policy change was engineered through the skilful development of alliances within the tripartite governing process. The subsequent endorsement by the G20, building on earlier work with the G8, was due to largely determined work by individuals working in the context of the fortuitous interest by France in having social protection on its G20 agenda.

In the following section this summary explanation is fleshed out and situated within a broader theoretical literature.

Theories of global social policy change: towards the ASID framework

In the search for an analytical framework for understanding global social policy formation and change, I have argued together with Stubbs (Deacon and Stubbs, 2013) that the attempt by Frank Moulaert and Bob Jessop (notably Moulaert and Jessop, 2006) to combine agency, structure, institutions and discourses (the ASID approach as they term it) may offer a way forward.[43] Referring to the problem of the relationship between agency and structure, which predates social science itself, they suggest (Moulaert and Jessop, 2006: 2) that:

> It is almost impossible to analyse any aspect of socio-economic growth and development without referring directly or indirectly to the actions that steer or interfere with these processes, the structures that constrain action, the

institutions that guide or hamper action and mediate the relation between structures and action, and the discourses and discursive practices that are part of these interactions.

They define the four key concepts as follows (2006: 2-3):

Agency is any type of meaningful human behaviour, individual or collective, that makes a significant difference in the natural and/or social worlds....

Structure comprises those moments of natural and/or social realities that, in the short or medium run and in a concrete spatial context ... cannot be changed by a given individual or collective agency....

Institutions ... can be considered as 'socialised structure', i.e., a relatively enduring ensemble of structural constraints and opportunities insofar as they appear in the form of a more or less coherent, interconnected set of routines, conventions, rules, sanctioning mechanisms, and practices that govern more or less specific domains of action.... [and]

Discourse is the inter-subjective production of meaning.

The concept of 'conjuncture' is also central to their framework. Thinking conjuncturally involves an examination of the different, and sometimes divergent, tendencies at work in a particular location at a particular moment in time. Using the ASID framework as 'a generic toolkit or heuristic that can be applied to all forms of social engagement with the natural and social worlds' (Moulaert and Jessop, 2006: 10) for the analysis of 'global social policy', offers rich possibilities.

Any understanding of (global) social *structure* is far from the rather functionalist notion of social structure found within much of 'world society theory' (Meyer and Hannan, 1979; Meyer and Jepperson, 2000; Abu Sharkh, 2004). I have counter-posed rather 'the framework of capitalism, patriarchy and a racially structured imperialism with its concomitant global social divisions of class, gender and ethnicity' (Deacon, 2007: 21), which would still be consistent with the ASID framework. At a global level, divisions between the securely employed and the 'informal sector' lie behind some of the structural imperatives of global social policy change. In terms of the contribution of *institutions* to the understanding of global social policy, the institutional legacy of intergovernmental organisations has some path dependency effects just as diverse welfare state institutional structures within single countries do. The tripartite governance structure of the ILO (Baccaro and Mele,

2012) has contributed to the continued emphasis on the desirability of countries adopting and retaining (reformed) Bismarkian–style PAYG pension systems. The World Bank's prime concern with global capital accumulation has, in turn, contributed to its promulgation of a pension system based on individual private savings' accounts. The limits of path dependency are clear, however, in the context of a longstanding concern with debates both within and between intergovernmental organisations (Deacon et al, 1997). *Agency* can be 'individual', and even 'idiosyncratic' (Moulaert and Jessop, 2006), and enables analysts to counter the primacy given to 'cultural processes, logics and mechanics' within 'world society theory'. Global social policy studies have argued that, at times, particular individuals can be important in pushing global and regional social policy ideas. The 'UN intellectual history project' (Emmerji et al, 2005) has traced the strong influence of Andrea Cornia and Richard Jolly of UNICEF in contributing to shifting the dominant global discourse from 'structural adjustment' to 'adjustment with a human face'. The same figures later influenced the UNDP in terms of developing measures of human and social development (the Human Development Report indicators) to challenge the World Bank's economic growth indicators. Too little has been written on the generational influences within global policy fora and institutions and it is also evident that the careers and biographies of civil servants (national, regional and global) matter in terms of preserving or changing institutions and policies. Perhaps the concept of '*discourse*' has proved to be most slippery in much of global social policy analyses. At the same time, a rather under-theorised sense that discourse, ideologies and ideas matter has been present throughout. One strand of my work has stressed the importance of understanding the shifting and sometimes contested policy debates within and between international actors and agencies (Deacon, 2007). Ideas about social policy and social change and their transnational contestation and promulgation by differentially powerful agencies (St Clair, 2006) and the role of epistemic communities and transnational networks (Stone and Maxwell, 2005) have also been addressed. Dostal's (2004) concept of 'organisational discourses' has been used by Mahon (2009) in her work on the OECD. Schmidt's (2008) focus on the importance of 'discursive institutionalism', which emphasises the scope for actors within institutions to challenge dominant discourses, is also relevant.

What is, of course, most complex, both theoretically and practically, is to assemble the four concepts together as an analytical approach in the context of any empirical study such as this one on the SPF. While it is important to question the determinist formulations of Sklair

(2002: 99) or Soederberg (2006) that the entire range of international organisations, the policies they formulate and the intellectuals working within and around them can be understood as a fraction of the global capitalist class, only challengeable by 'the multitude' (Hardt and Negri, 2005), seeing global social policy in terms of the condensation of processes of material struggles around gender, race, class and ethnicity, is both legitimate and desirable. Social policies at both national and global levels continue to be shaped by class, gender and ethnic interests and mobilisations and linked discourses concerning work (*who gets it*), family (*the role of women and how it is to be lived*) and nation/citizenship (*who belongs*) (Williams, 1995). The SPF story reflects some of these global contests of structurally determined interests.

Within the World Bank, as Sen (2004, 2006) has shown, arguments developed by feminists about the positive developmental effects of putting women at the centre of development by, for example, ensuring equal opportunity for girls in education and micro credit for women have become accepted, and therefore in some ways distorted of course, as mainstream. Sen (2004: 13) comments that 'the real struggle to transform the new discourse into effective policy change has to move on to the level of changes in institutions, laws, practices and norms.' In short, to be path creating in international institutions it is first necessary to change the discourse. It should never be forgotten, in this context, that 'established rules' can also be transformed, 'sometimes with major path-shaping effects, as individuals, groups, and other social forces reinterpret, resist, or overturn them' (Jessop and Neilsen, 2003: 8). The injection of the 'SPF' concept into ILO internal policy debates reveals a similar process.

The suggestion by Stubbs and I (Deacon and Stubbs, 2013) for a new synthetic analytical approach to global social policy theory is that the concepts and analytical tools that have been used to date within global social policy studies (Deacon, 2007) – 'complex multilateralism', 'policy advocacy coalitions', the 'politics of scale' – speak within the specific field of global social policy analysis to one or more elements of this broader framework. 'Complex multilateralism' focuses on the global *institutions* most concerned with social policy and addresses their capacity to act as *agents* to impede or impel change. While their policies may be framed to an extent by countries, they also exhibit autonomy, with their secretariats able to shift the discourse and in turn alter their global social policy prescriptions. Transnational 'policy advocacy coalitions' combine the *agency* of individuals and collectives and contribute to shifts in the dominant global *discourse* and in turn therefore to shifts in policy. The 'politics of scale' has drawn attention to the ways in which policy actors jump scale and link the global to the local and through sub-contracting become *agents* for *institutions* and help spread ideas.

Using ASID to explain the SPF

We turn therefore to the development of the ILO-, UN-, G20- and World Bank-endorsed SPFs global policy to illustrate how the ASID analytical framework, combined with the lower-level concepts of 'complex multilateralism', 'global policy advocacy coalition' and 'the politics of scale' can be helpful in advancing global social policy studies. The account proceeds through the four steps: structure, discourses, institutions and agency.

The *global social structural* context at the turn of the century was propitious for the development of such a policy. The expectation that the development of all economies would lead gradually to an industrial mode of production drawing more people into the ambit of formal employment and hence wage-related social security had long been thwarted. The decades of neoliberal globalisation had also facilitated a casualisation and flexibilisation of even formal employment. The world social structure was becoming increasingly polarised not only within countries between an increasingly rich minority upper class and an impoverished working and middle class but also between countries. The global financial system by 2008 had been found wanting, relying on lending money to people who could not afford to repay in order to prop up demand in a system of endemic overproduction. While, as I suggested earlier, I am not endorsing the formulations of Sklair (2002: 99) or Soederberg (2006) that international civil servants are busily seeking policies that prop up the global capitalist system, I am suggesting that these intellectuals working within these organisations were motivated to develop policies that would address the interests of those excluded from the perceived benefits of the global economy and the interests of those clearly negatively affected by its unjust workings.

This global social structural context and its associated global financial crisis gave rise to the possibilities that calls for a social floor under the global economy might find widespread support. At the same time the years of neoliberal globalisation had strengthened the structural power of global capitalism (Farnsworth, 2012) and weakened the power of labour unions, suggesting that the emerging contestations over interests were less likely to be couched in terms of capital and labour and more likely to be couched in terms of the privileged few and impoverished residents of the globe. More particularly, the specifics of the 2008/09 global financial crisis handed the ILO as, at that time, convenor of UNCEB the ideal opportunity to advance the case for a global SPF. The already existing cash transfer policies that had developed within Latin America and Africa as responses to the global social structural economic circumstances made this call plausible in the North and South.

Ranged against this seemingly immutable yet socially destructive global economy and its supporting discourse of the Washington Consensus within which the targeted poor would have their needs met by export-lad economic growth, micro credit and safety nets was the *idea and the emerging discourse* of a universal global social floor. Good ideas whose time has come have many parents. This story has reported some controversy over who it was who first suggested the idea that we needed to construct a floor under the global economy below which nobody would fall. Whether it was Juan Somavia or Wouter van Ginneken, both of the ILO, one its director, the other of its Social Security Department, is open to debate. What is certain is that the idea was a development from the outcomes of the 1995 Copenhagen Social Summit. The summit concluded with 10 commitments embracing poverty eradication, full employment and social integration. It also resolved a commitment to strengthen the framework of international cooperation and a commitment to create a (global) economic and political environment that would enable social development to be achieved. This was a wider commitment and one couched in more universalist terms than the subsequent watering down of this to the targeted and more limited MDGs of the follow-up summit of 2000.

Whether we take the Somavia formulation of February 2000: 'workers' rights aren't fringe benefits to be gained at a later date, or when the economic conditions are convenient, they constitute the "social floor" of the global economy below which no person should fall', or the van Ginneken formulation of March 2000: 'the concept of a global social floor can be extended to include the guarantee of some basic entitlements with regard to education, health and social protection', the concept became closely linked to and as we have seen subsequently developed and promulgated by the ILO. It evolved later within the ILO because the follow-up UN summit (Copenhagen plus 5) in 2000 was not a setting within which the idea could take route. The global social policy code or 'code of global best practice in social policy' of Gordon Brown (1999: 6) failed to make headway then because of the Global South's experience of the Structural Adjustment Programmes of the 1980s. The idea (of a global social policy code or global social floor) only resurfaced when it found an institutional home for its advancement after many countries in the Global South had developed their own SPFs. As a leading ILO ACTRAV member said, "we were saved by the social protection revolution in the South."

Part of the answer as to why the floor flew and the code fell is that by the time it became international soft law the floor had been drained of its content by some of those governments that had opposed the social policy principles in 2000. We have shown in effect how the idea, in order to stay alive, had to morf from a focus on universal social pensions, universal child benefits and specific health care access to a set of 'guarantees' to country-defined mimina and country-defined policies. The *idea*, however, rather than its *content*, was 'the thing' as current parlance has it. The idea of the 'social floor' became and is, in Jenson's (2012) terms, a 'quasi concept', which in global social policy discourse is used to empower some actors and disempower others. This is why so much has been invested in the historic battle between the quasi concept of 'safety nets' versus 'social floor'.

Despite this arguable watering down of the concept, the idea did stay alive and the global social policy debate within and between several international organisations did increasingly focus between 2005 and 2012 on how to realise SPFs in all countries. This happened because the idea took institutional root. It is to the *institutionalisation of the idea* that the analytical framework now turns. The problem, as has been noted at certain points in this account, was that the institution within which the idea took root was from the outset not predisposed by its history and governance structures to embrace the idea. One strand of the account has been to ask how did a tripartite labourist organisation come to embrace a social policy far removed from one that historical institutional analysis might have led us to expect. The ILO was designed to promulgate Bismarkian wage-related workers' social security standards. As van Ginneken[44] said, 'we never expected the ILO to become the vehicle for the social floor.' Baccaro and Mele's (2012) argument would have led us to expect that Somavia would have been defeated on this as he was on trying to open up the ILO governance structure to social movements. How then did path-dependent expectations become turned on their heads into path-breaking innovations?

It is the argument of this book that certain individuals both at the level of the ILO directorate and at the level of its Social Security department did change, to some extent, the practice of the ILO by first changing its discourse. Somavia was able to draw on the ILO's focus on work to get it to accept the concept of 'decent work'[45] one element of which was social protection. Cichon, appointed in 2005 as a less radical person than 'citizenship-income-Standing' was able to draw on very early ILO recommendations on health and living standards to win acceptance of his SPF policy so long as it was closely linked at all times with a two-pronged strategy to develop both a horizontal (the floor) and a vertical (social security) extension of social security. His use of the discourse of social rights, of practical feasibility and of economic affordability won over critics. His downplaying of the need for international funding, his fudging the issue of the social protection of unwelcome 'not normally resident' migrants and his willingness to embrace the arguably vacuous concept of SPFs in the plural made his policy shift acceptable to those who would otherwise have acted as they did in 2000 with regard to the social policy principles. The fact that the ILO now has a new clear policy whereby it recommends to all countries that they develop an SPF guaranteeing through the course of the life cycle that all residents are provided within a specific time period a guaranteed level of income security defined in relation to national poverty lines is a big policy shift for an ILO historically identified with promulgating conventions for workers.

The other institutional aspect of this story is the way the ILO has been used as an international institution to sell and win support for the SPF policy from other UN organisations and the G20. Indeed, given the initial obstacles placed in the way of Somavia to develop polices *within* the ILO more in keeping with the social movement-responsive UN summit of 1995 from where he arrived, it can be argued that Somavia stayed such a long time at the ILO because he felt he could use it to advance progressive policies concerned with globalisation *outside* the ILO and within the international community more generally. To this end he has indeed been very successful. The World Commission on the Social Dimension of Globalization involving two major progressive governments in the chair and drawing on an array of global talent was path breaking in its call for there to be a socioeconomic floor under the global economy. The Bachelet Report, again drawing on significant global talent, did influence the G20 in its adoption of the idea of the SPF. The 2009-12 flurry and ongoing processes of ILO–World Bank, ILO–IMF, ILO–UNICEF and ILO–UNDP meetings to advance the cause of policy synergy such that all international organisations including the international financial organisations sing to the same progressive global reformist song sheet, including about social protection, is impressive. The emergence of the SPIAC-B is a formal reflection of this in global governance terms.

This, then, is a story of a global social policy development that can be made sense of if we understand the (a) importance of the *global social structural* context within which it is set, making such a policy necessary, (b) the role of *ideas* in changing things and how global social policy discourses based on ideas can evolve especially when rooted in (c) *institutional contexts* that can be both path constraining but also are open to being path changing and can empower the ideas rooted in them. But it is also a story that would not have happened but that it was propelled by (d) *agencies and actors*. Who were these agencies? They were of two kinds. First providing a needed backcloth and point of reference to which other inside players could refer were the social movements both within countries and the cross-border social movements and INGOs that during the late 1990s and the early years of this century helped to bring into place a whole array of new social protection policies in Latin America, Africa, India and elsewhere. Perhaps allied to these, seeing the writing on the wall was the development of the policy within the ITUC of support for the SPF, which made its passage through the ILO less problematic. Also relevant was the push given for the development of universal social policies for a global era by the loosely networked epistemic communities that were to give rise in 2007 to the Campaign for a Global Social Floor. But also crucially important were the very few individuals, overlooked and undervalued international civil servants, who worked often tirelessly to advance the SPF policy both within and outside the ILO. We have named them in articles and reports we have referred to, in meetings convened by them. At the level of the ILO directorate focused mainly on external efforts was Juan Somavia and his social protection Cabinet member, Vinicius Pinhiero. At the level of the Social Security Department was Michael Cichon and his small band of policy analysts, working with a team drawn also from ILO Standards and Legal Departments.[46] Within UNICEF is Isabel Ortiz and her team. Without each of their efforts, motivated by global policy improvement, albeit laced at times for some with an eye to career advancement, the SPF policy would not have been achieved.

More precisely in terms of the role of *biography* I believe the story in the previous chapters has demonstrated:

- the significant role of Cichon, steeped in the internal politics of the ILO, which enabled him to keep alive the idea of a SPF Recommendation first muted in 2000, argued for by him and others with the launch of the Coalition for a Global Social Floor in 2007 and steered doggedly by him through the tripartite institution of the ILO between 2010 and 2012;
- the equally significant role of Samovia in being able to use his reputation as chair of the 1995 Copenhagen UN conference and

his position as director-general of the ILO to sell an even wider concept of the 'SPF' to the UN system in 2009 and advance the case further by asking his co-patriot to convene the Expert Committee leading to the publication of the Bachelet Report;

- the significant role of the young and ambitious Pinheiro as ILO sherpa in ensuring that the G20 gave full support to the SPF and establishing, according to the G20 mandate (which he wrote), better, if confusing, inter-agency coordination with which he was to become personally involved later with his appointment to the ILO office in New York;
- the existence of more than one individual driver within the ILO, which generated a degree of tension that had to be handled as when, for example, Cichon tried to keep the focus on the social transfers embodied in the four guarantees of the SPF Recommendation while Somavia (and Pinheiro), through the Bachelet Report, were selling a somewhat broader concept of the 'global social floor' involving also other goods and services.[47] Similar tensions arose with respect to how inter-agency cooperation might be enhanced and what emphasis should be given to global funding of the SPF;
- the biography of Isabel Ortiz, which was also central both in helping to drive the original Campaign for a Global Social Floor and in enabling the SPF-I to have real concrete support from UNICEF. Her early days as social security expert in the Asian Development Bank, followed by her work within UNDESA drafting social policy guidelines, fitted her for this supportive role.

The SPFs policy was thus not a policy of a government argued for in intergovernmental meetings. It was a policy of the fourth arm of the quadripartite structure of the ILO; the secretariat responding to the global social forces pressing in the direction of such a policy.[48]

Having argued that the ASID framework is a useful tool for enabling us to understand the development of this global social policy, let us not forget to add a dose of contingency, accident and luck. It was good fortune that placed Cichon in the driving seat of the Social Security Department in 2005. It was luck that Somavia was chair of UNCEB when the financial crisis broke in 2008. It was good fortune that the French presidency of the G20 determined upon social protection as an issue and certainly good fortune that the French government's representative at the ILO was who he was. It was associated good luck that the about-to-retire French-speaking member of Cichon's team in 2011 was on good terms both with the ILO sherpa and the Ministry of Labour in France. It was timely that the longstanding thorn in the side of the ILO's Social Security Department at the World Bank, Robert Holzmann, was replaced in 2010 by Arup Banjeri. It was no accident that Somavia, his social security Cabinet member and the resting place of the global SPF knowledge platform are all Latin American. In that sense the study has leant support also to those scholars who have argued for the role of contingency in shaping policy development (Trondal et al, 2010).

It is also possible to recast the explanation for the development of the SPF policy in the terms of the specific concepts of 'complex multilateralism', 'policy advocacy coalitions' and 'the politics of scale' used in earlier global social policy analysis (Deacon, 2007). Members of the 'policy advocacy coalition' for the global social floor used their relative autonomy within the ILO secretariat and worked within the framework of 'complex multilateralism' to win support from the global workers' organisation in alliance with a series of progressive governments to achieve the policy change. By 'jumping scale', global protagonists of the SPF such as HelpAge International had already found themselves acting within meetings of the Africa Union to inject ideas about universal social protection in the Africa Union's social policy framework for Africa, a factor influencing the African delegations to support the SPF at the ILO.

Other theoretical considerations

This case study is also a contribution to the renewed interest among international organisations scholars in the role of international civil servants. Marcussen and Trondal's (2011: 595, emphasis added) recent study of the OECD civil servants remind us of Mathiason's (2007) view that 'existing international organization research has largely ignored international bureaucracies as *autonomous* institutions and, in consequence, partly bypassed the study of international civil servants'. Their study points to the dual role of such civil servants (Marcussen and Trondal, 2011: 594):

> OECD officials mainly adopt two roles: the transnational epistemic role and the rule-following bureaucrat role. On one hand, they enact distinct transnational epistemic roles according to which their loyalty is directed towards science and knowledge.... On the other hand, however, current organisational reforms reward an entirely different role according to which OECD civil servants should be of

immediate operational value in the day-to-day handling of governance problems in the member states.

This study has illustrated how this tension is handled in this case with the civil servants in the Social Security Department both networked effectively into a global community of social protection experts and able to deftly negotiate a path through the institutional and external demands of, in this case, the ILO, to make a global policy contribution in keeping with the logic of their professional roles. The *autonomy* of the international organisation and of the civil servants inside it has been demonstrated.

In the same vein, as was mentioned earlier, one of the first books to be published in the context of the ILO Century programme notes in its review of all the existing texts on ILO history (van Daele, 2010: 38) that:

> In addition to the three constituent groups, the ILO is driven by the work of officials and experts, which in historical research are far too often represented as invisible and anonymous actors in international bureaucracy. Consequently their ideas and (non-) decisions through contacts and expert networks worldwide merit greater attention in historical research.

This contemporary history makes up a little for this lack of attention to the role of the so-called 'technical' secretariat and their space for autonomous action.

The results of this case study lend support also to those arguing within international relations theory that friendships matter. A recent conference on this theme[49] advertised itself by noting that:

> There is a growing body of literature that ... seeks to include the concept of friendship in the study of International Relations. In this sense, the conference picks up the threads of recent turns in IR [international relations] theory such as the sociological turn or the turn to Communitarian IR .The concept of friendship must not be limited to state actors or international organisations but typically involves domestic and transnational non-state actors as well.

This case study has shown the importance of trust won over time between key figures in the ILO, UNICEF, INGOs concerned with social protection and others, which has enabled the concept of the SPF to gain traction in many UN agencies and outside them.[50] The emerging closer relationship between the Social Security Department of the ILO and the Social Protection and Labour Division of the World Bank will be cemented and a closer working relationship developed around the SPF only if the leading figures 'get on'.

This study has certainly highlighted the value of the work of other analysts who have insisted on the importance of ideas as a factor in advancing international policy. Beland, in a series of articles and book (Beland, 2009; Beland and Cox, 2011; Beland and Orenstein, 2013), has stressed the role of ideas in shaping both national and global policies. Ideas here are defined as causal beliefs, symbols, theories, perceptions and lessons that underlie policy options and choices (Beland and Cox, 2011). In an article jointly with Orenstein (Beland and Orenstein, 2013: 1) he concludes: 'Ideas matter much more – and international organizations are far more flexible – than most structuralist accounts would predict.... International organizations frequently have shown themselves to be open to new ideas and approaches espoused by well-positioned policy entrepreneurs.' Indeed, using a discursive framework to criticise the realist principle–agent formulation where international organisations are merely the agents of government, he continues: (2003: 9): 'one of the most important sources of international organization ideas is not governments but individual policy entrepreneurs.' But he adds elsewhere (Beland, 2009: 702) that 'ideas only become a decisive causal factor under specific institutional and specific conditions'. This study of the SPF has reinforced these conclusions but also for an international organisation whose constitution might suggest that it would be the exception. While the policy entrepreneurs within the World Bank are relatively insulated from government, inside the ILO they are not especially when promulgating new policies. This study has shown that even inside the ILO, governments *react* to the Office proposals rather than drive them and that the Office proposals are derived from the ideas of a global ideas network. As Beland and Orenstein (2013: 2) suggest, 'the analysis of how ideas and discourses evolve within international organizations [is] one of the most important frontiers of global social policy theory.' It is my hope that this study has contributed a little to this task.

Reflections and prospects

Introduction

This final chapter does five things:

- It provides an assessment of the SPF Recommendation in its own terms as a piece of ILO policy and asks whether the ILO has really modified its prime focus on workers' social security and embraced a campaign for the social protection of residents. Will it be sustained within the ILO in the future?
- It asks to what extent the 'global social floor' or SPF-I has become really embedded in the UN system in the context of parallel debates and processes concerned with environmental sustainability (Rio plus 20) and with the broader UN development agenda planned for the period from 2015 after the 'expiry' of the initial MDG agenda.
- It discusses the further development of a global civil society campaign to realise SPFs in practice in countries. How will this new coalition take forward the work of the original Coalition for a Global Social Floor? Linked to this is the question of which of the two inter-agency coordination mechanisms (SPF-I and SPIAC-B) take forward the campaign at an official UN level? What will be the next ILO steps?
- It reports and discusses the very recent call being made to establish a global social protection fund and asks how this might operate.
- Finally, it returns to the broader question of complex global social governance and assesses the implications of this case study in global social policy formation for our understanding of the existing and future global social governance system.

Assessing the SPF Recommendation

The decision of the ILC in June 2012 to agree to a recommendation to its member countries that they should develop a SPF was historic. The SPF Recommendation is historic because, echoing and adding to some of the words of its main protagonist inside the ILO:

- it asserts that the ILO has a role in formulating social protection policy for residents and citizens, not just workers;
- it challenges the growth-first economists with the priority of social protection whatever the level of the economy;
- it argues for redistribution nationally and even in small measure internationally;
- it challenges the equity-efficiency trade-off economists with the case that equity supports efficiency;
- it posits a common interest between those formally employed with work-related benefits and those outside formal employment;
- it sees off the initial reservations of countries such as Canada, the UK and the US and won support from the wiser councils of France, a host of Latin American countries 'led' by Brazil, South Africa and elsewhere;
- it reverses the non-decision of 2000 when the UN refused to even consider defining a common set of social policy principles;
- when linked with the parallel process of creating both an SPF-I and a new SPIAC-B it contributes to a new policy synergy between global financial actors and global UN social agencies.

Having said all of that, what are the shortcomings? They are several. The compromises made necessary to win support for the SPF Recommendation meant that:

- the Recommendation is couched in terms of policy outcomes (the 'guarantees') rather than specific policy tools (such as universal pensions), leaving the fractious debate between those who would target and those who would provide universally unresolved;[51]
- the Recommendation is couched in terms of national responsibility with countries being urged to act with regard to their circumstances, which leaves enormous scope for backsliding;
- the Recommendation is couched in terms of guarantees for those normally resident and therefore raises the question of who is responsible for the social protection of those migrants not considered normally resident by countries;
- the watering down of the reference to international financial support to that being possibly necessary only initially and only in the poorest countries, flowing as it does with the fashion to stress to emphasise on national fiscal responsibility, undermines the case of those who still call for global taxes for global public goods.

More generally, the Recommendation's focus on the narrower SPF definition concerned with income support across the lifecourse plus access to affordable health care leaves there being no equivalent policy on the broader aspects of the UN's SPF definition, captured in the Bachelet Report, which embraced also access to water, sanitation and other social services. More critical too is Francine Mestrum (2012) who on the Global Social Justice website[52] analyses different proposals for a SPF. With regard to the new ILO policy, she asserts that '[i]n short, however positively the plans for a Social Protection Floor can be assessed ... if the SPF is limited to its minimal requirements, it will be compatible with Washington Consensus policies'. But here she ignores the twin-track approach of the SPF Recommendation, which is concerned to both extend social security coverage horizontally to the currently uncovered and extend it vertically to enhance the contributory wage-related social security benefits on workers both formal and informal.

This links to the possible criticism that it is indeed only a floor and therefore only focused on the poor people and that to focus on poor people is not the way to build inclusive welfare states. Elsewhere I argued, together with Cohen (Deacon and Cohen, 2011: 234), that 'For the past 30 years the dominant discourse in international development has been the "global politics of poverty alleviation", which focuses on the poor and seeks policies that lift populations out of poverty or protect others from falling into it.' What is needed instead 'a shift in the social construction of global poverty alleviation politics ... [replacing it with] a "global politics of solidarity" based on inclusion of the "middle class" in development policy. The new strategy would promote alliances between the poor and non-poor, especially the middle class, while making services and opportunities more available and more effective for all.' In other words, I argued (Deacon, 2011a: 89):

> [E]ffective functioning states which meet the welfare needs
> of their citizens and residents do so because they also meet
> the welfare needs of their state builders. In sum, a focus
> on the poor distracts from building cross-class solidarity. A
> focus on the poor undermines the middle class commitment
> to pay taxes. Countries need higher education as well as
> primary, city hospitals as well as rural clinics, and wage
> related pensions as well as social pensions and cash transfers
> to poor.

Within that context, how are we to judge the SPF? In its defence we would have to revert again to the same argument used by its ILO 'authors' and remind ourselves that the horizontal floor is intimately linked to the vertical stairway to wage-related social security. Thus, they acknowledged the possible criticism of a SPF focused only on poor people by saying that 'a social protection system that does not support higher benefit levels to a significant proportion of its population can lose the support of its own beneficiaries and contributors' (Cichon et al, 2011: 8). Regardless of the progressive merits of the SPF, if we are to rebuild developmental welfare states we need social policies that are much more than floors and much more than cash benefits.

So how does one assess the potential impact of this SPF Recommendation? Because it has the force only of soft law it is, like all other UN declarations and conventions on social rights, merely one point of reference to be used in the ongoing national and global struggles around the issue. Its existence adds strength to the arguments of those seeking to realise social floors in practice. It is a weapon to be deployed in discursive struggle. The national reports of progress against specific time horizons required under the terms of the Recommendation can add strength to campaigns. More than this, however, is the positive impact that this new policy will have on the way the ILO technical assistance to countries tries to help countries build such floors. And, given the increased cooperation that should be expected between the ILO, other UN agencies, the World Bank and the IMF is the positive impact that the new policy will have on coordinated support to countries. How this will pan out depends in part on the functioning of the new SPIAC-B.

Perhaps we should ask here what those who might otherwise have led the Social Security Department from 2005 would make of the way things have turned out. How might they view the development of the SPF policy? To what extent might they argue that for all its novelty this policy development built upon their separate legacies? Emmanuelle Reynaud (Javiliier et al, 2006) would have worked to develop ILO agreements with governments to secure the extension of social security by incorporating new voluntary and cooperative forms of insurance and micro-credit initiatives alongside state social security provision. Such plans 'bypass the conflict between hard and soft law in that, by defining a method for developing national plans, they make soft law complement hard law and enable it to be applied effectively in very different realities and situations' (Javiliier et al, 2006: xi). Reynaud might reasonably insist that his pre-2005 Department took the first steps to concretely build real SPFs in countries reflecting these diverse realities, something that the SPF Recommendation was forced to come to terms with when it added the s to floor. He might also have pointed to the fact that one of the showcase countries being exhibited as an example of a good SPF, Mozambique, had been one of the principal countries funded under the STEP programme, now ending, with which he and his close colleagues were associated. Indeed, it could be further argued that once the dust over the passing of this new soft law has settled, the reality of continuing technical assistance to countries will indeed be attempts to develop close cooperative agreements between the ILO and governments.

Equally, Guy Standing might reasonably insist that the guarantees to a liveable income across the lifespan that the SPF Recommendation hopes to ensure in effect builds on but does not acknowledge his conceptualisation of a citizen's or resident's income provided as of right. Where the difference lies is in relation to the terms under which such an income is provided to people of working age capable of working. For Standing those with a basic income would be free to seek to enhance it through work and work itself should become increasingly commodified, leaving social protection to be a provision for residents, not workers (Standing, 2011). Here of course he would have broken completely with the SPF strategy of linking the horizontal extension of social security to the vertical extension, with the horizontal as being seen merely as a *stepping stone* to the 'hallowed' worker's social security benefits. He would no doubt argue that the SPF Recommendation is rather platitudinous and contradictory. It still defends Convention 102, which he would argue to be sexist and labourist and out of touch with the precarious nature of work after globalisation (Standing, 2011). He might ask where does it stand on workfare, on conditionality, on means testing and on targeting?

Where do those who supported the original global new deal to secure a 'global social floor' go from here to build on the partial success of that campaign embodied in the Recommendation on SPFs? There are a number of aspects to this question, which are addressed in this and the next two sections of the chapter.

First there is the need to build within the ILO the procedures for monitoring and assessing progress. Little is likely to emerge in the short term as far as the formal procedures within the ILO are concerned. First, the SPF is a Recommendation and not a convention and so is not subject to the regular automatic obligatory reporting mechanisms surrounding conventions. Second, the Recommendation itself is very soft on its requirements for governments to report progress, something that the contact person for the ILO's Standards and Norms Department with the Social Security Department regretted.[53] However, progress on the ways in which governments have reacted to recommendations can be asked for by the governing body (Article 19, para 6(d) of the ILO constitution) and also under Article 5, para 1(c) of Convention 144 provision is made for 'tripartite consultations (within countries) at appropriate intervals to consider what measure might be taken to promote implementation … of … Recommendations to which effect has not been given'.

Whether there is a concerted effort by the ILO to track progress on the SPF Recommendation is to some extent up to the governing body and to the secretariat concerned with the Committee of Experts. It was the view of Alexandre Egerov, responsible for social security in the Standards and Norms Department, that when the next cycle arrived for an ILC focus on social security in 2018, the Committee of Experts would have, in preparation for this in 2017,[54] focused on its General Survey on Social Security *including* the SPF Recommendation. By then he felt, after four or five years from the SPF Recommendation being agreed upon that it would be time enough to assess whether the SPF had become an established part of government policy in a number of countries. Indeed, Egorov is hopeful that then will be the time to convert the Recommendation into a convention: "My vision is by 2019, the 100th anniversary of the ILO, there will be such a convention."[55]

Linked to this established reporting process is, in my view, the need to address the governance issue within the ILO to accommodate this new focus on the social protection of residents. While the ITUC might have seen the importance of supporting such a policy (so long as it dovetailed with Convention 102), the workers' and employers' bureaus within the ILO are, as we saw in Chapter Four, far from accepting the governance implications of this policy. Some mechanism needs to be found that goes beyond the current arrangements, which only provide for governments to involve civil society indirectly in their delegations and consultations. The reality of social partner dialogues and mechanisms in many countries and regional associations is far more complex than suggested by the formal tripartite structure recently reaffirmed within the ILO. The ITUC, and hence ACTRAV within the ILO, needs to find a more effective way of working alongside and with 'representatives of beneficiaries' who will increasingly be residents and not workers. At the time of writing the fairly new International Association of Economic and Social Consultative Bodies, which represents at a global level the newer forms of more representative bodies that embrace a wider civil society representation, with which many governments and regional associations of governments discuss economic and social policy, was seeking clarification of its provisional agreement to be recognised by the ILO.

If this opening up of ACTRAV to a wider civil society does not happen then, in terms of the future campaign to secure greater global social justice and reinforce a more effective 'global social floor', we may, despite Egorov's dream, need to recognise the rather fragile and fleeting association that the 'global social floor' concept has had with the ILO. It might then be argued that the ILO as a vehicle for advancing a global social floor was found wanting. We ended up not with a global social floor defined by access to universal social pensions and child benefits but with national social floors with creaking foundations. Perhaps all that has been witnessed in this book is a temporary alliance between the employers' and workers' bureaus in the ILO, forced upon them by a determined director-general and a driven head of social security, one of whom then left the ILO in September 2012 and the other now as of December 2012 retired. There is no guarantee that the new ILO director-general and the new head of social security will continue to carry as effectively the two torches of global social justice and global social policy synergy. Global social policy watchers will have to follow this up. Perhaps we will also have to look outside the ILO for the furtherance of the campaign. This is discussed in the following two sections.

Would the SPF become embedded in the post-MDG UN development agenda?

In Chapter Five we told a fairly positive story of how because of the determination of key members of the ILO secretariat and because of the political clout of the ILO's director-general, combined with the 'luck' of the 2008 global economic crisis and the fortuitous support of the French government during the 2011 G20 process, the concept of the 'SPF' came a long way. By 2012 it was ILO policy, it was UNCEB policy and it had brought into being a new SPIAC-B. It had broad civil society support. Yet also by the beginning of 2012 there were already concerns within the camp of supporters of the SPF that all might not be well in terms of the sustainability of this progress. At the meeting of the SPF-I hosted by UNICEF in New York on 31 January 2012, a number of concerns were expressed. First was the concern that the post-MDG consultation process designed to develop a new UN development agenda for after 2015 had been kicked off by UNDESA and the UNDP without explicit reference to the SPF as a possible element of this agenda. Second was the concern that this new development agenda might be overshadowed or dominated by discussions about environmental sustainability at the Rio plus

20 conference due to take place a day after the June 2012 ILC. This conference might stress the importance of ecological or environmental sustainability to the exclusion of social issues. Third was the concern that the UN secretary-general had just set out his own priorities at the start of his second five-year term of office and these also did not give space for the SPF. Fourth was even the concern that although a joint UNCEB-initiated SPF-I existed with good attendance at technical meetings by most agencies, the messages of the SPF had not yet been translated into the language of each UN agency so, in that sense, there was not wide UN ownership beyond the ILO and UNICEF. One of the four action points agreed at the 2012 SPF-I meeting was how to inject the SPF into these other processes and to strengthen UN ownership.

To start the process of thinking through the post-2015 development agenda within the UN system, the first step was given to the internal UN Task Force made up of spokespersons from over 50 UN agencies. It began its work in January 2012 with a zero draft (UN 2012a) prepared by UNDESA and UNDP staff drawing on a number of critical papers such as those of Gore (2010) and Fukuda-Park (2010). In its balanced review of the perceived positive and negative aspects of the MDG goals, it noted among the shortcomings of the MDG agenda that it was 'not explicit as what are to be seen as the *structural causes of poverty and social exclusion*, neither regarding the strategies and policy actions to be taken to address the structural causes to facilitate the achievement of the MDGs' (UN, 2012a: 4, emphasis added). It went on to suggest that 'critics have suggested that the MDGs have introduced an undue and mechanistic association of poverty reduction with economic growth with no reference to the structural causes of poverty and deprivation' (2012a: 7). The think piece asked: 'How to bring into the development framework questions of inequality, peace and security, global and national governance, human rights, sustainable development without overloading the agenda to the point of losing its operational value?' (2012a: 8).

After several video conferences and other forms of communication, the task team reported in May 2012 (UN, 2012b). Its executive summary is predictably bland but does suggest a future development agenda centred on 'four key dimensions of a more holistic approach: (1) *inclusive social development*; (2) inclusive economic development; (3) environmental sustainability; and (4) peace and security' (UN, 2012b: 2). It suggests that a high degree of policy coherence is needed to achieve this. The baton then passed to the High Level Panel on the Post-2015 Development Agenda whose membership and terms of reference was announced on 15 July 2012. In setting out the terms of reference the UN secretary-general sadly reorders the task team report, which had suggested inclusive social development as number one with economic growth as the number one mention; it commands the panel to make 'Recommendations on how to build and sustain broad political consensus on an ambitious yet achievable post-2015 development agenda around the three dimensions of economic growth, social equality and environmental sustainability; taking into account the particular challenges of countries in conflict and post-conflict situations' (UN, 2012c: 5).

Initial reaction from the Beyond 2000 Civil Society Campaign Group (Beyond, 2000, 2012) was critical of the terms of reference. It was 'surprised and disappointed that the ToRs [terms of reference] do not include a single reference to human rights'(Beyond 2015: 3). It did, however, 'welcome the HLP [High Level Panel] plans to set out key principles to reshape global partnership. One lesson learnt from the MDGs is the need to better deliver equity and equality, within but also between countries'(Beyond 2015: 4) .The panel must now consult widely and report initially in 2013.[56]

The beginnings of the post-2015 discussions therefore (a) do open up for debate the issue of *inequality and equity* rather than just poverty, (b) do open up a space for engaging in *policy recommendations* and not just targets and (c) do permit a *reordering of priorities* other than economic growth. But also they also muddy the waters with more intangible ill-defined concerns with *sustainability*. However, from the point of view of or concern with the future of the SPF it has to be pointed out that the ILO seemed to miss the chance to inject the SPF as a post-2015 policy priority in the initial discussions between UN agencies between January and May 2012.The ILO contact point was not even identified in the first official circulation from UNDESA–UNDP in contrast to most other UN agencies.[57] The SPF does not figure in the terms of reference of the High Level Panel. Unless the UN secretary-general says SPF as often as he used to say MDG, the prospect for the future of the SPF campaign might not be as great as hoped for.

In terms of the Rio plus 20 UN conference on sustainable development, concern at the January 2012 SPF-I meeting focused on the question of whether enough emphasis was give to the SPF as an element of a sustainable future in the zero draft outcome of the conference. Mention was made in paragraph 73 (UN, 2012d) although it was tacked on to a paragraph dealing mainly with green jobs: 'We stress the need to provide social protection to all members of society, including those who are not employed in the formal economy. In this regard, we strongly encourage national and local initiatives aimed at providing a social protection floor for all citizens.'

Disappointing was the final draft of the report of the High Level Panel on Sustainable Development, which the secretary-general had established to advise the conference. Chaired by the Presidents of Finland and South Africa it had been expected to clearly endorse the SPF as key to the social sustainability element of a combined policy of social, environmental and economic sustainability. Sadly, under the section on building resilience, it devotes attention to the SPF by referring to the four guarantees dismissively as 'aspirational goals for whose achievement many countries continue to strive, although few have yet met them' (UN, 2012f, para 131). Furthermore, it retreats in its recommendations, which are more likely to be read than the text, to the World Bank's preferred safety-net formulation. Thus, Recommendation 23 reads: 'Countries should work to ensure that all citizens are provided with access to basic safety nets through appropriate national efforts and the provision of appropriate capacity, finance and technology' (UN, 2012f, para 133). Words matter and defeat for supporters of the SPF can be registered by which ones are used.

In the event the outcome of the Rio plus 20 summit was generally regarded as a disappointment by activists lacking firm targets or clear commitments. Its 283 paragraphs read like a bad PhD thesis, mentioning every progressive idea on economic, social and environmental policy but setting firm obligations on none of them. The mention of SPFs was now relegated to one sub-paragraph (n) of paragraph 58 on the green economy, which should among 16 concerns 'address the concern about inequalities and promote social inclusion, including social protection floors' (UN, 2012e). In addition in a large section on action and follow-up we find paragraph 107:

> We recognize that promoting universal access to social services can make an important contribution to consolidating and achieving development gains. Social protection systems that address and reduce inequality and social exclusion are essential for eradicating poverty and advancing the achievement of the Millennium Development Goals. In this regard, we strongly encourage initiatives aimed at enhancing social protection for all people.

The worry, from the standpoint of those wishing to see a focus on the SPF as a key element of the post-MDG UN development policy and the Rio plus 20 agenda is not only that the SPF gets lost in the jumble of words but also, the vacuous concepts about sustainability will come to dominate the UN development discourse and further push the concrete proposals about SPFs off the headlines. Moreover, the term 'safety net' has not been obliterated from global discourse. The ILO, however, continues to press for social protection to be a key element of the Post 2015 agenda. The following overarching jobs and livelihoods goal would be appropriate and realistic (ILO 2012j:2):

'Upgrade the objective of full and productive employment and decent work as a central goal of the post-2015 development agenda (and) this goal should be supported through the implementation of social protection floors for poverty reduction and resilience.'

The ongoing campaigns to implement SPFs

The possibly fragile alliance between the 'Campaign for a Global Social Floor' concept and the ILO was always recognised by the head of the Social Security Department of the ILO. Indeed, van Ginneken, one of the earlier supporters of the concept of the 'global social floor' within the Social Security Department confessed[58] that "we never expected the ILO to be the place where this took off. It was the UN and the post-1995 Copenhagen debate which we were focused on."

It came as no surprise therefore that the driver of the SPF policy inside the ILO, the head of the Social Security Department, took time out to address in early 2012 the executive of the ICSW, the global civil society organisation that was very active at the time of the 1995 Copenhagen Summit, saying that 'by the summer 2012 the ILO's job would be done and the ICSW and other civil society organisations needed to follow up' by:

- building national SPF coalitions;
- mounting a SPF-I awareness-raising campaign;
- contributing to national SPF dialogues;
- undertaking stock-taking of existing SPF provision;
- helping countries develop SPF plans with budgets;
- monitoring progress towards the realisation of the SPF. (Cichon, 2012)

By taking this step he was straying far from the narrow confines of the tripartite modes of operation of the ILO and implicitly acknowledging the limitations of the ILO's reporting procedures as a way of sustaining the SPF movement.

The ICSW had already two years earlier agreed to build the SPF into its policy objectives and gave it active support. Thus, it was not unexpected that this meeting of the ICSW executive should agree to recommend to its wider membership that the SPF would become even more central to its work in the next four years. The ICSW agreed to make it a central pillar of its campaigning work. It was not alone in this. HelpAge International, which had been very influential in driving the case for social pensions across Africa and into the Africa social policy framework adopted in Namibia in 2009, was also a strong supporter. Within the broader UN focused NGO Committee for Social Development the SPF had already been adopted as a rallying call. Indeed, it launched in 2011 a global signature campaign calling on all governments to implement a national SPF and had within the first months gained signatures from 131 countries (NGO Committee for Social Development, 2012a).

These and other civil society actors came together in New York on the day after the SPF-I meeting of 31 January 2012 (to which some had been invited), and the day before the start of the annual meeting of the UN Commission for Social Development, which was to focus on poverty alleviation, to discuss strategy at the now-institutionalised Pre-Commission Civil Society meeting. This civil society forum was entitled 'The SPF-I – bridging the gap to poverty eradication' and was addressed by both Michael Cichon (ILO) and Isabel Ortiz (UNICEF) on behalf of the UNCEB's SPF-I. The statement read to the Commission by the NGO alliance following this pre-meeting argued that: 'All national budgets include an allocation of 4% of the Gross Domestic Product to a universal social protection floor for their citizens' (NGO Committee for Social Development, 2012b). The civil society campaign for the SPF was now in full swing even before the Recommendation had become formal ILO policy.

Next in March 2012, 14 NGOs from all over the world participated in a Friedrich-Ebert-Stiftung-convened workshop in Geneva entitled 'The ILO's social protection floor – lobbying for a strong recommendation'. A joint statement of NGOs was written to support the adoption of a strong, autonomous ILO Recommendation on the SPF. In the end, this joint statement was supported and signed by 59 NGOs from different parts of the world. As noted in Chapter Four, the statement was presented at the SPF committee at the ILC in June 2012. Generally speaking, the INGOs were happy with the form of the Recommendation but still had concerns about the 'consultation', as distinct from 'involvement' role foreseen for NGOs in the Recommendation. This was hotly debated at the ILC (Chapter

Four) but the trades union and employers' groups stuck to their view that the formal tripartite structures within countries should be the ones to develop national policies. They also had concerns about limiting access to the SPF to residents as defined by countries themselves, thus potentially excluding some migrants. Very soon after the June 2012 ILC Friedrich Ebert Stiftung convened a further meeting in Berlin on 25 September 2012 to consider the next steps. A Coalition for a Social Protection Floor (singular) was formed with the aims of raising awareness of the ILO Recommendation, creating a platform for learning experiences among civil society organisations worldwide, collaborating with national and regional social protection platforms and/or coalitions, and generally promoting the design, implementation, monitoring and evaluation of SPFs.

According to van Ginneken (2013), the three main issues for civil society and the way they are included in the ILO Recommendation are:

- the aforementioned concern about participation;
- the need to *represent* the interests and aspirations of beneficiaries *in policy making* alongside the 'normal' social partner;
- the implementation of the rights-based approach in actual SPFs, including the right of beneficiaries to 'dignity, equality and non-discrimination' and the right to 'accountability and transparent' processes;
- extending the universality of access to SPFs to cross-border movers.

Making sense of the several parallel steps currently (February 2013) being taken to advance the case for turning the ILO Recommendation into reality in countries was confusing even to a trained observer. This was because of the existence of the several fora and networks concerned with the issue both inside the ILO and UN system and outside it. On the one hand the work of the SPF-I continued to be reported on the GESS website[59] *managed from the ILO Social Security Department in Geneva.* No initiative to convene another UN SPF-I meeting has been taken. The last entry in August 2012 simple states: 'The Coalition members of the SPF Initiative play a consultative role and can provide technical and financial support to the national SPF processes. Although there are a variety of ways to implement national social protection floors, some generic activities have been identified as key milestones in the construction of national social protection floors.' At the same time the *ILO New York office*, acting as the secretariat of the SPIAC-B, announced, also on the GESS website, the agenda's for the second and third meetings of the board. The second meeting was held in Hyderabad on 29 October 2012. Its agenda excluded any explicit reference to the SPF probably in deference to the view of the World Bank that this cooperation board of which it is joint chair should address social protection systems more generally. This session would discuss concrete joint work in middle- and low-income countries that have already requested technical cooperation on social protection to more than one of the international organisations and/ or bilateral institution members of the board. The agenda suggested that preliminary discussions between the ILO and World Bank had already identified the possibility of combining actions in countries such as Ghana and Indonesia on a demand-driven basis. At the same time the agenda noted that the UNDP was to introduce the new Social Protection Gateway[60] while the ILO would present the social protection capacity-building online platform being developed by the International Training Centre in Turin.

The third meeting was convened on Feb 11th 2013 in the context of the Annual UN Social Development Commission in New York. Its agenda included inserting social protection in the UN Post 2015 agenda and collaboration between the World Bank and UN and bilateral agencies on social protection statistics. The main tabled paper (ECA, ILO et al. 2013:10) suggested that "If the new development framework uses a targeting approach with measurable indicators, goals related to social protection could be the following: (1) By 2030 all people have social protection at least at the level of national floors for social protection." Among the papers tabled was one by the Special Rapporteur on extreme poverty and human rights, Ms Magdalena Sepulveda and the Special Rapporteur on the right to food, Mr Olivier de Schutter (Sepulveda and de Schutter (2013)) on 'The need to include a rights-based approach to Social Protection in the Post 2015 Development Agenda'. In addition to calling for social protection to be included in the 'new MDGs' it referred to their earlier argument (see next section in this chapter) to establish a global fund for social protection. However no discussion took place with a view to lining up the SPIAC-B behind this proposal and no steps were taken to bring it into existence. It seems that whereas the concept of a global fund was played down by the ILO Social Security Department while the SPF Recommendation was being steered through the ILC (Chapter Four), it is now being played down within SPIAC-B in part because the concept clashes with the interests of the World Bank in *lending* money for building social protection systems.

Tensions and overlaps seemed to remain between the different players and initiatives that have peppered the story told in earlier chapters. It is noteworthy that the UNICEF-driven SPF-I web-based gateway[61] had not been updated since June 2012. Given that the SPIAC-B now undertakes much of the work of the UN SPF-I it is likely that it will not be reconvened and the web site will wither. The G20 initiated web site[62] has not provided information about the SPAIC-Board even though the G20 was formally central to its creation. Indeed the countries that had been give responsibility for the G20 work on Social Protection: Pillar 6, Resilient Growth (Australia, Indonesia and Italy) and on Pillar 9, Knowledge Sharing (Korea and Mexico) were not at the third SPIAC-B meetings, highlighting the problem the informal G20 with no permanent secretariat has in following through on initiatives. Which web site will prevail – the UNDP-initiated one, flowing from the G20, the UNICEF-driven one flowing from the UNCEB and the UNSPF-I or indeed the original ILO extension of social security one that had been agreed on in Turin in November 2009 as the SPF-I website, but now acting as the site for information about the SPIAC-B – is unclear. Probably the later but at the time of writing work is advancing on the creation of a SPIAC-B site within the ILO New York Office probably to be linked to the existing ILO's Partnership and Development Cooperation section of the ILO[63].

The invitation for the meetings of the SPIAC-B are extended to a large number of mainly Northern OECD member 'donor' countries, several international organisation and some INGOs including HelpAge International, Save the Children, the ICSW and Solidar. The active involvement of INGOs in the SPIAC-B and in the UNSPF-I reflects the earlier origins of their involvement in the Campaign for the Global Social Floor established in 2007. Michael Cichon's new role, even when still at the ILO, as president of the ICSW also ensured this merging of official UN agencies and INGOs in the continuing campaign for the floor. Time, and in particular the appointment of Michael Cichon's sucessor will clarify who the main movers will be and out of which institution they will operate and which web site will be *the* one to refer to. The rise and fall of the several web sites has reflected the parallel and not always well coordinated struggles of the key actors to influence the social protection floor agenda[64]. The rise and fall of the several coordinating centres: ILO Social Security Department in Geneva, UNSPF-I, SPIAC-B (ILO New York) reflected the same story of the overlapping and sometimes not perfectly coordinated influences of and roles played by Cichon, Somavia, Ortiz and Pinheiro

The ILO itself, however, *does* have a clear official strategy set out in a publication on the SPF, or Recommendation 202 as it is now known (ILO, 2012g), the rather grandly entitled *The ILO Strategy:*

Social Security for All: Building Social Protection Floors and Comprehensive Social Security Systems.

> The ILO's two-dimensional strategy provides clear guidance on the future development of social security in countries at all levels of development. Effective national strategies to extend social security, in line with national circumstances, should aim at achieving universal protection of the population by ensuring at least minimum levels of income security and access to essential health care (horizontal dimension) and progressively ensuring higher levels of protection guided by up-to-date ILO social security standards (vertical dimension). In line with national priorities, resources and circumstances, such two-dimensional strategies should aim at building and maintaining comprehensive and adequate social security systems. (ILO, 2012g: 1)

Guy Ryder's introduction to this strategy appropriately notes:

> [It] is the result of a decade of research, economic, fiscal and actuarial studies, legal analyses, tripartite consultations at global, regional and national levels, consultation and collaboration with our sister organizations in the UN system, dialogue with the international financial institutions as well as with a large number of civil society organizations and, most prominently, intense discussions during three sessions of the ILC (2001, 2011 and 2012). (ILO, 2012g: v)

– the story recorded in this book. By using the term 'comprehensive social security systems', November 2012 ILO Strategy Document is making an implicit reference to UNICEF's (2012) preferred formulation concerning social protection and is responding to the World Bank's view that the SPIAC-B is about more than the SPFs. The Social Security Department also prepared an action plan to support its implementation, approved by the ILO governing body in November 2012 (ILO, 2012h), which includes the view that:

> The Office will continue to actively collaborate with other relevant agencies and partners at global, regional and national levels to promote the implementation of the Recommendation, including through the SPF-I adopted by UNCEB (UNCEB SPF Initiative) (under joint leadership

of the ILO and the WHO) and the Social Protection Inter-Agency Cooperation Board, which was created upon the request of the G20 (under joint leadership of the ILO and the World Bank). (ILO, 2012h: para17, p 4)

Furthermore, in the new director-general's (Guy Ryder) preview of ILO programme and budget for the next few years (ILO, 2012i), support for the implementation of the SPFs was selected as one of the seven priority areas where resources of the ILO will be concentrated. Within this context the ILO has collaborated with the EU on an inter-regional conference on social protection.[65]

In terms of the new role for Michael Cichon as President of the ICSW he argued early in 2013 (Cichon 2013) that it was now the turn of civil society and the trade union movement to advance the cause of the social protection floor concept. International Organisations can only achieve so much. Calling for fiscal space to be created to fund social protection floors has to become a *national* issue. Significantly he argues (Cichon 2013:4)

'Political will on the national level can also not be created by international organisations, which are ultimately owned by national governments. These organizations have carried the ball as far as they could. The demand for social justice has to be articulated by the people themselves. The most likely representatives of people are civil society organizations, such as NGOs and independent trade unions. Civil society and trade unions are the natural agents of political will. They can build strong cases for more social justice through social protection. The global consensus on the Social Protection Floor provides moral guidance and legitimacy, as well as a political shield for national demands ... There is nothing that should stop national pressure groups from reminding national governments of that consensus whenever necessary and demanding the establishment or safeguarding of social protection floors at the national level.

The proposal for a Global Fund for Social Protection

One thing missing from the last stages of the campaigning process, and completely missing from the final ILO social security strategy document reviewed above (ILO, 2012g), has been the case for a Global Fund for Social Protection in poorer countries. This is the more remarkable given Michael Cichon's earlier commitment to developing the 'Global Social Trust' concept (Chapter Two). The emphasis on global funding withered during the course of the passage of the Recommendation through the ILO process. The fashion in development circles seemed to be to stress the importance of countries raising their own revenues for such provision to create sustainable social contracts. The continued wish of poorer countries to escape aid dependency added to the case for letting the issue drop. Then suddenly un-trailed by any of the main players in the ILO and INGO story came on 9 October 2012 the publication by Olivier de Schutter, UN special rapporteur on the right to food, and Magdelena Sepulveda, UN special rapporteur on extreme poverty (Schutte and Sepulveda, 2013) of the UN Human Rights Council's Briefing Note: *Underwriting the Poor: A Global Fund for Social Protection*. The note suggested (Schutte and Sepulveda, 2013: 3):

> the creation of a Global Fund for Social Protection (GFSP), to provide States the financial support needed to make social protection viable. The GFSP would provide two services: (1) it would respond to 'structural,' or endemic, poverty by providing support for States to meet basic social protection floors; and (2) it would serve as a reinsurance provider offering protection to the State against unexpected shocks to their social insurance systems.

The Briefing Note addresses the importance of impoverished states making every effort to meet their obligations to fulfil the UN Conventions on the Right to Food and to Social Security but then adds that more developed states too have an obligation to assist such states (Schutte and Sepulveda, 2013: 7):

> In regards to the right to social security, the Committee on Economic, Social and Cultural Rights has stated that '[d]epending on the availability of resources, States parties should facilitate the realization of the right to social security in other countries, for example through provision of economic and technical assistance. International assistance should be provided in a manner that is consistent with the Covenant and other human rights standards, and sustainable and culturally appropriate. Economically developed States parties have a special responsibility for and interest in assisting the developing countries in this regard.[66]

The Briefing Note argued that the first task of the Global Fund for Social Protection would be used to fill the gap between the cost of the SPF and the maximum available resources of states. Filling the gap would cost less than 2% of global GDP. In other words, it builds on the view that countries need to take responsibility for national taxation policy to secure the national social contracts involved in developing social protection systems by offering, in effect, matching funds to, say, double the national tax revenue raised for social protection purposes from a global fund.

While Magdelena Sepulveda, the UN special rapporteur on extreme poverty and human rights, one of the co-authors of this Briefing Paper, had worked together with the Social Security Department of the ILO on promoting the rights-based approach to social protection and ensured that the SPF Recommendation embodied a rights-based approach, the associated idea of a global fund had not been part of these collaborations.[67] It will be recalled (Chapter Three) that the global funding idea had been downplayed within the Social Security Department of the ILO given the view of the employers and some countries that the SPF should be paid for by states themselves. Indeed, in the very recent publication on social protection and human rights jointly authored by Sepulveda and Nyst (2012), there is no mention of the need for such a global fund. A second reason for the 'surprising' emergence (to the global social security community) of the call for a global fund was that the main 'father' of the idea had been the Briefing Note's co-author, the special rapporteur on the right to food. Parallel discussions have been ongoing within that community. Indeed, in October 2010, the World Committee on Food Security had requested the High Level Panel of Experts on Food Security and Nutrition to undertake studies on climate change and food security, and social protection for food security. So it was that on 22 June 2012, exactly when the ILO was agreeing to its Recommendation on the SPFs, the High Level Panel on Food Security and Nutrition produced its report entitled *Social Protection for Food Security* (FAO, 2012). Chaired by Steve Devereux of the Institute of Development Studies in Sussex, its first recommendation (FAO, 2012: 6) was that:

> Every country should strive to design and put in place a comprehensive and nationally owned social protection system that contributes to ensuring the realisation of the right to adequate food for all.... One possible model for the social protection portfolio is the 'Food Security Floor' as proposed for consideration in this report, which would

> identify a minimum set of appropriate social protection and
> other interventions that would realise the right to food in
> each country.

Devereux, in his presentation to the Committee on World Food
Security at the annual session held in Rome in October 2012[68] strongly
supported the idea of an international mechanism in support of the
SPF (as proposed by the Global Fund for Social Protection, which he
welcomed); so did the representative of the ILO.

This proposal for a Global Fund for Social Protection came too
late for inclusion on the SPIAC-B 29 October Hyderabad agenda.
However, Olivier De Schutter, the special rapporteur on the right to
food, did have a meeting at the ILO representation to the UN in New
York and it has been provisionally agreed that the issue of the Global
Fund for Social Protection shall be discussed within the inter-agency
framework. He has also commented that:

> [I]n preliminary discussions with various governmental
> delegates, the consensus seems to be that the initiative will
> indeed have most chances of succeeding if it is conceived as
> a way to support low-income countries in the establishment
> of social protection floors by matching funds (the support
> of the international community being proportional to the
> efforts made at national level), and by making access to the
> fund and to its reinsurance facility in particular conditional
> upon the beneficiary country taking certain measures to
> reduce the risks to which it is exposed, for instance by
> diversifying its sources of export revenues or adopting
> measures to support climate-resilient agriculture.[69]

A paper was tabled by them at the SPIAC-B third meeting in January
2013 (Sepulveda and de Schutter, 2013) but no substantive discussion
took place about how to advance the concept of the Global Fund
for Social Protection. Now that the SPF Recommendation is agreed,
perhaps the proposal for a Global Fund for Social Protection might find
support if there is the combined interest of the world food community
and the world social security community. Matching national funds
seems to be the way to go. The need to address the social protection
coverage of unwelcome migrants – those residents not recognised as
such by countries and who are therefore likely to be excluded from
national SPF coverage – is still missing from explicit focus in the Global
Fund for Social Protection proposal. Because of national resistance

to funding migrant social protection out of the public purse I have developed the argument that SPF coverage of such people should become an *entirely* regional or global responsibility financed by, say, regional sovereign funds from natural resource taxes, which would overcome national objections to financing such migrants (Deacon and Nita, 2011).

Finally, given that the Global Fund for Social Protection would only come into play if governments raised their own revenues, there is still the need for countries to be allowed the fiscal space to raise revenues for the SPFs. Of the several international organisation and INGO contributors to the campaign for the SPF, UNICEF has been the most vociferous in stressing this point to the IMF. A UNICEF paper by Ortiz et al (2011a) entitled *Identifying Fiscal Space: Options for Social and Economic Development for Children and Poor Households in 182 Countries* shows that there are alternatives to retrenchment of social expenditure, even in the poorest countries. The paper offers an array of options:

- re-allocating public expenditures;
- increasing tax revenues;
- lobbying for increased aid and transfers;
- tapping into fiscal and foreign exchange reserves;
- borrowing and restructuring existing debt; and/or
- adopting a more accommodative macroeconomic framework.

Michael Cichon, now as President of the ICSW, relieved of worrying about the impact of talking about global funding for fear of upsetting some countries can now line the ICSW up with the argument for such a fund. He argues (Cichon, 2013: 6)

> 'We can support the demand for a Global Fund for Social Protection that the UN rapporteurs for the right to food and human rights have jointly issued and help to ensure that the Fund concentrates on sponsoring national action to implement the SPF. We can support the International Financial Transaction Tax and demand that it help to feed the Fund and support the few countries that really cannot build floor levels of social protection by their own means. The most powerful tool in policy implementation is simply taking the first steps, without waiting for any form of global blessing. National pressure groups can be built, and national monitoring can begin now. The Global Fund could be

started by asking the members of the Global Civil Society Coalition on the SPF to contribute to a Fund that would allow us to support national policy making.'

He lends support to this point by referring to the NGO OGBL Solidarité Syndicale in Luxembourg which supports the testing of a new maternity and child support cash benefit in Ghana by contributions from the Luxembourg Trade Unions[70]. Here is going full circle and recalling the work he lead within the ILO in the early 2000s in trying to set up a global solidarity fund for social security using the Luxembourg-Ghana link as an experiment. (See Chapter Two).

The implications for global social governance

What does the account in this book imply for the suggestions I made in 2007 concerning the possible step-by-step reform and improvement in the functioning of the global social governance system? In *Global Social Policy and Governance* (Deacon, 2007: 143-4) I concluded that:

> At the global level there are a number of competing and overlapping institutions, all of which have some stake in shaping global social policy towards global social problems. This struggle for the right to shape policy and for the content of that policy is what passes for an effective system of international social governance.

Then I analysed the fragmentation and competition into different groupings of contestations. First, and most damagingly, the World Bank, and to a lesser extent the IMF and WTO, were in competition for influence with the rest of the UN system. The World Bank's health, social protection and education policies for countries were not always the same as that of the WHO, ILO or UNESCO respectively. Then again, the UN social agencies (WHO, ILO, UNICEF, UNESCO) did not always espouse the same policy as the UNDP or UNDESA. Moreover, the secretary-general's initiatives, such as the Global Compact or the Millennium Project, bypassed and sidelined the social development policies of UNDESA. The UNCEB did notionally bring together the chief executives of all the UN agencies and attempted to ensure policy coherence within the UN system, but in terms of global social policy this was frustrated by the fact that (a) the World Bank, IMF and WTO were present and (b) the five main social agencies were gathered in the company of a total of 26 agencies with very different briefs. Quite apart from conflict between the UN and World Bank and within the UN system, there was also the G8, G20, G77 and other groupings of countries. While the rich G8 continued to assume the right to make global policy, the newer G20 were struggling to forge a broader global consensus. Following this description I suggested (Deacon, 2007: 149-66) that certain reforms and developments were likely. I suggested that progress might be made over the coming years along seven dimensions. These were:

a) a strengthening of the UN's role in economic and social policy with moves to a One-UN, to agreed global social policy principles and a more influential ECOSOC;
b) greater inter-organisational cooperation, policy dialogue and synergy in the spirit of the report of the World Commission on the Social Dimension of Globalization
c) some changes in the architecture of aid to create a policy space for the Global South;
d) more global public–private partnerships, task forces, networks and ad-hoc initiatives;
e) reforms of the governance of the World Bank and WTO;
f) better management of global labour migration;
g) moves to constructive regionalism with a social policy dimension.

The story in this book certainly has relevance to propositions (a) and (b) and to a lesser extent (c) and (d).

In terms of the strengthening of the UN's role in economic and social policy, the moves to a One-UN, the furtherance of global social policy principles and a more influential ECOSOC, there are a number of points to be made. First, the combination of the ILO's SPF Recommendation and the UNCEB's SPF-I with its wider definition of an SPF is, in effect, a reversal of the earlier refusal of the UN system to agree to a common set of social policy principles. There may be disputes over the adequacy of the definitions and there is still the deference to national decision making but the world has taken a further step towards identifying some common social protection guarantees that states should provide. It could also be argued that the decision taken in April 2009 by the UNCEB to establish the SPF-I as one of eight responses the UN should have to the global economic crisis has strengthened the UN in global economic and social policy. However, there are a few caveats to be made. One is that although the UNCEB did take that decision it has not itself followed up on it and did not follow up on the other seven actions agreed. Indeed, the SPF-I has been advanced despite the UNCEB and not by it.

The subsequent development of the SPIAC-B involving other UN agencies is another step towards a UN speaking with one voice and one policy but this has been driven largely by the ILO and is not reflective of a broader UN push to strengthen itself. There have been no further moves by the UN secretary-general to build upon the earlier steps taken by Kofi Annan to institute the UN annual ministerial meetings or the Biannual Development Forum. Another caveat to be expressed is that the decision of the UNCEB to act in the field of global economic and social policy was overshadowed by the fact that (a) it was prompted to do so in part because the April 2009 G20 meeting had empowered an unreformed IMF to address the consequences of the economic crisis and (b) the subsequent UN conference called to address the global crisis in October 2009 proved to be a damp squib (Deacon, 2011a).

What my 2007 projections had not foreseen was that an alternative to the strengthening of ECOSOC was to be the strengthening of the role of the G20 as a new centre of global economic and social policy making. Catapulted to the centre of events by the 2008 crisis the G20 acted in 2009 and then went on in Seoul in 2010, Cannes in 2011 and Mexico in 2012 to rapidly develop a large portfolio of economic and social policies and commitments that demand a radical rethinking of how we characterise the global social governance system. The nine pillars of its development agenda agreed in Seoul became the vehicle that the ILO used to push the G20 to call for greater international coordination. Has the UN come out weaker or stronger from the actions of the G20? Pascal Lamy noted already in 2009 that he saw

> a new triangle of global governance emerging that we need
> to strengthen. On one side of the triangle lies the G20,
> providing political leadership and policy direction. On
> another side lie member-driven international organisations
> providing expertise and specialised inputs whether rules,
> policies or programmes. The third side of the triangle is
> the G-192, the United Nations, providing a forum for
> accountability.[71]

From the account given in this book it seems that while the aspiration to G20 accountability through the UN has yet to be realised, the UN social agencies have been strengthened by the decisions of the G20. We noted the workings of the G20 development group, which in its short life had required the ILO, the UNDP, the IMF the World Bank and other social agencies to report on a whole raft of issues. Regarding the ILO in particular it was called upon to be involved in a report to finance ministers on job creation (with the IMF, OECD and World Bank), a report to employment ministers on the Task Force on Youth Unemployment and several related issues connecting employment, social protection and growth (with the OECD and IMF), a report for the development working group on skills development (with the OECD, World Bank and UNESCO) and a report for the development working group on private investment and job creation (with the UNCTAD, UNDP, World Bank and OECD). This is both remarkable and unprecedented. It remains to be seen whether the agencies can continue to work together and deliver and whether the G20 continues to follow up this agenda.

This development has its critics. Herman (2011: 2) has argued that the G20 is the wrong international forum for development:

> In all, the G20 development initiative seems to have usurped discussions that could have been held in more inclusive intergovernmental forums. They have also swept decision-making into a private club that meets behind closed doors, following the practice of the earlier Group of 8. In response, a group of non-G20 governments formed, seeking to bring the voices of smaller countries into this new decision-making process, as well as set limits to its arrogation of global authority. This Global Governance Group, comprising 28 developed and developing country governments, thus requested in a letter circulated at the United Nations that any further work undertaken by the international institutions at the request of the G20 be first approved by the governing bodies of those institutions and that the G20 cover the un-programmed cost of the additional analytical and subsequent applied work to be performed (Global Governance Group, 2011).

This brings us neatly to the related 2007 prognosis that there would be greater inter-organisational cooperation, policy dialogue and synergy in the spirit of the report of the World Commission on the Social Dimension of Globalization (ILO, 2014b). While I think my earlier characterisation of the system of global social governance as being one within which international organisations *competed* with each other for the right to shape global social policy and for the content of that policy still has value, within the past few years in the context of multiple attempts to rethink global economic policy in the wake of the crisis there has arisen a call for more effective *cooperation* between such agencies. Indeed, global policy synergy is now at the top of the agenda. As we have seen in this book there was the path-breaking Cannes G20 summit where the call was made in paragraph 31, for '*international organizations, especially the UN, WTO, the ILO, the WB [World Bank], the IMF and the OECD, to enhance their dialogue and cooperation, including on the social impact of economic policies, and to intensify their coordination* (G20, 2011b). This drive we showed was very much led by Somavia at the helm of the ILO. In my view this does not imply a reversion to a neat division of labour where the WHO does health, UNESCO does education and the IMF does fiscal policy for example. It rather calls for more intense discussion between the authorised social agencies on the one hand and those primarily concerned with the trade and the economy on the other so that in future global and national economic and trade policies are developed so that economic activity returns to its rightful place as the servant of sustainable social goals. The need is to re-inject the concerns of the real economy (jobs) and to re-inject social concerns (social protection) into the consideration of economic policy. It implies that the global social floor becomes an objective of economic policy.

This implies a reversion of what I had earlier suggested in 2007 was a mission creep of the World Bank and IMF into the territory of the social. *Now what is required is a reverse mission creep of the social agencies into the territory of the economic.* Conventional pure economic analysis and forecasting and modelling have been found wanting. Debates about alternatives are now the order of the day. UNICEF, for example, has a long and honourable tradition in this regard. The work of Richard Jolly and his colleagues published as *Adjustment with a Human Face* (Cornia et al, 1987) did a huge service in the 1980s and 1990s in drawing attention to some of the negative social consequences of the economic orthodoxy of the time. The excellent initiative, with which UNICEF colleagues had been centrally involved, of launching the email dialogue on *Recovery with a Human Face* (UNICEF, 2010a) followed in that same tradition. Recent UNICEF papers pointing to the negative social impacts of current post-crisis IMF interventions in countries are very valuable. The ILO's work with the IMF to show and ensure that there is fiscal space for the funding by countries of national SPFs is what is required. My point is that there is now a need for the social agencies to engage directly with the economic to refashion overall economic and social policy that works in tandem. The job of economics cannot be left to the economists. The social agencies have to gear themselves up to be able to address the economic.

A different aspect of the way in which global social governance has been developing was addressed in my 2007 book. It noted that we might be witnessing a shift in the *locus* and *content* of policy debate and activity away from those more formally located within the official UN and World Bank policy-making arenas to a set of practices around networks and projects, which, in some ways, bypass these institutions and debates; policy making has become projectised and task-centred and based on networks and alliances. This development was drawn attention to by one the referees for this book, who reasserted that:

> The world of global policy making involves the enormous expansion or multiplication of policy statements, position papers and so on, in the context of a decline in the number of permanent international civil servants with a loyalty to one organisation and its causes. We live in a world of out-sourcing, of flexible identities, of revolving doors, and of networked epistemic communities. The book needs to reflect that perhaps better than it appears to do so far; the author needs to explicitly address whether a new post-modern policy world is emerging in which there is a hyperactivity of proposals, partnerships, and innovative ideas which, actually, lead to almost no change on the ground.

There are two aspects to this: whether this case study of the emergence of the SPF policy reflects such hyperactivity by networked but disconnected members of an epistemic community and whether its outcome – the SPF policy – leads to no real change within countries. It is clear that informal alliances between unaccountable free-floating professionals wedded to some notion of a global social floor provided a backdrop to this policy story. In that sense the story lends support to the view of Mosse (2011: ix) that 'global policy is shaped by interests, strategies, professional rivalries or insecurities within relatively small communities of which for a time we may also have been members'. However, the work of this alliance in this case (the Campaign for a Global Social Floor) *did* become focused on changing *formal policy* of one or more UN agency and certainly in the case of the ILO the policy had to be argued through something approaching a global democratic process. It is the bringing together of that floating network or 'small community' into partnership with the formal policy-making processes of the ILO and the UN that is the distinguishing feature of this development. That said, loyalty to one or other UN agency as *the* agency within which to work to secure the subsequent goal of laying down SPFs has not been the hallmark of the story. It just so happened that the ILO standard-setting process at a certain conjuncture provided the opportunity to shift global social policy thinking.

In 2007, reflecting then, in effect, on the concerns of my referee, I suggested that:

> A key question is how intervention in these tasks and projects and networks might be anything other than opportunistic or self interested or pragmatic ... principles that guide these actors become important.... There is a case, therefore, for not only the networks and partnerships focused on short-term projects and tasks but also for longer-term *global political alliances* that might fashion sets of principles and steer members of the task forces. (Deacon, 2007: 158)

I believe that a significant legacy of the story told in this book is *the establishment of a global set of social policy principles, which will endure and can guide the disparate actors of today and tomorrow.* The SPFs Recommendation represent such a set of principles.

However, set against that it has to be noted that as this book with its focus on the ILO closes, the focus and locus of the activity of this networked Global Advocacy Coalition moves on to the new SPIAC-B, which might or might not become important and to the INGO coalition lead by the ICSW. The leading actors in this play *have* moved on: the director-general of the ILO has retired, the head of social security moves on to become president of the ICSW, the driving force for the floor within UNICEF resigns. No permanent replacement has yet been made to replace Michael Cichon at the ILO. If my analysis, which has focused attention on these and other key biographies, is even partly accurate then we should indeed expect less 'hyperactivity of proposals, partnerships, and innovative ideas' around global social protection policy in the next years. The global circus may alas move on to 'global policies for sustainability'. In the short term, precisely because biography is important, there is the leadership (and website) confusion described earlier in this chapter.

As to the second half of my referee's concern, let us wait and see if the sound and fury on the global stage about SPFs impacts in time on the ground, as Cichon would now wish in his new role, so that such floors are solidly built within countries funded in part from global revenues. There is some reason to hope, precisely because this process concluded in more than a 'hyperactivity of proposals, partnerships, and innovative ideas'. It concluded in a major piece of new international soft law with, quoting the new ILO director-general, 'bite'.

Endnotes

[1] In many cases I have substantiated my text by reference to the specific person who informed me about the topic being discussed. Of course, the substantiation is open to the charge that I have relied on a partisan opinion. I have tried to avoid this by checking with other informants or the published record. In other cases it is precisely the partisan nature of the observation that is of interest. In some cases where I have simply referred to an unnamed informant this is in deference to the fact that the informant would not want to be associated in public with the opinion expressed.

[2] This account is an edited version of the one first published in Deacon (2007: 138-40).

[3] Information for all Latin American countries can be found at www.ipc-undp. org/PageNewSiteb.do?id=123&active=3

[4] Interview, September 2011.

[5] The account here of Guy Standing's involvement in the debate about how to 'extend social security' starts around 2000. A case can be made that in an earlier phase of ILO policy making in Geneva he had already been very active in trying to lay the foundation for an alternative universal income security approach for social protection. For the Kreisky Commission on European Employment he wrote an ILO Working Paper (Standing, 1988) effectively advocating basic income and a social floor. He also had several articles in the *International Labour Review* pushing for universalism. At that time the-then Social Security Department was opposed to a universal, unconditional approach, and Colin Gillion, its head, was actually favouring targeting through means testing (Deacon, 2007: 65). During the period as head of the East European Team in Budapest (1992-94), Michael Cichon worked in his team. Standing wrote and spoke on the need for a universal basic security approach in the 'transition countries' and disagreed both with Robert Holzman in the World Bank and with Collin Gillion and Michael Cichon, then in favour of a Bismarkian approach to social security in the ILO (Deacon, 1997: 99-100). Standing was brought back to Geneva to be director of labour market policies and, in the period 1994-96, conflict between his views and those of the Social Security Department continued. He was not employed in the ILO from 1997 until 1999. Although still persona non grata inside the ILO, Somavia, the incoming director-general, asked him to be on his 'transition team' and for six months he worked with the others in the team on a planned restructuring of the ILO. His main role was to coordinate the restructuring of the social protection sphere and argued that the ILO should revise all its social security

conventions and recommendations, beginning with what he regarded as the sexist and labourist Convention 102 of 1952, a policy to which those in the existing Social Security Department were opposed.

[6] Interview, February 2012.

[7] www.basicincome.org/bien/

[8] Interview with Wouter van Ginneken, October 2011.

[9] www.ilo.org/public/english/protection/secsoc/areas/policy/gst.htm

[0] V. Pinheiro, email communication, 18 October 18 2011.

[11] Interview with Wouter van Ginneken, October 2011.

[2] Interview October 2011.

[3] I am instancing here the fact that even Bill Gates was about to report to the G20 in Cannes on the possibilities of such a tax and that the President of the European Commission had advanced the idea in a policy paper concerning Commission funding.

[4] Interview with the deputy director of ACTRAV, January 2012.

[5] Interview with Egorov, December 2011.

[6] Interview with Egorov, December 2001.

[7] Indeed, the workers' social security contact person offered me the view that she steered the conference to its positive conclusion (interview, 13 September 2011).

[8] A member of ACTRAV commented that the ILO's Global Extension of Social Security (GESS) website has all these links with agencies such as Save the Children with whom the ILO had major disputes regarding child labour, for example.

[9] Personal communication.

[20] Much of the information in this and the next paragraphs is drawn from verbal presentations given at two seminars convened at the ILO in November 2011. The first was by John Kirton, co-director of the G20 research group when delivering the paper cited as Kirton (2011) and the second was a joint presentation by Stephen Pursey, ILO Policy Integration Branch and Vinicius Pinheiro, of the director-general's Cabinet, when speaking to the presentation cited as ILO (2011i).

[21] Interview with Christian Jacquier, September 2011.

[22] www.g20.utoronto.ca/2010/g20seoul-development.pdf

[23] www.brettonwoodsproject.org/print.shtml?cmd(884)=x-884-569017

[24] www.g20.utoronto.ca/2011/2011-cannes-dwg-111028-en.pdf

[25] It was significant that this ILO in-house meeting was not attended by anybody (except the health specialist) from Cichon's Department so focused were they on the upcoming ILC. Indeed, some of the activities resulting from the G20 process that Pinheiro had been so instrumental in setting in train, such as the G20 call for more coordination between agencies, came as a surprise to Cichon and his colleagues.

[26] www.siteresources.worldbank.org/SOCIALPROTECTION/

Resources/280558-1274453001167/7089867-1279223745454/7253917 -1291314603217/SP-L_Strategy_Concept_Note_web.pdf

[27] This quotation, taking from the penultimate draft circulated on 16 March, is exactly the same as in the final version published in April.

[28] Email communication, 27 March 2012.

[29] The European Commission, in typical sub-contracting mode, put out for tender the task of advising it on how it should incorporate social protection into its development work. IBF International Consulting won the contract. (The ILO, of course best placed to advise, does not bid for this type of work.) The European Commission's (2011) Consultation Paper D.3/NT/AMD (2011) 1458287 invited responses between December 2011 and February 2012. These were compiled by IBF and reported by Commander et al (2012). They concluded (2012 :12) that while '[t]he UN Social Protection Floor concept ... attracted quite wide support and was seen as a useful mobilizing framework for social protection policy ... [there were] concerns over the ability of governments to fund such schemes'. However, the final version (European Commission, 2012, section 8) regarded the SPF 'as a well defined basis on which to build coordinated and where possible, joint support for social protection with partner countries who decide to adopt them'.

[30] Email communication, 27 March 2012.

[31] www.imf.org

[32] www.guardian.co.uk/world/2011/sep/25/austerity-measures-irreversible-impact-unicef , www.brettonwoodsproject.org/art-567212 , www.twnside.org.sg/title2/resurgence/2010/237/cover07.htm , http://globalhealthequity.blogspot.com/2011/10/unicef-austerity-measures-threaten.html , www.socialwatch.org/node/12288 , www.un.org/en/development/desa/policy/wesp/wesp_archive/2011wesp.pdf

[33] This issue of the mandate of the ILO and UNICEF encroaching on that of the IMF was an issue of contestation.

[34] This referenced a note by Griert Cattaert, ILO New York: *An interagency Social Protection Floor website,* April 2011 relating to the UNSPF-I site that UNICEF staff were working on about to launch.

[35] Minutes of the follow-up meeting to the G20, 2 December 2011, ILO Washington Office, attended by the ILO, World Bank, UNDP, UNICEF, UNDESA and PAHO (in lieu of WHO).

[36] In the event it had not been convened by the time the writing of this book was finished (February 2013).

[37] www.socialprotectionfloor-gateway.org

[38] Email to SPF-I members, 23 April 2012.

[39] www.ilo.org/gimi/gess/ShowLibrary.do?sid=3

[40] www.socialprotection.org

[41] The revised name and acronym were agreed at the first meeting of the SPIB on 2 July 2 2012.

[42] http://web.worldbank.org/WBSITE/EXTERNAL/TOPICS/EXTSOC IALPROTECTION/0,,menuPK:282642~pagePK:149018~piPK:149093~t heSitePK:282637,00.html

[43] The following paragraphs are based on an article written myself and Paul Stubbs (Deacon and Stubbs, 2013). I am very grateful for the long collaboration with Paul that has enabled me to get a better grip on explaining rather than just advocating global social policy change.

[44] Interview June 2012

[45] The use of the term 'work' rather than 'labour', Standing claims, was his one success in the ILO.

[46] Cichon's counterpart within the Standards and Norms Department, Alexander Egorov, who was the person responsible within that department for overseeing the ways in which the ILO obtained reports from countries about their social security policies and their implementation of ILO conventions and responses to ILO recommendations should perhaps be added to this list of actors. By 2010 he had been working in that field within the ILO for 15 years and had his own conception as to how ILO recommendations and conventions might be improved. These conceptions were to become clear in the report of the Committee of Experts on the Application of Conventions and Standards (ILO, 2011l), Part III of which in 2011 focused on a General Survey of Social

Security Instruments, which was reported on in Chapter Four. That report, penned largely by Egorov, expounded the case for a human rights-based social floor, building also on the 'forgotten' 1944 recommendations in the following terms (ILO, 2011l: 21-2):

> The persistent realities of poverty and informality call for drafting a new blueprint for the development of social security in the twenty-first century, equipping it with more effective means to alleviate poverty. The idea of underpinning the world economy by a global social security floor has the potential of once again changing the social security paradigm, the ways and means with which social security is going to be provided in the coming future, moving away from the risk-based towards more integrated forms of social protection.

[47] This in turn explains the rather odd final formulation in the Recommendation that 'guarantees should ensure at a minimum that, over the life cycle, all in need have access to essential health care and *to basic income security which together secure effective access to goods and services* defined as necessary at the national level (ILO, 2012d para 4, emphasis added).

[48] It is this formulation and the emphasis on the role of individuals that has caused much tension and disagreement between myself and the ILO regarding an acceptable final version of this text. The final official report produced by the ILO (ILO, 2012g) to publicise the SPF Recommendation devotes several pages to listing all the members of the social protection committees that sat in 2011 and 2012. It does this in celebration of the fact that the SPF Recommendation was the outcome of this tripartite process. If the account in this book is only partly accurate, this was not the case. The tripartite process *endorsed and refined* the ideas of key individuals within the fourth arm of the ILO – the secretariat – none of whom are listed or acknowledged personally in the final report. In that report there is some recognition that other actors have been important but the fiction of the central role of the committee members is retained. Thus, it says:

> This document is the result of the work and commitment of hundreds of people who contributed to the formulation of the strategy in governments, in workers' and employers' organizations, in academia, in civil society and in international organizations, including the International Labour Office. It is impossible to name them all. Those who served as members of the social security committees of the 100th and 101st Sessions of the International Labour Conference are listed at the end of this document. It is they who held the final discussions and adopted the strategy and the Recommendation as representatives of all those who contributed to its development. We thank them all.

A final note; in terms of the emphasis I have given to key named players I too do not want to take anything away from the dedicated contribution of the other members of the several teams within the ILO secretariat who worked on this Recommendation in the Social Security, Standards and Legal Departments as well as in the ILO directorate. In that sense it was a team effort.

[49] International conference 'Friendship in International Relations, 24 February 2012, Weatherhead Center for International Relations, Harvard University, Cambridge, MA, USA.

[50] It is significant that the retirement email sent to colleagues within and outside the ILO by Cichon was sent to 150 or more members of the global social protection epistemic community in many agencies and countries.

[51] Seeking a positive gloss, one ACTRAV member suggested that positing defined outcomes was a way of challenging, for example, defined contribution pension policies.

[52] www.globalsocialjustice.eu

[53] Interview with Alexandre Egorov, 6 February 2012.

[54] Whereas historically the Committee of Experts focused on the same topic as the Committee on Standards in the same year, from now on the Committee of Experts will report one year earlier to facilitate better-informed discussion by the ILC's Committee on Standards.

[55] Egorov interview, December 2012. In 'his' experts report for the 2011 conference (ILO, 2011l) on page 12 is a drawing of a Greek temple; the base is represented by R67 and R69, the Recommendations from 1944; the next step up to the temple is Convention 102, the hallowed Social Security Convention, the pillars of the façade are numbered (as if in a museum) C121, C128, C130 and C168, representing the vertical improvements in social security entitlements. The roof of the temple is unfinished.

[56] In parallel to setting up the HLP, the UN secretary-general took the step of establishing the Sustainable Development Solutions Network (SDSN) on 9 August 2012 (www.un.org/millenniumgoals/beyond2015.shtml), which 'will provide global, open and inclusive support to sustainable-development problem solving at local, national, and global scales. The SDSN will work together with United Nations agencies, other international organizations, and the multilateral funding institutions including the World Bank and regional development banks, to mobilize scientific and technical expertise to scale up the magnitude and quality of local, national and global problem solving, helping to identify solutions and highlighting best practices in the design of long-term development pathways'. Professor Jeffrey D. Sachs, special advisor

to UN secretary-general on the MDGs, will direct the project with the core aim of creating an open, inclusive and world-class global network of expertise and problem solving. The network will comprise mainly universities and scientific research institutes, but will also tap technical expertise within technology companies, science foundations and academies of sciences and engineering. Columbia University's Earth Institute will serve as the secretariat for the network.

[57] This initial 'error' seems to have been remedied by May 2012 with the production of the joint ECA, ILO (2012) think piece within which SPFs are argued to be an element of post MDG agenda.

[58] Interview, February 2012.

[59] www.social-protection.org/gimi/gess/ShowTheme.do?tid=2527

[60] www.socialprotection.org/

[61] www.socialprotectionfloor-gateway.org/

[62] www.socialprotection.org

[63] www.ilo.org/pardev/lang--en/index.htm

[64] 'GESS' is linked to Michaels Cichon's long and sustained campaign inside the ILO Social Security Department. It became www.social-protection.org when the long established Extension of Social Security activity became the Global Extension of Social Security under his leadership. The socialprotectionfloor-gateway.org site reflected the wish of Isabel Ortiz to bring UNICEF into the fold. The probably short-lived G20 www.socialprotection.org site reflected the ambition of Vinicius Pinheiro, using the G20 route to secure a Social Protection Secretariat.

[65] www.social-protection.org/gimi/gess/RessShowRessource.do?ressource Id=35028

[66] Committee on Economic, Social and Cultural Rights (2008) *General Comment 19: The Right to Social Security*, para 55, UN Doc E/C.12/GC/19, 4 February.

[67] Magdalena Sepulveda, special rapporteur on extreme poverty and human rights, email communication, 17 October 2012.

[68] www.fao.org/fileadmin/user_upload/hlpe/hlpe_documents/CFS39/ HLPE_Social_Protection_Report-CFS39-Devereux-15-Oct-12.pdf

[69] Gaëtan Vanloqueren, senior advisor to the UN special rapporteur on the right to food, email communication, 17 October 2012.

[71] www.wto.org/english/news_e/sppl_e/sppl132_e.htm

References

Abu Sharkh, M. (2004) 'Fighting child labor: what works and why', paper presented at the conference 'Transnational Risks and Civil Society', Potsdam.

Baccaro, L. and Mele, V. (2012) 'Pathology of path-dependency? The ILO and the challenge of new governance', *Industrial and Labor Relations Review*, 65 (2): 195-224.

Barrientos, A. and Hulme, D. (2008) *Social Protection for the Poor and Poorest in Developing Countries: Reflections on a Quiet Revolution*, BWPI Working Paper 30, Manchester: Brookings World Poverty Institute.

Behrendt, C. and Hagemejer, K. (2009) 'Can low-income countries afford social security?, in Townsend, P. (2009) *Building Decent Societies: Rethinking the Role of Social Security in Development*, Basingstoke: Palgrave.

Béland, D. (2009) 'Ideas, institutions and policy change', *Journal of European Public Policy*, 16 (5): 701-18.

Béland, D. and Cox, R.H. (eds) (2011) *Ideas and Politics in Social Science Research*, New York, NY: Oxford University Press.

Béland, D. and Orenstein, M. (2013: forthcoming) 'International organizations as policy actors: an ideational approach', *Global Social Policy 13*.

Beyond 2015 (2012) *Beyond 2015 and GCAP comments on the set up and Terms of References of the High-Level Panel of Eminent Persons on the Post-2015 Development Agenda* . http://beyond2015.org/sites/default/files/Beyond%202015%20GCAP%20HLP%20ToRs%20analysis_0.pdf

Brown, G. (1999) 'Rediscovering public purpose in the global economy', *Social Development Review*, 3: 3-7.

Bhatt, E. (1994) 'Long Way to Go', in *ILO Visions of the Future of Social Justice: Essays on the Occasion of the ILO's 75th Anniversary*, pp. 41–5. Geneva: ILO.

Center for Economic Policy Research (2009) *IMF shouldn't get the woney without reform*, Washington, DC: Center for Economic Policy Research, www.cepr.net/index.php/op-eds-&-columns/op-eds-&-columns/imf-shouldnt-get-money-without-reform/

Cichon, M (2012) 'Power Point Presentation on SPF to ICSW Executive Committee'. Paris. 23-24th January.

Cichon, M (2013) 'It is our turn now: Civil society, the labour movement and the stewardship of the social protection floor', *ICSW Global Cooperation Newsletter* January 2013.

Cichon, M. and Hagemejer, K. (2007) 'Changing the development policy paradigm: investing in a social security floor for all', *International Social Security Review*, 60 (2-3): 169-96.

Cichon, M., Behrendt, C. and Wodsak, V. (2011:9) *The UN Social Protection Floor Initiative: Turning the Tide at the ILO Conference*, Germany: Freidrich Ebert Stiftung.

Clements, B., Gupta, S. and Nozaki, M. (2011) *What Happens to Social Spending in IMF-Supported Programs?*, IMF Staff Discussion Note SDN/11/15, Washington, DC: International Monetary Fund.

Coalition for a Global Social Floor (2007) founding document.

Commander, S., Davies, M. and Zaman, C. (2012) *Social Protection in EU Development Cooperation: Report of the Key Results of the Consultation with Stakeholders*, Brussels: IBF International.

Cornia, G., Jolly, R. and Stewart, F. (1987) *Adjustment with a Human Face*, Oxford: Clarendon Press.

Daly, M. (ed) (2002) *Care Work: The Quest for Security*, Geneva: International Labour Office.

Deacon, B. (2000) 'The future for social policy in a global context: why the south now needs to take the lead', *Futura*, 2000: 65-70.

Deacon, B. (2007) *Global Social Policy and Governance*, London: Sage Publications.

Deacon, B. (2010) Globale Soziale Strukturen, Institutionen, Akteure und Diskurse Ein Theorieansatz zur Globalen Sozialpolitikforschung" Zeitschrift fur Sozialreform, 56 (2)

Deacon, B. (2011a) 'Global social policy responses to the economic crisis', in K. Farnsworth and Z. Irving (eds) *Social Policy in Challenging Times*, Bristol: The Policy Press.

Deacon, B. (2011b) 'After the Cannes G20: UNICEF's Contribution to the Global Dialogue on the Social Impact of Economic Policies', Comment on UNICEF's Economic and Social Policy Programme, included in the *Pratolino IV Report : UNICEF Global Social and Economic Policy Consultation November 2011-February 2012*, www.unicef.org/socialpolicy/files/Pratolino_Report_IV_18July2012_eversion.pdf/

Deacon, B. and Cohen, S. (2011) 'From the global politics of poverty alleviation to the global politics of social solidarity', *Global Social Policy*, 11 (2-3): 233-49.

Deacon, B. and Stubbs, P. (2013) 'Global social policy studies: conceptual and analytical reflections', *Global Social Policy*, 13 (1): 5-23.

Deacon, B. and Nita, S. (2013) 'Regional social integration and free movement across borders: The role of social policy in enabling and preventing access to social entitlements by cross-border movers European Union and Southern Africa compared', *Regions and Cohesion*, 3 (1):

Deacon, B., Stubbs, P. and Hulse, M. (1997) *Global Social Policy: International Organisations and the Future of Welfare*, London: Sage Publications.

Dorfman, M. and Palacios, R. (2012) *World Bank Support for Pensions and Social Security*, background paper for the World Bank 2012-2022 Social Protection and Labor Strategy, Washington, DC: World Bank.

Dostal, J.M. (2004) 'Campaigning on expertise: how the OECD framed EU welfare and labour market policies – and why success could trigger failure', *Journal of European Social Policy,* 11: 440-60.

ECA, ILO, UNCTAD, UNDESA, UNICEF (2012), *Social protection: A development priority in the post-2015 UN development agenda. Thematic Think Piece*

Emmerji, L., Jolly R. and Weis, T.G. (2005) 'Economic and social thinking at the UN in historical perspective', *Development and Change*, 36: 211-35.

European Commission (2011) *Public Consultation: Social Protection in EU Development Cooperation: Issues Paper*, Brussels: European Commission.

European Commission (2012) *Social Protection in EU Development Cooperation*, COM (2012) 446, Brussels: European Commission.

FAO (Food and Agriculture Organization) (2012) *High Level Panel of Experts, Social Protection for Food Security*, a report by the High Level Panel of Experts on Food Security and Nutrition of the Committee on World Food Security (CFS), Rome: FAO, www.fao.org/cfs/cfs-hlpe

Farnsworth, K (2010), *Social versus Corporate Welfare*, London: Palgrave

Ferguson, C. (1999) *Global Social Policy Principles: Human Rights and Social Justice*, London: Department for International Development.

Foli, Rosina and Béland, Daniel. (2012). *International Organizations and Ideas about Poverty in Sub-Saharan Africa*. Saskatoon: Johnson-Shoyama Graduate School of Public Policy (unpublished paper).

Fukuda-Park, S. (2010) 'Reducing inequalities – the missing MDG: a content review of PRSPs and bilateral donor policy statements', *IDS Bulletin*, 41 (1): 26-35.

G8 (2007) *Dresden Meeting of the G8 Ministers of Labour: Chair's Summary.*

G8 (2008) *Japan G8 Labour Minister's Final Communiqué.*

G20 (2010a) *G20 Multi-Year Development Action Plan: Mapping of Responsibilities of Countries and International Organisations.*

G20 (2010b) *Seoul Summit Communiqué Annex II: Multi Year Action Plan on Development.*

G20 (2011a) *G20 Meeting of Labour and Employment Ministers in Paris 26-27 September 2011: Communiqué.*

G20 (2011b) *G20 Heads of State Meeting in Cannes, 3-4 November 2011: Final Communiqué.*

G20 (2011c) *2011 Report of the Development Working Group to Cannes Summit,*

G20 (2011d) *French Priorities for G20.* www.g20.utoronto.ca/summits/2011cannes.html

G20 (2012a) *Conclusions of the G20 Labour and Employment Ministers,* Guadalajara, Mexico, 17-18 May.

G20 (2012b) G20 Development Working Group (DWG): Growth with Resilience Pillar, *Interagency Coordination on Social Protection,* note submitted to the 2nd meeting of the G20 DWG, 19-20 March.

G20 (2012c) G20 Development Working Group (DWG): Growth with Resilience Pillar, *Proposal for a G20 Knowledge Sharing Platform on Social Protection,* draft, 15 March.

G20 (2012d) G20 Development Working Group (DWG): *Progress Report of the Development Working Group* (to Mexico Summit).

G20 (2012e) *G20 Heads of State Meeting in Mexico, 19 June, Final Communiqué.*

Gates, B. (2011) *Innovation With Impact: Financing 21st Century Development,* a report by Bill Gates to G20 leaders, Cannes Summit, November.

Global Governance Group (2011) Letter dated 27 May 2011 from the Permanent Representative of Switzerland to the United Nations addressed to the Secretary-General, United Nations General Assembly, Document A/65/857.

Gore, C. (2010) 'The MDG paradigm, productive capacities and the future of poverty reduction', *IDS Bulletin,* 41 (1): 71-9.

Graham, C. (1949) *Safety Nets, Politics and the Poor,* Washington, DC: Brookings Institute.

Hagemejer, K., Cichon, M. and Behrendt, G. (2011) ILO comments on the World Bank's strategy concept note 'Building Resilience and Opportunity: The World Bank's Social Protection and Labour Strategy 2012-2020', 21 March.

Hall, A. and Midgley, J. (2004) *Social Policy for Development,* London: Sage Publications.

Hardt, M. and Negri, A. (2005) *Multitude: War and Democracy in the Age of Empire,* London: Hamish Hamilton.

Held, D. (2004) *Global Covenant: The Social Democratic Alternative to the Washington Consensus*, Cambridge: Polity Press.

Herman, B. (2011) *G20: Wrong International Forum for Development*, www.socdevjustice.org/mediapool/96/965703/data/G20_on_development_pre-summit_2011.pdf

Hirsch, M. (2011) *Secu Objectif Monde Le Defi Universel de la Protection Social*, Paris: Parti Stock, www.editions-stock.fr

Holzmann, R., Robalino, D.A. and Takayama, N. (eds) (2009) *Closing the Coverage Gap: The Role of Social Pensions and other Retirement Income Transfers*, Washington, DC: World Bank.

ILO (International Labour Office) (1995) *'Report of the Director General: Fifth European Regional Conference'*. Geneva: IL.

ILO (2000a) *Income Security and Social Protection in a Changing World*, Geneva: ILO.

ILO (2000b) *Social Security: Issues, Challenges and Prospects*, report VI to the 89th International Labour Conference, Geneva: ILO.

ILO (2001) *Social Security: A New Consensus*, Geneva: ILO.

ILO (2002a) *Global Social Trust*, Geneva: ILO, www.ilo.org/public/english/protection/secsoc/downloads/policy/feasibility.pdf

ILO (2002b) *Provisional Record of the 90th Session of the ILC*, Geneva: ILO

ILO (2004a) *Economic Security for a Better World*, Geneva: ILO.

ILO (2004b) *A Fair Globalization: Creating Opportunities for All*, Report of the World Commission on the Social Dimension of Globalization, Geneva: ILO.

ILO (205a) *Independent Evaluation of the In Focus Programme on Socio-Economic Security (IFPSES)*, Geneva: ILO.

ILO (2006) *Social Security for All: Investing in Global Social and Economic Development: A Consultation*, Issues in Social Protection Discussion Paper No. 16, Geneva: ILO.

ILO (2008) *Social Security Policy Briefings: Paper 3: Can Low-Income Countries Afford Basic Social Security?*, Geneva: ILO.

ILO (2009) *Manual and Strategic Framework for Joint UN Country Operations*, Geneva: ILO/World Health Organizations.

ILO (2010a) *Extending Social Security to All*, Geneva: ILO.

ILO (2010b) 2nd Interagency Meeting on the SPFI, workshop report, November.

ILO (2011a) *Social Security for Social Justice and a Fair Globalization*, ILO Conference Report IV, Geneva: ILO.

ILO (2011b) 'Conclusions regarding the recurrent discussion on social protection (social security), in International Labour Conference, *Provisional Record, Sixth Item: A Recurrent Discussion on the Strategic Objective of Social Protection … Report of the Committee for the Recurrent Discussion on Social Protection*, Geneva: ILO.

ILO (2011c) *Social Protection Floors for Social Justice and a Fair Globalization (IV (I))*, report to the 101st Conference (including a questionnaire on the social protection floor), Geneva: ILO.

ILO (2011d) *Social Protection Floor for a Fair and Inclusive Globalization*, report of the Advisory Group chaired by Michelle Bachelet, Geneva: ILO.

ILO (2011e) *Bachelet Report G20 Version*, Geneva: ILO.

ILO (2011f) *Towards National Social Protection Floors: A Policy Note for the G20 Meeting of Labour and Employment Ministers*, Paris, 26–27 September, prepared by the ILO in collaboration with the OECD, Geneva: ILO.

ILO (2011g) *Follow-Up to the Discussion on Social Security at the 100th Session of the International Labour Conference (2011): Plan of Action*, GB.312/POL/2, Governing Body 312th Session, November 2011: Policy Development Section: Second Item, Geneva: ILO.

ILO (2011h) *Governing Body 312th Session, November 2011: High Level Section, Policy Coherence in the Multilateral System*, GB.312/HL/1, Geneva: ILO.

ILO (2011i) 'ILO and G20: dawn at Cannes?', presentation by ILO Sherpas to the ILO, 23 November.

ILO (2011j) 'Strategies for the implementation of social protection floors: a knowledge sharing platform and a mechanism to improve inter-agency coordination', non-paper, for discussion and consultation.

ILO (2011k) *Building Resilience and Opportunity: The World Bank's Social Protection and Labor Strategy 2012-2020*, ILO comments on the World Bank's strategy concept note, Geneva: ILO Social Security Department.

ILO (2011l) *Social Security and the Rule of Law. Report of the Committee of Experts on the Application of Conventions and Recommendations, Report III (part 1B)*, Geneva: ILO.

ILO (2011m) *Provisional Record, Third item: Report of the Committee on the Application of Standards*, International Labour Conference 2011, Geneva: ILO.

ILO (2011n) *Communication and Capacity Building: Social Protection Floor Initiative: Outcome of 3rd Interagency Meeting on the SPF*, Geneva: ILO.

ILO (2012a) 4th Inter-Agency Technical Meeting on the CEB Social Protection Floor Initiative, 31 January.

ILO (2012b) *Social Protection Floors for Social Justice and a Fair Globalization* (summary of member's responses to questionnaire and office commentary), Report IV (2A) to International Labour Conference 2012, ILC.101/IV/2A, Geneva: ILO.

ILO (2012c) *Proposed Recommendation Concerning National Floors of Social Protection*, Report IV (2B) to International Labour Conference 2012, Geneva: ILO.

ILO (2012d) *Recommendation Concerning National Floors of Social Protection (Social Protection Floors Recommendation), 2012 (No. 202), International Labour Conference, 2012*, Geneva: ILO.

ILO (2012e) *Draft Report of the ILC's Social Protection Floor Committee*, Geneva: ILO.

ILO (2012f) 1st Social Protection Inter-Agency Cooperation Board Meeting, www.social-protection.org/gimi/gess/ShowProject Ressource.do?ressourceId=31230&pid=1625

ILO (2012g) *The Strategy of the International Labour Organization: Social Security for All: Building Social Protection Floors and Comprehensive Social Security Systems*, Geneva: ILO.

ILO (2012h) *Follow-Up to the Adoption of the Resolution Concerning Efforts to Make Social Protection Floors a National Reality Worldwide*, matters arising out of the work of the 101st Session (2012) of the International Labour Conference, Geneva: ILO.

ILO (2012i) Governing Body: *Preview of the Programme and Budget Proposals for 2014–15*, GB.316/PFA/1, Geneva: ILO.

ILO (2012j) ILO framework for the post-2015 development agenda: Jobs and livelihoods at the heart of the post-2015 development agenda. (www.ilo.org/global/about-the-ilo/media-centre/statements-and-speeches/WCMS_193483/lang--en/index.htm

ILO–IMF (2012) *Towards Effective and Fiscally Sustainable Social Protection Floors*, 10 May, Geneva: ILO, www.ilo.org/gimi/gess/ RessShowRessource.do?ressourceId=30810

ILO–UNDP (2011) *Inclusive and Resilient Development: The Role of Social Protection*, a paper prepared by the ILO and UNDP for the G20 development working group, 2010-11.

IMF (International Monetary Fund) (2010a) *Exiting from Crisis Situations*, Washington, DC: IMF, www.imf.org/external/np/pp/ eng/2010/020410.pdf

IMF (2010b) *Strategies for Fiscal Consolidation in the Post-Crisis World*, Washington, DC: IMF, www.imf.org/external/np/pp/ eng/2010/020410a.pdf

IMF (2010c) *Oslo Conference Calls for Commitment to Recovery Focused on Jobs* Press Release No. 10/339 September 13, 2010

IMF–ILO (2010) *The Challenges of Growth, Employment and Social Cohesion*, a paper for the joint ILO–IMF conference in cooperation with the office of the Prime Minister of Norwa.

IOE (International Organisation of Employers) (2011) *The Concept of the Social Protection Floor: Explanatory Note for Employers*, Geneva: IOE.

ITUC (International Trade Union Confederation) (2010a) Vancouver resolution on extending social protection and ensuring occupational health and safety, 2nd World Congress, 21-25 June, 2CO/E/6.12 (final).

ITUC (2010b) Resolution on the ILO, 2nd World Congress, Vancouver, 21-25 June, 2CO/E/6.8 (final).

ITUC (2011) 'ITUC comments on the SPF-I report', www.ituc-csi. org/IMG/pdf/SPF.pdf

Javiliier, J.-C. Regent, S. and Reynaud, E. (2006) 'social protection and decent work: new prospects for international labor standards: foreword', *Comparative Labor Law and Policy Journal*, 27 (2): ix-x.

Jenson, J. (2012) 'Social innovation: gadget, concept, mobilising notion', paper presented at the RC 19 Conference, Oslo, Norway, 23-26 August.

Jessop, B. and Neilsen, K. (2003) 'Institutions and rules', *Research Papers on Institutional Network Theory*, 11: 1-11.

Kirton, J. (2011) *G20* 'Development governance, 1999-2011: increase, institutionalization, impact' paper presented at a Knowledge Sharing Conference entitled 'The Global Development Agenda after the Great Recession of 2008-2009', Employment Policy Department, ILO, Geneva.

Kohler, G. (2011) *The Challenges of Delivering as One: Overcoming Fragmentation and Moving towards Policy Coherence*, Working Paper 100, Geneva: Policy Integration Department, ILO.

Kulke, U. (2007) 'The present and future role of ILO standards in realizing the right to social security', *International Social Security Review*, 60, 2-3: 119-41.

Leisering, L. (2009) 'Extending social security to the excluded: are social cash transfers to the poor an appropriate way of fighting poverty in developing countries?', *Global Social Policy*, 9 (2): 246-72.

Leutelt, M. (2012) 'HelpAge's engagement in spreading social pensions in the global south: slow and steady wins the race?', paper presented at the RC 19 Conference, Oslo, Norway August.

Liebert, N. (2011) *No Social Justice without Social Protection: What can International Development Cooperation Do to Make the Social Protection Floor Initiative Work?*, Bonn, Germany: Freidrich Ebert Stiftung.

Mahon, R. (2009) 'The OECD's discourse on the reconciliation of work and family life', *Global Social Policy*, 9: 183-204.

Marcussen, M. and Trondal, J. (2011) 'The OECD civil servant: caught between Scylla and Charybdis', *Review of International Political Economy*, 18 (5): 592–621.

Mathiason, J. (2007) *Invisible Governance: International Secretariats in Global Politics*, Bloomfield, CT: Kumarian Press.

Mestrum, F. (2012) *Social Protection Floor: Beyond Poverty Reduction*, Global Social Justice website, www.globalsocialjustice.eu/index. php?option=com_content&view=article&id=223:social-protection-floor-beyond-poverty-reduction&catid=5:analysis&Itemid=6

Meyer, J.W. and Hannan, M.T. (1979) 'The world educational revolution', in Meyer, J.W. and Hannan, M.T. (eds) *National Development and the World System*, Chicago, IL: University of Chicago Press.

Meyer, J.W. and Jepperson, R.L. (2000) 'The "actors" of modern society: the cultural construction of social agency', *Sociological Theory*, 18: 100-20.

Mkandawire, T. (2005) *Social Policy in a Development Context*, Basingstoke: Palgrave.

Mosse, D. (2011) *Adventures in Aidland*, Oxford: Berghahn.

Moulaert, F. and Jessop, B. (2006) 'Agency, structure, institutions, discourse', Conference Proceedings: European Association for Evolutionary Political Economy Conference, Istanbul, Turkey, http://demologos.ncl.ac.uk/index.php

NGO Committee for Social Development (2012a) *Can You Hear Us: Voices from Around the World in Support of the Social Protection Floor Initiative*, New York, NY: NGO Committee.

NGO Committee for Social Development (2012b) *Pathways to Poverty Eradication: Civil Society Perspective 2012*, New York, NY: NGO Committee, www.ngosocdev.net/index.php/2012-commission-on-social-development/

Orenstein, M. (2008) *Privatizing Pensions: The Transnational Campaign for Social Security Reform*, Princeton, NJ: Princeton University Press.

Ortiz, I. (2007) *Social Policy Guidance Notes*, New York, NY: UNDESA.

Ortiz, I. and Cummins, M. (eds) (2012) *A Recovery for All: rethinking Socio-Economic Policies for Children and Poor Households*, New York, NY: UNICEF.

Ortiz, I., Chai, J. and Cummins, M. (2011a) *Identifying Fiscal Space: Options for Social and Economic Development for Children and Poor Households in 182 Countries*, Social and Economic Working Papers, New York, NY: UNICEF.

Pal, K., Behrendt, C., Léger, F., Cichon, M. and Hagemejer, K. (2005) *Can Low Income Countries Afford Basic Social Protection?*, Issues in Social Protection Discussion Paper 13, Geneva: ILO.

Plant, R., (1994) Labour Standards and Structural Adjustment in Hungary, *Occasional Paper 7, Project on Structural Adjustment.* Geneva: ILO.

Reynaud, E. (2006) 'Social security for all: global trends and challenges', *Comparative Labor Law and Policy Journal*, 27 (2): 123-51.

Rodgers, G., Lee, E., Swepston, L. and Daele, V. (2009) *The ILO and the Quest for Social Justice 1919-2009*, Ithaca, NY and Geneva: Cornell University Press and International Labour Office.

Ryder, G. (2006) 'Social security for all – a human right must become reality', in *Social Security for All: Trade Union Policies: Labour Education 2006/4*: 1-9.

Schmidt, V.A. (2008) 'Discursive institutionalism: the explanatory power of ideas and discourse', *Annual Review of Political Science*, 11: 303-26.

Schutte, O. and Sepulveda, M. (2013) *Underwriting the Poor: A Global Fund for Social Protection*, UNHRC Briefing Note 7, Geneva: UN Human Rights Council.

Sen, G. (2004) 'The relationship of research and activism in the making of policy: lessons from gender and development', paper presented at the 'UNRISD Conference on Social Knowledge and International Policy Making', Geneva.

Sen, G. (2006) 'The quest for gender equality', in Utting, P. (ed) *Reclaiming Development Agendas*, Basingstoke: Palgrave.

Sepulveda, M. and Nyst, C. (2012) *The Human Right Approach to Social Protection*, Finland: Ministry for Foreign Affairs of Finland, http://formin.finland.fi/public/default.aspx?contentid=250472&nodeid=34606&contentlan=1&culture=fi-FI

Sepulveda M and de Schutter O (2013) *'The need to include a rights-based approach to Social Protection in the Post 2015 Development Agenda'* Office of the High Commission for Human Righs.

Sklair, L. (2002) *Globalization: Capitalism and its Alternatives*, Oxford: Oxford University Press.

Soederberg, S. (2006) *Global Governance in Question*, Oxford: Oxford University Press.

Somavia, J. (2000) 'The future: a global deficit of decent work', *New Perspectives Quarterly*, February, www.digitalnpq.org/global_services/nobel%20laureates/11-02-00.HTML

St Clair, A.L. (2006) 'Global poverty: the co-production of knowledge and politics', *Global Social Policy*, 6: 57-77.

Standing, G. (1988) *European Unemployment, Insecurity and Flexibility: A Social Dividend Solution* (with a preface by Ralf Dahrendorf), Labour Market Analysis Working Paper No. 23, Geneva: ILO, (revised April 1989).

Standing, G. (2008) 'The ILO: an agency for globalization?', *Development and Change*, 39 (3): 355-84.

Standing, G. (2011) *The Precariat: The New Dangerous Class*, London and New York, NY: Bloomsbury Academic.

Standing, G. and Samson, M. (eds) (2003) *A Basic Income Grant for South Africa*, Cape Town: University of Cape Town Press.

Stone, D. and Maxwell, S. (eds) (2005) *Global Knowledge Networks and International Development*, Oxford and New York, NY: Routledge.

Supiot, A. (2006) 'Position of social security in the system of international labor standards', *Comparative Labor Law and Policy Journal*, 27 (2): 113-213.

Trondal, J., Marcussen, M., Larsson, T. and Veggeland, F. (2010) *Unpacking International Organisations: Multiple Roles in Compound Bureaucracies*, Manchester: Manchester University Press.

UN (United Nations) (1995) *Copenhagen Declaration and Programme of Action* Adopted by the World Summit for Social Development. Copenhagen 6-12 March.

UN (2012a) *Post-2015 United Nations Development Agenda: Preliminary Review of the Contribution of the MDG Agenda. Zero Draft*, 6 January.

UN (2012b) *UN System Task Team: Report: Realizing the Future we Want for All*, New York, NY: UN, www.un.org/en/development/desa/policy/untaskteam_undf/unttreport_summary.pdf

UN (2012c) 'UN secretary-general appoints high-level panel on post-2015 development agenda', UN Press Release, www.un.org/millenniumgoals/Press%20release_post-2015panel.pdf

UN (2012d) *The Future We Want: Rio plus 20 Draft Outcome Document*, New York, NY: UN

UN (2012e) *The Future We Want, Rio plus 20 Outcome Document*, New York, NY: UN, www.uncsd2012.org/content/documents/727THE%20FUTURE%20WE%20WANT%20-%20FINAL%20DOCUMENT.pdf

UN (2012f) *Resilient People, Resilient Planet: A Future Worth Choosing*, report of the High Level Panel on Global Sustainability, New York, NY: UN, www.un.org/gsp/sites/default/files/attachments/GSPReport_unformatted_30Jan.pdf

UNCEB (United Nations Chief Executives Board) (2009a) *The Global Financial Crisis and its Impact on the Work of the UN System*, UNCEB Issue Paper. April.

UNCEB (United Nations Chief Executives Board) (2009b) *The Global Financial Crisis and its Impact on the Work of the UN System*, Draft UNCEB Issue Paper. February. (CEB/2009/HLCP-XVII/CP.1.).

UNDESA (United Nations Department of Economic and Social Affairs) (2012) *The Future We Want – Zero Draft of the Outcome Document* (of the Rio plus 20 UN Conference on Sustainable Development), www.uncsd2012.org/rio20/content/documents/370The%20 Future%20We%20Want%2010Jan%20clean%20_no%20brackets.pdf

UNICEF (United Nations Children's Fund) (2010a) *Recovery for All*, New York, NY: UNICEF, www.unicef.org/socialpolicy/files/ Recovery_for_All_5_August_2010_for_e-distribution_FINAL(1). pdf

UNICEF (2010b) *Prioritizing Expenditures for a Recovery with a Human Face: Results from a Rapid Desk Review of 86 Recent IMF Country Reports*, New York, NY: UNICEF, www.escr-net.org/usr_doc/ Prioritizing_Expenditures.pdf

UNICEF (2010c) *Prioritizing Expenditures for a Recovery for All: A Rapid Review of Public Expenditures in 126 Developing Countries*, New York, NY: UNICEF, www.unicef.org/socialpolicy/index_56435.html

UNICEF (2012) *Integrated Social Protection Systems: Enhancing Equity for Children*, New York, NY: UNICEF, www.unicef.org/socialprotection/ framework/

van Daele, J. (2010) 'Writing ILO histories: a state of the art, in van Daele, J., Garcia, M.R., can Goethem, G. and van der Linden, M. (eds) *ILO Histories: Essays on the International Labour Organisation and its Impact on the World during the Twentieth Century*, Berne, Germany: Peter Lang.

van Ginneken, W. (ed) (1999) *Social security for the Excluded Majority: Case Studies of Developing Countries*, Geneva: International Labour Office.

van Ginneken, W. (2000a) 'The extension of social protection: ILO's aim for the years to come', Paper presented at the DFID–ODI inter-agency seminar on social protection, Easthampstead Park, 22-23 March.

van Ginneken, W. (2000b) 'The extension of social protection: ILO's aim for the years to come', in Conway, T., de Haan, A. and Norton, A. (eds) *Social Protection: New Directions of Donor Agencies*, London: Department for International Development, www.odi.org.uk/ resources/docs/2233.pdf van Ginneken, W. (2004) 'The Global Campaign on Social Security and Coverage for all', paper presented at the international conference entitled 'Globalization and the Welfare State? World Society, Transnational Social Policy and "New Welfare States" in Transitional Countries', Hanse Institute for Advanced Study, Delmenhorst, Germany, 8–10 February.

van Ginneken, W. (2012) ILC SPF committee proceedings, day 5, INGO report (email communication, 5 June).

van Ginneken, W. (2013) 'The role of civil society: outline for paper 5 of the *International Social Security Review* special double issue for 2013.

Voipio, T. (2011) *From Poverty Economics to Global Social Policy*, Kuopio: University of Eastern Finland, http://epublications.uef.fi/pub/urn_isbn_978-952-61-0260-3/urn_isbn_978-952-61-0260-3.pdf

Williams, F. (1995) 'Race/ethnicity, gender and class in welfare states: a framework for comparative analysis', *Social Politics*, 2: 127-159.

Wimann, R., Voipio, T. and Ylonen, M. (eds) (2006) *Comprehensive Social Policies for Development in a Globalising World*, Helsinki, Finland: Ministry of Foreign Affairs of Finland.

World Bank (1990) *World Development Report: Poverty*, Washington, DC: World Bank.

World Bank (1991) *Assistance Strategies to Reduce Poverty*, Washington DC: World Bank. World Bank (1992) *Poverty Reduction Handbook*, Washington DC: World Bank.

World Bank (2011) *Building Resilience and Opportunity: The World Bank's Social Protection and Labour Strategy 2012-2020* (first draft), Washington, DC: World Bank.

World Bank (2012a) *Resilience, Equity and Opportunity: The World Bank's Social Protection and Labor Strategy 2012-2022* (third draft for review), Washington, DC: World Bank.

World Bank (2012b) *Resilience, Equity and Opportunity: The World Bank's Social Protection and Labor Strategy 2012-2022*, (final draft) Washington, DC: World Bank.

World Bank (2012c) *Resilience, Equity and Opportunity: Consultations Report*, Washington, DC: World Bank.(http://go.worldbank.org/GJBLQ8IYM0)

World Bank (2011b) *Social Protection & Labor Strategy Advisory Group: First Meeting, Paris, April 27 and 28, 2011* (http://go.worldbank.org/2G20ARIYQ0)

Index

Please note: 'SPF' refers to 'social protection floor'